THE END OF THE FRENCH INTELLECTUAL

THE END OF THE FRENCH INTELLECTUAL

From Zola to Houellebecq

Shlomo Sand

Translated by David Fernbach

VERSO

This English-language edition first published by Verso 2018
First published as *La fin de l'intellectuel Français?*
© La Découverte 2016
Translation © David Fernbach 2018

1 3 5 7 9 10 8 6 4 2

Verso
UK: 6 Meard Street, London W1F 0EG
US: 20 Jay Street, Suite 1010, Brooklyn, NY 11201
versobooks.com

Verso is the imprint of New Left Books

ISBN-13: 978-1-78663-508-2
ISBN-13: 978-1-78663-511-2 (US EBK)
ISBN-13: 978-1-78663-510-5 (UK EBK)

British Library Cataloguing in Publication Data
A catalogue record for this book is available from the British Library

Library of Congress Cataloging-in-Publication Data

Names: Sand, Shlomo, author. | Fernbach, David, translator.
Title: The end of the French intellectual? : from Zola to Houellebecq /
  Shlomo Sand ; translated by David Fernbach.
Other titles: Fin de l'intellectuel français? English
Description: London : Brooklyn, NY : Verso Books, [2018] | Includes index.
Identifiers: LCCN 2017050264 | ISBN 9781786635112
Subjects: LCSH: Intellectuals – France – History. | France – Intellectual life.
Classification: LCC DC33 .S2513 2018 | DDC 305.5/520944 – dc23
LC record available at https://lccn.loc.gov/2017050264

Typeset in Adobe Garamond Pro by Hewer Text UK Ltd, Edinburgh
Printed in the UK by CPI Group (UK) Ltd, Croydon, CR0 4YY

In memory of Simone Weil, André Breton and Daniel Guérin

Contents

Preface: The Intellectual as Object – a 'Selfie'?   ix

Introduction: The City and the Pen   1

Part One: Intellectuals in the Torment of the Century

1. The Dreyfus Affairs:
    Human Rights or Author's Rights?   39

2. From Voltaire to Bourdieu:
    Who Are the 'True Intellectuals'?   67

3. Marx and His Descendants:
    Symbolic Capital or Political Capital?   101

4. The Discreet Charm of Fascism:
    Flirtation or Love Story?   135

5. Twilight of the Idols:
    The Critical Intellectual Domesticated?   167

Part Two: Islamophobia and the Intellectuals' 'Rhinoceritis'

6.   From Houellebecq to *Charlie Hebdo*:
      Submission or Humour?   203

7.   From Finkielkraut to Zemmour:
      Decadence or Xenophobia?   235

Acknowledgements   265
Index   267

The Intellectual as Object – a 'Selfie'?

'I'm an intellectual myself,' Lambert said. 'And it annoys me when people make that word an insult. They seem to think that an empty head means they've really got balls.'

Simone de Beauvoir, *The Mandarins*, 1954

What we do know is that speech is a power, and that a group of people, somewhere between corporation and social class, are well enough defined by the fact that to a varying extent they wield the nation's language.

Roland Barthes, 'Authors and Writers', 1960

The last forty years have seen the publication in Paris of several dozen books and articles on the presence and status of intellectuals. It will not demonstrate much originality on my part if I maintain that nowhere else have so many works been devoted to intellectuals and the intelligentsia. True, debate about 'the intellectuals' is not exclusively French; a number of studies of the subject may be found in other countries. But in terms of quantity, their production is far from equalling the Parisian crop.

It is not an easy task to search for the cause in specifically French factors. Many have tried to do so, appealing to circumstances and

factors arising from political philosophy, ethics, history and sociology. Only a small minority of these works are at all convincing.
The majority of scholars and commentators have adopted the
idea that the age of great intellectuals is over, supplanted by the
age of summaries. This hypothesis may indeed be well founded,
and it is something I shall re-examine. But first of all, we must
recognize the halo of nostalgia that surrounds these long elegies
over the classic intellectuals. After all, we all grew up in the
immense shadow of these 'great' figures! If we are wise, we are
aware that our own shadows will be smaller and more short-lived.
It might even be said, perhaps wrongly, that we who remain are
like the mannerists at the end of the Renaissance, which we are
trying vainly to preserve, imitate, or even plunge back into.

I am not certain this little book will make a real contribution
to deciphering the double enigma of the intellectual: the specificity of France, and the disappearance (or not) of 'great' intellectuals. But having long been bothered by these questions, I felt
the need to put my fragmentary reflections in order. In the
following pages, my intention is not to write the nth history of
intellectuals in France. There are already enough of these, and
exemplary ones at that.[1] I simply wanted to cast a few beams of
light on certain periods and forms of discourse, selected in this
brief particular history.

A mandarin self-portrait

All writing bears in its recesses signs from which a self-portrait
can be sketched, but it is clear that the autobiographical dimension will be all the more prominent in any account of intellectuals. There will be nothing surprising, therefore, about finding in
the discussions of the present book indications of a personal

---

1   Two books I would particularly recommend are Pascal Ory and Jean-François
Sirinelli, *Les Intellectuels en France: de l'Affaire Dreyfus à nos jours*, Paris: Armand
Colin, 1986; and Michel Winock, *Le Siècle des intellectuels*, Paris: Seuil, 1997.

character, both conscious and, one might imagine, involuntarily lurking behind supposedly scientific definitions. Despite the impartial tone I have sought to give this presentation, these indications express my unease about some of the contents included in the concept of the 'intellectual'.[2]

To start with, a confession! I am today a historian by profession, but my desire to become an 'intellectual' goes back a long way. I dreamed of it already in my youth. More precisely, like many others, I had the ambition early on to be a writer; in other words, to write stories. I grew up in a home where neither of my parents had finished primary school and they were barely literate. Yet both of them loved to read, and my father was in the habit of respectfully caressing the few books in his library. His relation to the written word was one of veneration, perhaps a belated echo of a childhood in a Jewish family in Eastern Europe. And as himself a communist, he repeated to me more than once Lenin's motto: 'Learn, learn, and learn again!' It is understandable then that I detested learning and hated school; I was expelled from high school at the age of sixteen.

In actual fact, my passion for reading stopped me doing my homework. Even at school, I hid away to read during classes, to the point that more than once the teacher sent me out of the room. The fine and varied literature that I read was almost all in translation: from classic works by Jack London, Victor Hugo and Charles Dickens, to detective stories by Arthur Conan Doyle, Agatha Christie and Georges Simenon, not to mention fascinating pornographic books. I also appreciated the biblical stories that contained all three genres. Thanks to this daily reading, as well as my night-time dreams, I managed to escape for a moment from the poor immigrant quarter of small-town Jaffa, and joyously sail off to magical countries.

---

2   I have already offered some autobiographical elements in the foreword to my book *The Words and the Land: Israeli Intellectuals and the Nationalist Myth*, Los Angeles: Semiotext(e), 2011.

One book, however, played a decisive role in my trajectory, substituting for the naïve model of the writer, as I conceived this in my early youth, the figure of the intellectual that I would go on to worship in the following years. In due course, I came across Simone de Beauvoir's famous novel *The Mandarins*, published in 1954 and translated into Hebrew at the end of the decade. It was towards the mid-1960s that I read it, though I no longer remember the exact year. However, I have kept a clear memory of its extraordinary characters, who moved between literary writing, journalism and political action, between sexual freedom and humanist morality. I was bowled over by the romantic levity of the world of those who lived from writing, by the idealization of their intellectual commitment in the service of just causes, and against the enchanting backdrop of the City of Light.

I was at this time a young manual worker, employed in a factory producing radio sets, for whom the idea that it was possible to live from writing and continue to be admired by the working-class left formed part of an unattainable dream. Thanks to, or because of, the snobbery that then affected me, I identified with the Parisian 'mandarins', whom I envied and desperately aspired to resemble. In this way, I clearly sought to differentiate myself from the people around me and from my wretched living conditions. I gave free rein to my mental frustrations by writing poems that very fortunately were never published.

Rereading the same novel years later, I could not contain my surprise at having been bewitched at this time by such flat characters, and by discussions and controversies that had so little credibility. Subsequently, I preferred to the 'progressive' intellectuals of *The Mandarins* the powerful reactionary intellectuals who torture themselves in Dostoevsky's *The Possessed*, or the conservative ones who haunt Thomas Mann's *The Magic Mountain*. If the literary aura of the author of *The Mandarins* faded relatively early for me, I still continued to admire for many years 'Robert Dubreuilh' (Jean-Paul Sartre) and 'Henri Perron'

(Albert Camus), the two most prominent 'mandarins', naturally along with 'Anne Dubreuilh', the novelist.

Camus initially aroused my strong enthusiasm. His modest origins made it easier for me to identify with this indecisive character. His mother, like mine, had been a housemaid. His intransigent moral stand against Stalinism seduced me right away. For a short period, *The Plague* was both a stimulus and a support for me in my activity in a small political group, isolated and aware that any hope of victory was out of reach. The preference for revolutionary syndicalism that Camus expresses in *The Rebel* gave a direction to my rebellious inclination, and was subsequently a factor in my choice of George Sorel's critique of Marxism as the subject of my doctoral thesis.[3] I also remember having been a little perturbed by the nostalgia and 'philosophical' idealization of the luminous 'Mediterranean spirit' that Camus expresses at the end of this essay, despite himself having always preferred to live in Paris, the cold centre of the 'intellectual universe'.

My admiration for and identification with Perron/Camus did not last very long. The new reality in Israel after the Six-Day War of 1967, during which I fought in Jerusalem, taught me what it means to occupy and dominate another people, and pushed me towards the radical left. As well as Camus's anti-Stalinism, which I had cherished, I now discovered his benevolent attitude to Israel when it took part in the Franco-British aggression against Egypt in 1956. On top of this, his position towards the Algerian demand for independence, despite being less brutally colonialist than that of the socialists, was still a prevarication. His idea that national independence was for the Algerians a 'purely emotional response' and a demonstration of the 'new Arab imperialism' chilled the blind admirer that I had been.[4]

---

3   Shlomo Sand, *L'Illusion du politique. Georges Sorel et le débat intellectuel 1900*, Paris: La Découverte, 1985.

4   Albert Camus, *Algerian Chronicles*, Cambridge, MA: Belknap, 2014, pp. 137–8.

Rereading *The Outsider*, that 'anti-solar' novel which I had never really liked, I discovered a certain arrogant tone. The comparison between Camus's 'Killing an Arab' and Orwell's 'Killing an Elephant' emphasized the abyss that separated the son of colonists with his tattered language from the critic of British colonialism with his steely gaze. To my eyes, it was Orwell who better deciphered the link between the sense of absurdity and a historical situation that could develop this to an extreme.[5] There was also the unfortunate declaration in Stockholm in 1957, when Camus was awarded the Nobel Prize, which shocked me when I was confronted with it for the first time: 'I believe in justice, but I would defend my mother before justice.'[6]

I recall having immediately thought of an imaginary situation, perhaps unfairly, that I have tried in vain to wipe from my mind to this day. Camus, the fine intellectual, drives his mother to hospital in an ambulance, at full speed in order to save her, and on the way runs over two Arab children playing innocently in the street. Of course, two children are not enough to sum up the cruel struggle of a movement for national independence, but justice, despite its application being always difficult, and despite, as everyone knows, always coming second after self-interest, is supposed by definition to be universal. An intellectual ready even

---

5   Camus's admirers do not like to be reminded that *The Outsider*, published in Paris in 1942, had no problem obtaining the authorization of the Propaganda Staffel. It was only the following year that the writer made connections with the Resistance.

6   This declaration appeared in a report by Dominique Bermann for *Le Monde*, dated 14 December 1957. In a letter to the paper on 19 December, Camus corrected a number of points, without however denying the authenticity of his expression. 'I would again like to add, on the subject of the young Algerian who questioned me, that I feel closer to him than to many French people who talk of Algeria without knowing it. He knew what he was speaking of, and his face was not one of hatred, but one of despair and unhappiness. I share this unhappiness, his face is that of my country. Which is why I wanted to give this young Algerian publicly, and just to him, personal explanations that I had previously been silent about, and that your correspondent faithfully reproduced.' The desire of certain of Camus's commentators to retroactively 'correct' his phrase has long seemed to me quite ridiculous.

for a moment to disregard this, despite being driven by an extraordinary sincerity, and to declare it publicly, moved by an egoism of family, tribe, religion, nation or class, could no longer serve as a model for my young eyes, imbued with an excess of morality.

With today's distance, Camus's hasty and incautious assertion about justice strikes me as having a premonitory aspect. Two decades after he spoke, the universalism of intellectuals in general, and Parisian intellectuals in particular, significantly declined, giving way to thoughts and attitudes that have always characterized the intellectual right, to which Camus did not want to belong and did not see himself as belonging.

I remained for a long time an enthusiastic and faithful supporter of Dubreuilh/Sartre. Although his long novels never convinced me, his short stories and essays, peppered with philosophical insights (even if I must confess having never managed to finish reading *Being and Nothingness*) and with steely and precise political and psychological reflections, made me a kind of 'provincial existentialist'; this was fashionable in Israel in the 1960s, when we still knew nothing of structuralism. After my working day, I would devour in the evenings all the writings by the great little man of Montparnasse that were available in Hebrew – a man who, for me, embodied not an idea but rather the standard of a group. His inconstant positions on Stalinism confused me; on the other hand, his unambiguous commitment against the war in Algeria, then against that in Vietnam, was a great help to me in clarifying my ideas about Palestine.

Much later, when I was a doctoral student in Paris in the late 1970s, the discovery of Sartre's rather unheroic action during the German Occupation created the first cracks in my image of him. Subsequently, the petty quarrels at the court of the sick philosopher, sadly dragged along by the mad ideas of his last secretary, Benny Lévy, further degraded in my eyes the aura of an intellectual 'lighthouse'. In 1982, two years after his death, when Israel invaded Lebanon to definitively 'eradicate' the Palestinian resistance, Simone de Beauvoir and the couple's friend Claude Lanzmann lent their support to this war, while Benny Lévy enrolled at a Talmudic school (later on he emigrated comfortably to Jerusalem, a city where a third of the inhabitants have been deprived of citizenship and sovereignty for nearly fifty years). Pathetic old age drew new and deep wrinkles on the glorious faces of the Left Bank intellectuals.

The residue of my idealization of Parisian intellectuals was finally exhausted by another event that I have already related elsewhere in part, and the account of which I now have the opportunity to complete, in the context of the present examination of the 'intellectual' conscience. In 1985, three years after the massacres at Sabra and Shatila by Christian Phalangists, but made possible, as is well known, by the Israeli army's control of Beirut, Claude Lanzmann's long documentary film *Shoah* was released. From then on, and more than ever, all reference to the immense and terrible crime of the Nazis would put all other 'more commonplace' crimes of the present into the shadows.

By way of promoting the film, Simone de Beauvoir wrote an introduction to the screenplay, full of emotion, which was published in parallel. I already knew at this time that under the Nazi Occupation the author of *The Mandarins*, in order to continue teaching at a Paris lycée, had signed a document attesting that she was not Jewish. She made a brief reference to this in her memoirs published in 1960: 'I found putting my name to this repugnant, but no one refused to do so; the majority of my colleagues, like myself, had no possible alternative.'[7] Neither more nor less. A laconic but precise phrase, as 'the majority' signed, but not all. Henri Dreyfus-Le Foyer, for example, teaching at the Lycée Condorcet, did not sign and was dismissed in

---

7   Simone de Beauvoir, *The Prime of Life*, London: André Deutsch and Weidenfeld & Nicolson, 1963, p. 369.

1940. His post was subsequently taken by Sartre, on his return to Paris from a prisoner-of-war camp in 1941.

What irritated me was not so much the 'declaration of Aryan status', as I will never know whether I might not have acted similarly so as to continue earning my living. The last straw was the subsequent discovery that de Beauvoir had contributed to Radio Vichy in 1943. True, her work consisted in writing programmes on the music hall, but these were broadcast side by side with less inoffensive programmes such as *La milice vous parle* . . . Which did not prevent her, contrary to Albert Camus, Paul Valéry and François Mauriac, from refusing to sign the petition against the death sentence on Robert Brasillach. Nor from spelling out, in her memoirs, 'By trade, by vocation, I attach an enormous importance to words . . . There are words as murderous as gas chambers.'[8]

Words can also be designed to mask a large number of 'petty details'. The lack of many disturbing points, in such a copious and detailed autobiography, reveals the limits of authenticity of many intellectual poses in the field of the Paris mandarinate. Of course, Simone de Beauvoir and her partner were not 'collaborators', but neither were they as portrayed in *The Mandarins*, the heroes of my youth. In a time of crisis and misfortune they were very typical Parisians, more keen on getting by and publishing their work than on Resistance activity (de Beauvoir's later descriptions of their vain attempts to 'organize' seem rather ridiculous and little credible). With the Liberation they became figureheads of the Resistance, thanks in particular to their literary talent, their brilliant skill in deciphering the spirit of the time and their ability to construct a media image for themselves. This accumulation of symbolic capital was carried out in the form of an exchange: they became fellow travellers of the communist movement, which had justly emerged from the war with an aura of

---

8   Simone de Beauvoir, *Force of Circumstance*, London: André Deutsch, 1965, pp. 29–30.

heroism. In exchange for this spectacular convergence, the couple provided the communists with a cover-up or alibi for the crimes of Stalinism.

Defying the myths

A short while before his death in 2006, I visited the historian Pierre Vidal-Naquet for the last time. Ill and weak, he had difficulty standing up. I wanted to thank him for all the help he had given me. The conversation was particularly warm. Vidal-Naquet suddenly changed the subject of discussion and asked me why, in my book *Le XXe siècle à l'écran*, I had been so critical towards the film *Shoah*, which he had much appreciated. I tried to explain to him the various historical and cinematic reasons for my criticism. But this did not satisfy him, and he insisted on knowing whether there was not a more specific factor that explained why I had taken such a cutting and aggressive position. I immediately replied, 'Because of Bianca Lamblin. She didn't appear in the film, and certainly not by accident.' He understood immediately (his parents had died in the camps), asked me to help him get up, and embraced me with tears in his eyes. I left immediately after, and sadly had no further chance to see him again.

Readers will certainly ask who this Bianca Lamblin was. When they were lycée teachers, Jean-Paul Sartre and Simone de Beauvoir shared a number of female students in their love triangles. One of these, who appears under the name of Védrine in Simone de Beauvoir's letters and diaries, was Bianca. In a letter of 10 December 1939, the author of *The Mandarins* traces the following portrait of her:

> She cries before a wailing wall that she builds with her own busy hands, that she often builds to protect the positive riches she fiercely wants to defend . . . Something of the old Jewish usurer in her, who cries out of pity for the client he is driving to suicide. She is terribly 'self-interested' – with generous ideas

that she feels passionate about and that exclude the interests to which she clings. But, such as she is, with the unpleasant quality of a Jewish businesswoman, I like her and find her very interesting.[9]

From reading this extract, it is clear that Bianca Lamblin, née Bienenfeld, was of (Polish) Jewish origin, as distinct from three other lovers, Nathalie Sorokine and Olga and Wanda Kosakiewicz. She was accordingly the only one to be forced to find refuge in the 'free zone' of southern France in 1941. The couple's emotional and sexual relations with the young woman had come to an end in the course of 1940, and the two 'mandarins' paid no attention to their former lover during the four years of the Occupation: not a single message, telegram or phone call to a woman who had been forced to flee on account of her origin. Nor did the couple seek to inquire as to her situation when they went to the south on vacation, during the school holidays. The ardent discussions on authenticity and existentialism in the cafés of Saint-Germain-des-Prés left them no time to take an interest in the existential danger experienced by their abandoned and persecuted lover, whose grandfather and aunt were murdered in the camps. Yet despite everything, Bianca remained to the end of her days in love with her mistress, whose charismatic authority, in the Weberian sense of the term, continued to grow after the war.[10]

If we abstract from the particularities of time and place, this story seems almost banal. Yet the fact that the intellectual who signed a declaration that she was Aryan acted in such a casual

---

9   Simone de Beauvoir, *Wartime Diary*, Champaign, IL: University of Illinois Press, 2008, p. 188.

10   In her memoirs, Simone de Beauvoir confines herself to the following dry remark: 'Bianca had spent a year hidden in the Vercors with her parents and husband' (*Force of Circumstance*, p. 17). Following the posthumous publication of the couple's correspondence, Bianca Lamblin ventured to write a bitter and accusatory autobiography: *Mémoires d'une fille dérangée*, Paris: Balland, 1993.

and inhuman way towards her former lover, who unlike de Beauvoir could not declare herself to be of pure race, finally shattered the residue of intellectual and moral esteem that I had long preserved for my Parisian heroes. The attempted breast-beating of these intellectuals after the war, because of their sense of guilt and their bad conscience, and the extraordinary generosity they showed for the rest of their lives towards anyone of Jewish origin, did not reconcile me with them (and still less with those who exploited this generosity). Bad conscience is certainly a mark of civilization and morality that has to be preserved, but in no way does it form a preventive insurance against the stupidity, hypocrisy and cynical exploitation of a painful past. Unfortunately it can serve to justify new injustices.

I admit I particularly deplored the fact that the film of Claude Lanzmann, one of Simone de Beauvoir's two male lovers of Jewish origin (the other being Nelson Algren), failed to mention even by allusion the fate of Bianca and her kind in France: those fortunate enough to be saved, and those interned in Drancy while awaiting transportation to Auschwitz. The fact Lanzmann's *Shoah* leads the viewer to believe that the persecution of Jews (and of Jews alone) only took place east of the Rhine, and particularly in Poland, a country so 'unintellectual' and anti-Semitic, is in no way an accident.[11] And it is hardly surprising that the author of *The Mandarins*, just like the majority of her kind, had no difficulty expressing enthusiastic support for a film which so well agreed with the image that Parisian literati wanted to give of themselves, increasingly 'philo-Semitic' in a united Europe that claims its 'Judeo-Christian civilization'. How different from the 1940s!

---

11   The fact that a French film such as *Shoah*, made in 1985, could have ignored the role of the Vichy state in this catastrophe, converges with the tendency subsequently expressed by the Franco-Israeli rabbi Alain Michel in his book *Vichy et la Shoah. Enquête sur la paradoxe français* (Paris: CLD, 2012), with a preface by Richard Prasquier, president of the Conseil Représentatif des Institutions Juives de France (CRIF). Éric Zemmour drew on this book to undertake a partial rehabilitation of the Vichy regime in *Le Suicide français* (Paris: Albin Michel, 2014).

The accumulation of little truths is able to corrode and challenge great mythologies. Many young readers' heroes are bound to lose their aura when their readers reach maturity. The myth of the intellectual that I forged for myself at a relatively young age pressed me to acquire knowledge, stimulated my political commitment and opened the gates of writing to me. But it was shaken when I myself became a kind of petty intellectual. In other words, I was an academic who was not content to teach and write books, but from time to time made incursions into the public arena to denounce the holders of power and creators of political lies. For a while I signed petitions for peace in the Middle East; and in this way I tried to exploit the prestige that used to attach to high academic qualifications in order to convince those without such qualifications of the correctness of my positions. And as there were always other intellectuals to express positions different from mine, these protests reciprocally neutralized one another, enabling politicians to continue shaping public opinion as they liked.

The particular reason why I chose the profession of historian is that I had comprehensively failed, as a left-wing activist, in my attempts to change the course of history. During the first years of my career, I made a serious effort to separate my historical work from my political positions. Yet I was clearly aware of the impossibility of this task, and never thought that history was a science. All the same, when I taught, I found myself stifling the explicit criticisms I was nurturing about historical decisions and developments; I sometimes even defended the actions of people I found repugnant, and too often played devil's advocate.

The principle of pedagogic pluralism is no doubt correct, but I know today that mine was also pervaded by a fearful conformism, bound up with my still unstable institutional situation. I had come from a disadvantaged social background and, knowing that university work provided for upward social mobility, I more or less consciously sought constantly to internalize the borders between the possible and the impossible, between what was authorized and what was forbidden. I think this is a socio-psychological process familiar to almost all those who join an apparatus of knowledge production: as Pierre Bourdieu put it very well, an institution where they are 'dominated within the dominant class'. I waited to feel more secure before I ventured to introduce into my historiographical work the treatment of subjects more pertinent for the development of historical consciousness. The positions I took up became more critical and incisive, but also more hesitant, and in this way I hoped to become a bit better as a historian. I was clearly not certain about this at all. Even if I freed myself from a good number of conceptual apparatuses deeply implanted in the culture by which I had been shaped, I believe that there remain in me many images and words that are loose and deceptive, and that I will perhaps never manage to escape from. Is my role as historian to continue reproducing them? Doesn't the critical intellectual within me have the duty of trying to deconstruct them, in order to produce a more sophisticated understanding? Should I not persevere and face up to any kind of taboo that brakes or stifles the capacity to think ahead?

Despite the successive disappointments I have just mentioned, it seems the romantic representation I made for myself in my youth of the intellectual in general, and the Parisian intellectual in particular, still lies concealed within me, in the deep folds of my consciousness.

My extended stays in Paris, in the context of my study and research, enabled me to meet a number of 'indigenous' intellectuals, thanks to whom I managed better to decipher the mysteries of intellectual debate in the City of Light. I thank them with all my heart, and I know how much I remain in their debt. I decided, however, to dedicate this book to three intellectuals whom it was clearly impossible for me to meet: Simone Weil, André Breton and Daniel Guérin, some of that handful of people in the literary world who managed, in the face of the storms of their era and its terrible dilemmas, to hold firm to their political positions and express values to which I refer still today in my reflections and actions. Like George Orwell, another of my intellectual references, they held their ground in the face of the three greatest crimes of the century: Western colonialism, Soviet Stalinism and German Nazism, not absolving any of these by any kind of philosophical justification on the basis of liberalism, nation or class. They steered clear of any compromise, even temporary; and in this way, they escaped the ideological traps into which so many others fell.

In our day, the traps are no longer the same, and we have to live through new conflicts without nostalgia for the battles of the past. However, inasmuch as we do not have a replacement moral arsenal at our disposal, we are forced to draw on moral elements from various earlier worldviews. I have in mind, above all, a critical approach based on a universal foundation, a premise that is nowadays increasingly rare. This same critique must be aware that any universalist representation is also the bearer of personal motivations, which should be brought to light with the greatest transparency.

The City and the Pen

But Paris is in actual fact all of France. The rest is just a great suburb of Paris . . . The whole of France is a desert, at least in intellectual terms. All that is distinguished in the provinces emigrates early on to the capital, the focus of all light and all brilliance.

Heinrich Heine, *On France*, 1833

Five years would be just about long enough after our first book for us to be shaking hands with all our confrères. Centralization has grouped us all in Paris . . . It is Paris to which writers from the provinces, if they are well-off, come to practise regionalism; it is Paris where the qualified representatives of North African literature have chosen to express their nostalgia for Algiers.

Jean-Paul Sartre, *What Is Literature?*, 1947

In France, the age of collective intervention by intellectuals began in the late nineteenth century, when the liberal–democratic space, with its national culture, had reached an advanced stage of establishment and expansion. Following the achievement of male suffrage in the 1870s, and the birth of compulsory education in the 1880s, an autonomous collective intellectual of a new kind slowly constituted itself, which accompanied political life for almost a century and gained a privileged status in the French cultural field.

In the eighteenth century, the monarchical state had not hesitated to imprison Denis Diderot, the architect of the *Encyclopédie*. Jean-Jacques Rousseau was prosecuted by the Paris *parlement*, and the Marquis de Sade, despite becoming a writer in prison, was not permitted any remission of his sentence. When Victor Hugo felt threatened, however, the state did not take up his challenge to arrest him, and he chose exile instead.

The status of the Parisian intellectual was further consolidated at the turn of the twentieth century. Émile Zola was indeed condemned to prison in 1898, but unlike Oscar Wilde, imprisoned only two years before in England, the French authorities refrained from arresting the writer and allowed him to take refuge abroad. And in 1960, when Jean-Paul Sartre publicly appealed to French soldiers to refuse to serve in Algeria, and many voices were raised to demand that the existentialist philosopher be prosecuted in accordance with the law, General de Gaulle, as is well known, replied, 'You do not imprison Voltaire.'

A more recent episode was quite strange, at least for someone not native to France and not knowing the rules of the French capital. On 16 November 1980, Louis Althusser strangled his wife on the premises of the École normale supérieure. According to the law, anyone having committed such a crime should immediately be arrested, even if they are considered mentally ill. In the latter case, they are to be examined by a psychiatrist from the prefecture of police, and only then sent to a psychiatric institution by police authority. This rule of law, however, which applies to every citizen of the republic, made an exception for the famous Marxist philosopher. All parties involved, including the justice minister, Alain Peyrefitte, himself a former student of the École normale supérieure, ignored the law, so that the philosopher was directly admitted to the Sainte-Anne hospital without spending even an hour under arrest.[1]

The particular relationship to intellectuals, and perhaps also the Cartesian legacy, would not allow the supposition that a philosopher of Althusser's status could have deliberately committed a murder; so he had to be automatically considered mentally unbalanced. Althusser spent nearly four years in hospital, and was then able to return home. Shortly before his death in 1990, he wrote an autobiography in which he complained at not having had the possibility of defending himself as a legal subject.[2]

French exception . . . or just Parisian?

The particular status of Parisian intellectuals is a phenomenon that has been repeatedly studied. In a society where the level of language itself amounts to an ideology, and cultural distinction still competes with social distinction, the 'producers of high culture' have always enjoyed eminent privileges.

We might say that in the French capital, intellectuals have inherited both the role of court jester, able always to say whatever was in their minds without being punished, and that of priest, serving as intermediary between the believer and divine truth. Nor has France ever forgotten that, since the great epoch of the Enlightenment, the prestige capital built up by men of letters made Paris for many years the cultural epicentre of the Western world. It could even be maintained that in Paris today, intellectuals have long been the last aristocrats. And if the monarchist tradition has been replaced by a popular thirst for authoritarian and paternalist presidents, a deep nostalgia for knights and musketeers, seemingly foreign to bourgeois values, has also contributed to the prestige of this modern 'nobility of mind',

---

1   Not long after leaving the École normale supérieure, Alain Peyrefitte had written a book about it: *Rue d'Ulm. Chroniques de la vie normalienne*, Paris: Fayard, 1946.

2   Louis Althusser, *The Future Lasts a Long Time*, London: Chatto, 1993.

who confront dangers and brandish their sharpened pens to defend truth and justice.

With due precaution, we might add that Paris is distinguished by the fact that it was there that intellectuals became conscious of themselves. If we borrow from Karl Marx the famous distinction between a 'class in itself', in other words an objective sociological fact, which human subjects are not necessarily aware of belonging to, and a 'class for itself', when subjects see themselves as forming part of a group and act in the context of this identity and according to its demands, we can conclude that it was in the French capital that intellectuals appeared for the first time as a 'class for itself'.

This does not mean that Parisian intellectuals ceased to speak in the name of others. Their status, like that of politicians, depends on their recognition by the rest of society as representatives of the general interest. Nor should we lose sight of the fact that France in the Age of Enlightenment was the place where men of letters created an agora in which a hegemonic discourse with a universal essence was developed. At the threshold of the twentieth century, intellectuals once again organized collectively in Paris to take back possession of a public arena already well configured and very widely recognized.

The status of the intellectual in a national culture is clearly dependent on the nature and dimensions that this grants the public sphere.[3] By 'public sphere', I have in mind the public field of debate, which in a liberal democracy is open despite its relations of dependence with the apparatuses of the state and/or big capital, enabling it to maintain various levels of autonomous dialogue in relation to these powers. Through the intermediary of the press, books, cultural institutions and other forms of communication, a public opinion is formed and intervenes in

---

3   I take this term from Jürgen Habermas, *The Structural Transformation of the Public Sphere: An Inquiry into a Category of Bourgeois Society*, Cambridge, MA: MIT, 1991, despite rejecting some of the 'ideal' meanings that he attributes to it.

decisions taken by governments. In France, this space has taken on specific characteristics, and continues to assume them.

Any attempt to decipher the role of intellectuals in France must start from the following postulate: the public sphere here is more homogeneous and more centralized than in any other liberal democracy, and the origin of this cultural and linguistic homogeneity lies in the long effect of absolute monarchy. The transition from administrative language to national language, in the seventeenth and eighteenth centuries, took the form of a slow centrifugal process from an urban centre to the provincial margins. Besides, if for the kings of France, as for other sovereigns, the language and culture of the majority of their subjects was of little importance, the accumulation of financial capital at the level of the supreme leadership of the kingdom was accompanied by a growing accumulation of symbolic cultural capital, powerfully channelled towards the capital city.

It is scarcely surprising, therefore, that the Great Revolution began with a revolt in Paris, before being transformed into the 'French Revolution'. Similarly, Paris played an unprecedented role, and one without equivalent, in the fashioning of national culture, which only really began to crystallize in the nineteenth century. True, this national construction from the centre towards the periphery is also found in other societies, but in France it was conducted continuously and in the same direction, in a far more significant and striking fashion; and this tendency has lasted a long time.

It is not only high politics that is decided in Paris, but also all the strategies, novelties and changes in the fields of cultural creation. By way of comparison, in Great Britain we find quite a high degree of centralization, but not equalling that of France. Oxford, Cambridge and even Edinburgh have maintained a power and effect in relation to London. In the United States, Germany or Italy, the morphology of the public sphere has a radically different shape: establishments of higher education, newspapers, reviews and periodicals, publishing houses and high cultural creation have always existed here in a far more dispersed and pluralist manner, whereas in France everything is essentially limited to Paris.

In the United States, an important book may be published in Boston, Los Angeles, Washington, DC, New York or Chicago; in Germany, it could appear in Berlin, Frankfurt, Hamburg or Heidelberg; in Italy this could be Rome, Milan, Turin or even Naples. In France, a major work can only be published in Paris, for the simple reason that prestigious publishing houses are located in the capital and nowhere else.

The intellectual currents that have stamped their mark on Western culture, such as symbolism, surrealism, existentialism or structuralism, were not born in France but in its capital. These artistic expressions and magnificent currents of thought, like many others, appeared in the Parisian press, in periodicals established in Paris and in books that were published there. Their impact was clearly widespread in all French cities, and even in other centres of culture across the world, but only after they had been elaborated and fashioned in a restricted geographical space. This abundance of original production has always maintained a metropolitan character.

As a result, to clarify the specificity of the intellectual in France, it is necessary to start by defining him or her as a *Parisian* intellectual. Young intellectuals, writers, essayists and professors have certainly emerged from the provinces, but they have soon been attracted by the magnetism of the capital, an obligatory move for access to the pinnacle of their power and intellectual maturity. If one of them had not been educated at a Parisian lycée, they would join some prestigious Paris institution at university level, the pinnacle being the École normale supérieure on the rue d'Ulm. The summit of republican pedagogic elitism has always been fundamentally Parisian. In the determining stage of the production of ideas, positions and sensitivities, the public sphere of the man or woman of letters is not genuinely French; it is the effervescent and dynamic zone of a great metropolis, or even just certain districts of this. Thus, the intellectual polemic around the trial of Alfred Dreyfus, far from having been a storm in a teacup, was essentially a squall in the Paris public arena rather than a series of events of national scale.[4]

French intellectuals have always quarrelled among themselves, banded together, reacted to one another and frequented the same salons, cafés and restaurants where their potion is distilled. Everything remains in the Parisian intellectual family – not only the symbolic capital, but also the disputes and hatreds, alliances and reciprocal homage. With a journalistic lightness of tone, Hervé Hamon and Patrick Rotman traced in the early 1980s a group portrait of this intellectual centralism that is precise, well targeted, and somewhat provocative.[5] Paris has always known talented intellectuals, some brilliant, original and very prolific, others more superficial, their sole advantage being excellence in their mastery of language. It has not always been easy to distinguish between these, particularly on account of the all-powerful rhetoric that echoes speedily throughout the national territory and even beyond its borders.

A basic sociological fact has to be noted. Across the rest of France the intelligentsia has almost always lived and acted as a receptacle of the ideological products and cultural symbols received from Paris, which it has gone on to diffuse to wider

---

4   There were of course provincials among those who signed petitions, especially professors and students, but the lines of cleavage between the hostile camps, and the struggles of ideas, were established by the Paris nerve centres. On the subject of the provincial petitioners, see in particular Christophe Charle, *Birth of the Intellectuals: 1880–1900*, Cambridge: Polity, 2015, pp. 152ff. It should also be spelled out that the wave of popular Judeophobia at this time was not just a Parisian phenomenon but affected the whole of the country.

5   Hervé Hamon and Patrick Rotman, *Les Intellocrates. Expédition en haute intelligentsia*, Brussels: Complexe, 1981. The negative reactions of the Parisian press and, a contrario, the favourable reception in provincial media, well reflected this geocultural syndrome.

strata. As distinct from political figures, the Left Bank intellectuals have not had to share their absolute power with any other intellectual centre in France. Their hegemony has not been threatened from another source. They were not content with planting themselves on the highest summit; they were the mountain in the middle of a plain.[6]

It has been an irony of fate that the writings of Parisian scholars devoted to intellectuals, their status, and their relationship to politics and government have in most cases ignored this geocultural aspect, or made only a very marginal reference to it. When you live in a bubble, it is hard to see the world outside. They have generally seen themselves as the intellectuals of France as a whole, rather than a group of agents specially selected, at the heart of a ruling capital. It was quite natural that they should identify Paris with France. There has been no specific sociology of Parisian intellectuals, let alone a comparative history with other intellectual centres across the world.

The ability to understand the specific character of intellectuals in France, and the dynamic of the relationships that animate them, depends above all on perceiving their urban concentration and their manner of lasting domination of public opinion in the whole of the country. Concentration is a synonym of strength, density creates quality, while physical proximity to power (a section of politicians were also their former students) has engendered self-confidence and self-importance. With time, however, this contributed to the decline of the Parisian writing 'star', a decline still more rapid than that of their counterparts in other Western countries. When a bubble bursts, it deflates very quickly. All that is left for those in the bubble is to grumble about the difficulties of modernization, to investigate the problems of their

---

6   The fact that there have been in the past writers such as Jean Giono, sociologists such as Jacques Ellul or, in our own time, singular philosophers such as Jean-Claude Michéa who have insisted on living away from Paris, in no way changes the fact that there has never been an intellectual centre that competed with the capital.

wronged identity, or else the constant threat of communist or Islamic totalitarianism to their freedom of creation and the 'French way of life'.

Intellectuals and intelligentsia

Intellectuals are not of course an exclusive feature of the French capital. To judge from the many works and studies whose title includes the term 'intellectual', one may readily conclude that in the twentieth century intellectuals were present in almost all public forums, or alongside every apparatus of power in the modern nation-states. In fact, works of history, sociology, and even philology of the intellectuals have been published for many years in a number of languages, and occupy several shelves in university libraries. We know far more today on the status of intellectuals, not only in the Western world or the communist world of yesterday, but also their social and cultural position in the countries of Africa and Asia.[7]

It might be useful to open debate on the problematic of the intellectual with the preliminary question – why 'intellectuals'? Why not simply the better defined professional categories, such as writers, philosophers, poets, historians or artists? Why does the French language, and other languages in its wake, have the need for a common denominator for all the 'accredited' producers of knowledge and culture, despite their means of expression being so different?

The response is broadly contained in the central concept that I have used to formulate this question. There has always been a certain common foundation for the producers of symbolic goods, differentiating them both from producers of material goods and from the holders of political power. These differences, and the specific characteristics of the learned strata,

---

7   See Christophe Charle, *Les Intellectuels en Europe au XIXᵉ siècle. Essai d'histoire comparée*, Paris: Seuil, 1996.

became still more marked in the nineteenth century with the developing division of labour. This meant that linguistic cultures had need for new inclusive denominations, which appeared at different times.

As I shall show in the first chapter of this book, the concept of the 'intellectual' only entered current usage in the late nineteenth century. It had certainly been used already for a long time as an adjective, and was used just once as a noun by both Claude Henri de Saint-Simon and Ernest Renan. But a period of latency was needed for it to become a usable term, generally employed. The concept was popularized in the context of the events that followed the military trial of Alfred Dreyfus, and the widening of this usage was a direct effect of the ensuing political and legal battles. It is important to emphasize that the term 'intellectual' did not initially appear as a neutral professional category, but rather as an ideological expression par excellence. Certain of those who first used it did so in the form of an insult, while others began on the contrary to give it a positive and sympathetic connotation. In actual fact, this ambivalence has lasted until our own day, and the use of the term remains contested and problematic. It is hard to find 'scientific' distancing in the field of research devoted to 'intellectuals'. The majority of those who write on the subject either view themselves as intellectuals or, on the contrary, explicitly reject belonging to such a category and vigorously resist the idea that the term might be applied to them.

To characterize and define the expression 'the intellectuals' is not an easy matter. Its usage has always been multiform, to the point that any attempt to arrive at an unambiguous definition that would integrate all the meanings affixed to the word over a century strikes me as bound to fail. Each national culture has added new variations to it, and historical circumstances have brought a continuous evolution. In some times and places the term is replaced by synonyms. Thus the somewhat older word 'intelligentsia' successfully competes with it in various languages, while in Germany there is the notion of *Geistmenschen*.[8]

In any case, I believe it is by writing its history, and examining the various uses the term has found, that we obtain the best definition of the 'intellectual' and are best able to understand its multiple facets. The major part of the analyses contained in this book will deal with interpretations inherent to the concept of the 'intellectual', in parallel with presenting the different images that have been imposed on it. This is in no way a guarantee to the reader that he or she will have acquired at the end of this exercise a less ambiguous notion than they already had beforehand. The importance I attach to a clear and precise conceptual apparatus does not necessarily make me a zoologist, and the attribution of labels and classification of genera is not my main object of interest.

We can however start by pointing out a double usage that generates confusion and misunderstanding. On certain occasions, the term 'intellectual' serves to denote those scholars who, after gaining notoriety chiefly in the humanities but outside of their particular professional field, address the broad public or the government with a political and moral proclamation. Several historians have adopted this usage, which has likewise been popularized in the media, and it is why those scholars who view themselves as 'pure' scientists in no way recognize themselves in this definition.

In other cases, particularly among sociologists, the concept is applied to all those groups whose profession it is to produce or diffuse works of culture. From the tribal sorcerer, through the prophet or priest, down to modern philosophers, writers, and

---

8   On the German use of the term and the status of *Geistmenschen*, see Dietz Bering, *Die Intellektuellen. Geschichte eines Schimpfwortes*, Stuttgart: Klett-Cotta, 1978; Jürgen Habermas, 'Heinrich Heine und die Rolle des Intellektuellen in Deutschland', in *Eine Art Schadensabwicklung. Kleine politische Schriften VI*, Frankfurt: Suhrkamp, 1987, pp. 25–54. See also the excellent article by Hans Manfred Bock, 'Histoire et historiographie des intellectuels en Allemagne', in Michel Trebitsch and Marie-Christine Granjon (eds), *Pour une histoire comparée des intellectuels*, Brussels: Complexe, 1998, pp. 79–109.

the last of today's journalists and professors, this criterion lumps together the ensemble of 'mental workers' in a single specific social stratum which, in the human division of labour, is regularly engaged in organizing and diffusing a knowledge capital or in examining moral norms. Despite sometimes arousing reservations, and not really being accepted by the wider public, this latter approach is no less legitimate than that which sticks to a narrow use of the term. Which is why, even if most of the debates discussed in this book turn around the 'intellectual' as producer of 'high culture', who intervenes in the public arena to defend politically explicit positions, I have been led here and there to expand the concept to the educated class as a whole. The 'weight' of politics is widely expressed in almost all cultural creation and diffusion, even among people persuaded that it does not pertain to their field.

I have sometimes used the term 'intelligentsia' as an alternative to 'intellectuals'; the varying use of these terms is a subject in itself, and has already given rise to a copious literature. To make an absolute distinction between them seems to me today artificial and problematic. In general, I have always preferred to reserve 'intelligentsia' for the wider strata of diffusers and duplicators of culture, and keep 'intellectuals' for the producers of the 'deep symbols' that formalize public language. However, I have not always been strictly coherent in this distinction, which remains dependent on the historical context in which a particular debate is inscribed.

In fact, the dividing line between 'high' intellectuals and 'low' intelligentsia is elastic and mobile, and the internal hierarchy of the various categories of producers of culture has always been an object of confrontation and negotiation. The balance of forces between different groups is constantly evolving, as is the level of prestige within each of them, giving rise to new images and previously unknown scales of evaluation. For example, many non-Western societies view those who have completed secondary education as forming part of the intelligentsia, and, until the last third of the twentieth century, university graduates almost every-where saw themselves as 'naturally' forming part of the cultural elite. The rapid democratization of higher education over the last few decades, however, has deeply modified the marks of cultural distinction, with the result of blurring the boundaries of member-ship of those groups viewed as embodying an elite.

Having been a professor of history for many years at the University of Tel Aviv, I know from experience how in our day the devaluing of the status of the traditional human and social 'sciences', in the intensified division of labour, can increase and intensify internal struggles. The residues of a declining symbolic capital in subjects such as philosophy, history, sociology or litera-ture are at stake in tough confrontations, which sometimes end in disillusion and frustration. It seems that there is no longer sufficient prestige capital to be calmly shared, as in the early twentieth century; nor is the situation any better on the side of writers and poets. It is said that, when he was asked why he was leaving the university to become secretary of state, Henry Kissinger replied that he had had enough of politics. The grain of truth in this joke relates to the academic milieu, rather than the personal ambitions of the honourable professor. To become the foreign-policy architect of the leading world power was far more attractive than teaching international relations to a new genera-tion of students. It is in no way surprising that a good number of university intellectuals have regularly turned towards the spheres of politics or the media, with the aim of accumulating a new prestige capital.

The American sociologist Lewis S. Feuer has suggested an excellent way of defining the difference between intellectuals and politicians. The former wield influence, the latter wield power.[9] If we leave aside the direct forms of power that, for example,

9 Lewis S. Feuer, 'What Is an Intellectual?', in Aleksander Gella (ed.), *The Intelligentsia and the Intellectuals: Theory, Method and Case Study*, Beverly Hills: Sage, 1976, pp. 47–58.

teachers wield over their students (by assessments), newspaper editors over journalists (by setting salaries) or publishers over writers (by the very fact of publication), it would appear that intellectuals act mainly in the world of symbols, and not directly in the system of social relations. For the most part, as distinct from those with political responsibility, they do not exercise any power over people. They do not fix the level of taxes, they do not vote on laws or decide on foreign policy. Contrary to bosses in the world of production and exchange, they do not give other people any immediate directive to be carried out. What they produce above all are knowledge, symbols and particular brands of images and values. Some of them elaborate, modify and diffuse these, for which they receive their reward from various cultural establishments and institutions.

Their impact on the consciousness of their fellows, or among wider circles of the public, is what essentially determines their status. It follows that their power derives principally from the symbolic capital they have managed to accumulate. This capital is clearly not a 'thing' but a social relation, and in this respect it resembles financial capital. We might say that to a certain degree the patterns of thought of the consumers of intellectual production are banks in which this important capital accumulates. Its symbolic power can be measured by academic qualifications, the awarding of prizes, the number of references and citations, the volume of publications, and many other practices current in the stock exchange of esteem and fame.

The level of prestige or, in other words, the potential for 'influence' of these intellectuals is what makes for their margin of autonomy in relation to the institutional or economic powers. Their degree of dependence or independence vis-à-vis the powers of the cultural field, or other powers such as politics or big capital which, though located outside the cultural field, are nevertheless always a part of it, is a function of the level of charismatic authority they have managed to establish. The advent and expansion of national democracies over the last 150 years has placed new functions on the shoulders of all learned strata, on top of the accumulation of knowledge and the various services they already rendered to the state: the invention, fashioning and transmission of national memory and culture, and in tandem with this, the manufacture of a stable democratic ideological consensus around the central institutions of power. The nation-state and the democratic principle could not have functioned or become a reality without the active mediation of accredited cultural agents, and this is one of the sources of their importance in the process of political modernization.

This importance, however, was not enough to establish the autonomy of the cultural field vis-à-vis the apparatuses of the nation-state. The relative autonomy of the intellectual only managed to develop in the liberal democracies where a plurality of institutional, political and economic powers was maintained, and where the state did not succeed in totally absorbing civil society. It is good to remember that, in 'totalitarian democracies' (to use the old and pertinent expression of Bertrand de Jouvenel and Jacob Talmon[10]), the ruling bureaucracy has needed an educated class who not only organize and institutionalize knowledge but also produce the hegemonic national consciousness and ideologies, while at the same time assuring their defence.

The existence of state socialism in the twentieth century, in its various forms, was made possible by the foundation of a national culture and an ideological consensus no less structured than those which accompanied the development of liberal democracies. In the 'popular democracies', and other authoritarian democracies in the Third World, the learned provided their cultural goods while being happy to enjoy socio-economic privileges; the struggle for a wider autonomy of their specific cultural field scarcely led to significant results. The lack of stable traditions that could provide

---

10   See Bertrand de Jouvenel, *Du pouvoir. Histoire naturelle de sa croissance*, Geneva: Éditions du Cheval Ailé, 1947, pp. 313–42, and Jacob Talmon, *The Rise of Totalitarian Democracy*, Boston: Beacon Press, 1952.

political conflict with legitimacy, and the absolute economic dependence of the learned on the apparatus of the nation-state, rather than that of the market, almost demolished any possibility of collective intellectual struggles to win an independent presence and acquire more influence.

In the liberal democracies, on the other hand, relative autonomy became a marker of intellectual activity. The pluralism that enabled the masses to replace the ruling political elites, from time to time and to a certain extent, made these broadly dependent on a public sphere that was open to debate. It is in this space, which particularly includes the press, periodicals, literature, higher education establishments, the audio-visual media and social media networks, that a substantial part of political opinion is elaborated, a fact that obliges the ruling political personnel to have at their disposal a docile intelligentsia, and also to collect spontaneous favours from the cultural elites. The intervention of intellectuals in the public arena expresses a relative freedom of action that generates this autonomy, an object of pride for all intellectuals in the liberal world. It is on the basis of this relative autonomy that the image of the critical intellectual was constructed.

The majority of intellectuals are perceived in public opinion as figures prepared to challenge, independent of and outside a state that they do not hesitate to oppose. The prestige capital acquired in the West by such individuals as Émile Zola, Romain Rolland, Jean-Paul Sartre, Bertrand Russell, George Orwell or Noam Chomsky has created the impression that talented literati have always fought against injustice and arbitrary rule. Knowing the major role that scholars play in the formalization of the collective imaginary, the reputation of the critical intellectual became widespread. The ancient world was also enlisted in support of this view: Socrates of Athens, the Hebrew prophets and the first Christian missionaries of the Mediterranean civilization appeared to many as distant ancestors of the contemporary intellectual. Did these Biblical figures and ancient Greeks not challenge the despots of their day? Did they not risk their lives to defend truth and justice? Any original creator who enriched our culture by their great works had also to appear as a figure who preached amending the ways of exercising power and reducing arbitrariness. Ethics and aesthetics were intertwined, and the social group that produces 'beauty' and 'wisdom' for our culture was naturally perceived as its enlightened and moral section.

Jean-Paul Sartre is seen as the most emblematic and famous critical intellectual of the twentieth century. His creative work spread across a number of fields, as philosopher, playwright, novelist, essayist and editor of a prestigious periodical. This authentic Renaissance man sold more books of philosophy than any other philosopher, and his plays also attracted a wide public. Perhaps he was not as great a philosopher as he was said to be in his day, and his plays often suffer from excessively abstract verbiage, but his economic independence and high level of autonomy (was it a coincidence that, like Émile Zola and André Gide before him, he was never a professional academic?) enabled him to take up bold critical positions that powerfully reinforced and magnified his celebrity. His attacks on the misdeeds of French colonialism conferred on him the aura of a modern 'prophet', which aroused a great deal of jealousy. He was perhaps the only intellectual who could allow himself to refuse the Nobel Prize for Literature (Boris Pasternak did too, but against his will).

Thomas Mann was not only one of the most important and famous writers of his century; he regularly expressed his opinion on the political course of the world. If during the First World War the future author of *The Magic Mountain* proclaimed himself a German patriot, proud and conservative, he preferred exile when the Nazis came to power, and only returned to his homeland after the fall of the Third Reich. His publications against Hitler's Germany made him a symbol of anti-totalitarian *Aufklärung*, and cast a beam of dignity on the German intellectual tradition. Goethe had clearly found an authentic twentieth-century heir.

Bertrand Russell was perhaps the most brilliant intellectual in the British cultural world. A philosopher who came from an aristocratic milieu, and whose early writings brought him great fame when still a young man, he soon turned to social problems and did not stint at sharp criticism of the ruling classes. During the First World War, he left the comfortable ivory tower of the university and courageously adopted a minority point of view that led to his imprisonment. In the 1960s he still marched at the head of demonstrations to demand the banning of nuclear weapons, surrounded by many who could have been his grandchildren – if not great-grandchildren.

We could continue to list these 'great names' who brought glory to the history of relations between intellectuals and power in the modern era, names that, in the age of nations, conferred the aura of cultural producer while showing that men of reason and intellect have laboured to limit the power of the nation-state by the counterweight of higher moral norms. The halo of romanticism that undoubtedly surrounds the intellectual professions was maintained by the bearers of 'high' culture by way of hundreds of publications and works of research. And yet, a detailed examination of the history of relations between intellectuals and the authorities, as well as a study of the balance of forces within the various intellectual fields, reveals a picture of the modern man of letters that is not always flattering.

Between morality and power

It is worth noting right away that the 'great names' mentioned above enjoyed a process of idealization which left a certain number of their actions in the shadows.

Jean-Paul Sartre, for example, while valiantly battling against the moral corruption that was inherent to colonial oppression, was also one of the main intellectuals to have sought for several years to defend the criminal practices of the USSR. The great German liberal writer Thomas Mann, who left to settle in

Switzerland as soon as Hitler came to power, was prepared to return to his beloved homeland despite the establishment of the Nazi regime. He feared that his publications might be banned, and was also concerned for his substantial wealth if he did not return to Germany. He finally gave in to the strong pressure of his pacifist daughter Erika and his radical son Klaus, who spurred him to give up this idea. Reluctantly he remained in exile. Bertrand Russell, one of the great pacifists of the century, seemed to suggest in 1948 that a threat of a preemptive nuclear strike might be justified to block the expansion of communism. He wrote letters stating that it was morally justified and better to go to war against the USSR using atomic bombs while the USA possessed them and before the USSR did.[11]

It was not at all certain that if these or other intellectuals had been in charge of twentieth-century politics, it would have been conducted in a significantly more responsible or rational manner. Jacques Prévert was perhaps not completely wrong when he wrote in 1946, 'Intellectuals should not be allowed to play with matches.'

We should also take care not to view critical or dissident literary figures as typical representatives of intellectual elites as a whole. Since the start of the nineteenth century, the majority of scholars in the liberal West – professors of philosophy and history, writers, poets, essayists, journalists, etc. – lent their support to colonial conquests and took pride in the territorial gains made by the states to which they belonged. It is well known, for example, how the cream of English university graduates enthusiastically enlisted in the service of the empire, seeing this as an important and obligatory first step on a career. When the anti-colonial wave broke in the wake of the Second World War, and was met by

---

11   For example, in May 1948 he wrote to Walter Marseille, 'Communism must be wiped out . . . I don't think the Russians will yield without war'. See Ray Perkins, 'Bertrand Russell and Preventive War', in Alan Schwerin (ed.), *Bertrand Russell on Nuclear War, Peace, and Language: Critical Historical Essays*, Westport: Praeger, 2002, p. 6.

bloody warfare designed to stem the tide, only a small minority of the intellectual world took a clear stand against the long repression conducted by the West against the Third World.

The famous images of the May 1933 book-burnings in the streets of Berlin remained engraved in the memories of many throughout the twentieth century. The visual message was strong and clear: totalitarianism against the book, the barbarism of an excited and ignorant crowd against intellect and culture. It was easy to lose sight of who actually were the book-burners and enthusiastic spectators around the bonfires. They were not uneducated illiterates from the poor quarters of Berlin, nor down-trodden workers solely preoccupied with ensuring the subsistence of their families in a period of harsh economic crisis. These gleeful incendiaries were students, whose main occupation was to study and read other books. What they particularly set out to do was purge their libraries of works that they deemed to be insufficiently 'German'; it was in the universities that the fires were lit. Several professors took part in the proceedings, or at least watched them, while university rectors spoke with strong emotion. Before Nazism gained its first impressive successes among the citizenry of Weimar Germany, it had won the elections of the student associations, whose members all belonged to the middle and upper classes.

A good number of German intellectuals chose exile in the 1930s, but the great majority of scholars remained where they were and continued to faithfully serve the Thousand-Year Reich and its eternal racial nation. Careful examination of the list of German exiles shows that the majority of these were of Jewish origin, or else had expressed pacifist or radical-left views; in other words, they were declared enemies of Nazism. Thomas Mann, considered a pure 'Aryan' and far from a man of the left or a pacifist, was thus not a 'natural' representative of liberal or conservative intellectuals, which is the impression often given by history books written for the 'general reader'. Despite the anti-intellectual image commonly associated with Nazism, it is worth remembering that many eminent scholars – such as Werner Sombart, Ernst Jünger, Carl Schmitt, Gerhart Hauptmann and Gottfried Benn – supported their powerful nation-state, and indeed adjusted very well to the Hitler regime. Even the writer Erich Kästner and the pacifist film director Georg Wilhelm Pabst, despite their critical views of Nazism, preferred to remain in Germany and compromise with the 'new order'.

Hundreds of philosophy professors whether Nietzschean or neo-Kantian, teachers of history and archaeology whether idealist or positivist, physicists and biologists, continued to publish and teach without a problem. Some of them even became enthusiastic Nazis.[12] Martin Heidegger, the preeminent philosopher of the Weimar period, whom a growing consensus today tends to view as the most important philosopher of the twentieth century, was appointed rector of Freiburg University in 1933. He joined the Nazi Party at this point, and remained a member until the end of the war.[13]

Just as the majority of British and French intellectuals were not anti-colonialist, so the majority of educated Germans were not anti-Nazi, and indeed a wide stratum of the 'enlightened' Western intelligentsia showed no opposition to totalitarianism. The blindness of many literary figures in relation to the USSR, and what took place there in the 1930s and early 1950s, is glaring today, and has been documented in many publications.[14] The

12   On the question of scientists, see Benno Müller-Hill, *Murderous Science: Elimination by Scientific Selection of Jews, Gypsies, and Others in Germany, 1933–1945*, New York: Cold Spring Arbor Laboratory Press, 1997.

13   See Victor Farias, *Heidegger and Nazism*, Philadelphia: Temple University Press, 1991; Hans Sluga, *Heidegger's Crisis: Philosophy and Politics in Nazi Germany*, Cambridge, MA: Harvard University Press, 1994; and Trawny Peter, *Heidegger et l'antisémitisme. Sur les 'Cahiers noirs'*, Paris: Seuil, 2014.

14   See the pioneering works of David Caute, *Communism and the French Intellectuals 1914–1960*, London: Deutsch, 1964, and *Fellow-Travellers: A Postscript to the Enlightenment*, London: Weidenfeld & Nicolson, 1973; and Jeanne Verdès-Leroux, *Au service du Parti. Le Parti communiste, les intellectuels et la culture (1944–1956)*, Paris: Fayard/Minuit, 1983, and *Le Réveil des somnambules. Le parti communiste, les intellectuels et la culture (1956–1985)*, Paris: Fayard/Minuit, 1987.

fact that the Stalinist regime appealed to humanist progressive principles brought it widespread sympathy in intellectual milieus. Seen from afar, revolutionary politics was perceived as the logical application of a coherent and perfect theory. The abstract ideas of communism, associated with the universal values of equality and fraternity between peoples, were seductive to intellectuals, including a number who never became communists themselves. George Bernard Shaw, as well as Beatrice and Sidney Webb, expressed their admiration for Stalin's five-year plans. Berthold Brecht, Pablo Neruda and Louis Aragon saw Stalin as the 'sun of the people' and Soviet communism as the realization of human rationalism.

Even in the USSR, the majority of the intellectual elite supported the repressive regime. The physicist Andrei Sakharov and the writer Alexander Solzhenitsyn were not typical representatives of intellectual *Homo sovieticus*. Hundreds of professors in the humanities and social sciences, along with journalists, writers, filmmakers and other cultural producers, showed themselves faithful supporters of the totalitarian dictatorship. This support for a revolution that had devoured its children and massacred millions of peasants was not limited to those of average education: from Vladimir Mayakovsky to Nikita Mikhailov, from Sergei Eisenstein and Maxim Gorky to Ilya Ehrenburg, the elite of Soviet literati and artists offered their talents to the greatest nation-state apparatus of the twentieth century, and sought to adapt their cultural creativity to the taste of the all-powerful rulers.[15]

The situation was no different in the 'people's democracies'. Apart from recurrent confrontations between the state and a few

---

15   In 1931, just when a deadly collectivization was in full swing, Gorky published a polemic against those Western intellectuals who dared to protest against what was happening in his country. In particular, he wrote: 'Never have intellectuals shown their weakness so clearly, and their indifference to life so shamelessly, as in the twentieth century, so full of tragedies created throughout the world by the cynicism of the ruling classes' (Maxim Gorky, 'Réponse à un Intellectuel', available at Marxiste.fr). The humanist writer clearly did not think of including himself in the category of intellectuals having shown this 'indifference to life'.

isolated creative figures, the struggle to liberalize political culture and the autonomy of the intellectual field remained relatively marginal in relation to cultural production as a whole. Revolts and protests may well be imprinted in social memory, but the number of dissidents was actually quite negligible. We should recall that in the 1960s, the period when the totalitarian tendency of communist power in China was at its height, it was the intellectual youth from universities and high schools who acted as the spearhead in imposing a form of terror over the whole population. The great Cultural Revolution that shook China and caused large-scale massacres was a political project with little cultural about it, applied in the main by a new generation of young intelligentsia.

In the West, it was precisely during the most totalitarian years in China that intellectual youth expressed sympathy for Maoism and the Red Guards. In Paris in particular, the pro-Stalin fashion of 1945–56 gave way to the Maoist one that attracted thousands of students. And it was the École normale supérieure that most frenetically expressed the aspiration to repeat on the banks of the Seine the totalitarian actions of the Cultural Revolution: the most rigid activists, who distributed the most ridiculous Maoist pamphlets, were recruited from the prestigious elite institution of the rue d'Ulm. Philippe Sollers, soon to be an up-and-coming writer, Julia Kristeva, an original researcher, and Serge July, future editor of the newspaper *Libération*, mouthed the language of revolutionary contradiction, idolizing the father of the Chinese Revolution and crying their contempt for 'reformist traitors'. Those who would later call themselves the 'new philosophers', and many others who took up their ideas and popularized them, came from precisely this Maoism then in vogue. Intellectuals such as André Glucksmann, Benny Lévy, Bernard-Henri Lévy, Jean-Claude Milner, Blandine Kriegel, Alain Finkielkraut, Pascal Bruckner and many others changed their ideological banner in the course of time. They were 'revolutionaries', warm admirers and champions of a totalitarian regime, when Maoism seemed in the process of imposing itself on a large part of the world. When its star declined, and with the advent of neo-conservatism, they abandoned this 'revolution' to become sycophants of the 'anti-totalitarian' bourgeois order, while maintaining the same intolerance and self-satisfaction.[16]

It is a constant surprise that such major French intellectuals as Jean-Paul Sartre, Simone de Beauvoir, Michel Foucault or Jean-Luc Godard, who had supported the protests of the rebel generation of the late 1960s, were able to fix their choice precisely on the current with the most totalitarian tendency (Foucault was still able to rally to the final totalitarian squall of the century, the Islamic Revolution in Iran).[17] Why did these thinkers, and others with them, not prefer the less authoritarian and more rational currents of political revolt? Why did they bring themselves to sympathize with movements that organized a cult, and whose affinities with a distant dictatorship and its oppressive practices were visible to the naked eye?

One of the answers to these questions may perhaps be found in the observation of the complex relationships that exist between intellectuals and power. The widespread image of the reticence of intellectuals towards state power and its arbitrary side seems simplistic and unsatisfactory. The world of symbols is the central object of the activity of intellectual elites, which frequently arouses tensions or frustrations towards the castes that hold power and are perceived as major decision-makers of the fate of the real world. The aspiration to free themselves from dependence on power and expand their autonomy has also played a notable part in the ambivalent relationship between the world of the intellect and that of political decisions.

---

16   On this tendency, it is useful to refer to the interview with Gilles Deleuze in the supplement to no. 24 of the bi-monthly *Minuit*, May 1977, and to François Cusset, *La Décennie. Le grand cauchemar des années 1980*, Paris: La Découverte, 2006.

17   See Michael Scott Christofferson, *French Intellectuals Against the Left: The Antitotalitarian Moment of the 1970s*, New York: Berghahn Books, 2004.

The desire to share power has always been a fairly widespread mental component. The Platonic image of the philosopher-king has haunted the dreams of a good number of writers. When intellectuals are offered the opportunity to cross the lines, they are found not only as counsellors to the prince, but also as political figures to whom the taste and habits of power are not foreign, particularly outside of the West. True, the will to power may always be interpreted as a sincere aspiration to reform and improve the world, and it would be wrong to reject such an explanation out of hand. Yet it is still pertinent to judge intellectuals in terms of concepts that combine their desire for power and their aspiration to participate in it. We may thus suppose that the fundamental contradiction and gap in values that appeared between the sovereign and the philosopher in the twentieth century had the effect of leading the latter's dreams to drift towards substitute powers located in other places. The strong attraction to the dictatorships of Stalin, Mao or Castro was able, to a certain extent, to serve as substitute for a banal local impotence.

Any attentive observer of the political and moral attitudes of intellectuals in the twentieth century will note that only a few of them have been able to preserve a clear and balanced judgement on the situations of distress that attend their age. This sad reality, however, should not lead to a misjudgement that would attribute to intellectuals a greater share of blame in the century's tragedies than to other mortals.

Given their eminent and hegemonic place in the process of examining norms, it should be a requirement that producers of 'high culture' rise above their fellow citizens. They are in fact the people whose written expression creates the compass needle that will aid future generations in forging their moral judgements, and they are also deemed to know more than others, given that a section of them earn their living by producing 'truth'. Nevertheless, if we leave aside the romantic conception that would see the man or woman of letters as an idealist in search of public good, it becomes possible to grasp the problematic of the intellectual in a fashion both less normative and less demanding.

Intellectuals, and the educated stratum as a whole, are no less moral than other humans, but neither should they be expected to be any better. Just as there has never been a causal link between cultural refinement and moral behaviour, so it is useless to seek a simple and direct relationship between the privileged status of the intellectual in society and their political 'turpitudes'. Many intellectuals supported the Nazis; others – mainly those on the left and certain religious figures – opposed them at the risk of their lives. Students certainly formed the vanguard of the Nazi breakthrough, but the White Rose group that formed against Nazism in splendid isolation was also made up of young students. Many university and high school students took part in the Chinese Cultural Revolution of the 1960s, but it was also students who ten years later marched on Tiananmen Square and defied the tanks sent to repress their new demands for freedom and political pluralism.

In the Western metropolises, the groups who protested against colonial conquests were not made up of trade unionists or socialist workers; they were most often minorities from intellectual milieus.[18] In the United States, it was not truck drivers, waiters or shopkeepers who went to demonstrate against the war in Vietnam, but writers and the student youth. The voices raised against nationalist wars, dictatorships and racism came almost always from the intelligentsia and rarely from political mass movements. Many intellectuals also paid with their lives in the harsh battles for freedom or social justice.

A certain incisive anti-intellectualism has again made itself felt, seeking only to expose the 'treason' of the intellectuals, their weaknesses and mistakes – in large part as a reaction to the

---

18   Except the Confédération générale du travail (CGT) in France, which was active against the war in Indochina in the early 1950s.

romantic adoration and idealization that formerly attached to their status. In fact, a global critique that presented intellectuals as either enemies of tradition or hostile to progress arose along with the very appearance of the term, and would last until the end of the twentieth century. In 1906, Charles Péguy began to sharpen his critique of the 'party of intellectuals', aimed among others at the entire university professoriat.[19] Biting condemnations of intellectuals were countless throughout the century, from Édouard Berth, a follower of Georges Sorel and author in 1914 of a virulent pamphlet *Les Méfaits des intellectuels*,[20] through to Noam Chomsky, who characterized the educated classes in 1986 as 'the most indoctrinated, most ignorant, most stupid part of the population'. 'There are very good reasons for that,' he added.[21]

Over the years, many politicians have certainly expressed contempt for literati, but the heart of the critique of the producers of 'high culture' has come from typical intellectuals themselves. Why did these individuals suddenly decide to condemn their peers and cease to see them as legitimate colleagues? Contrary to a widespread idea, this kind of attitude does not come from self-hatred. The majority of intellectuals have nothing against the image that the mirror shows them, and self-criticism is rarely found in their own writings. If we leave aside writers' jealousies, anti-intellectualism is most commonly fuelled by ideological disagreement. Opposition to the value judgements contained in a political position is a stimulus to discrediting the professional status of competitors, and thus to challenging the totality of the functions of the intellectual in society. However, critical discourse on intellectuals sometimes also develops for

---

19   See Simone Fraisse, 'Péguy et la Sorbonne', *Revue d'histoire littéraire de la France*, vol. 3, 1970, pp. 416–34.

20   Édouard Berth, *Les Méfaits des intellectuels*, Paris: Marcel Rivière, 1914.

21   Speech given in Nicaragua in 1986, quoted in Bruce Robbins (ed.), *Intellectuals: Aesthetics, Politics, Academics*, Minneapolis: University of Minnesota Press, 1990, p. 101.

other reasons, and in complex circumstances, as the first chapter of this book will seek to clarify by close examination of the French intellectual field over a long period.

In the second chapter of this book I shall seek to present certain forms of discourse characteristic of leading intellectuals, chiefly in Paris, from Voltaire in the eighteenth century to Pierre Bourdieu in the twentieth. These forms can in fact help us to better understand the origins of the development of anti-intellectualism. The third chapter, which describes the relationships of various Marxists to intellectuals, also includes an analysis of certain characteristic anti-intellectual approaches. There is always an evident tension in Marxism between, on the one hand, theories that see the organized working class as a universal subject, by which revolutionary change will be accomplished, and, on the other hand, a reality that confers on intellectuals an almost total hegemony over the formation of the political and historical consciousness of the masses. We shall see that certain Marxists actually tried to legitimize this hegemony.

Public intellectuals

Given that these two chapters deal mainly with types of discourse that have taken shape in the European continent, and above all in Paris, it seemed desirable to tackle in this introduction, at least with some general reflections, the critical debate concerning intellectuals in the English-speaking world (to which I shall return briefly in the fifth chapter). Discourse on intellectuals in the British and American public sphere developed later than in France or Italy, but its importance has steadily grown, to the point that the 'intellectual' seems by the end of the twentieth century to have emigrated to those national cultures that refused in the past to recognize the existence of such. Beyond the significant difference in the relationship towards scholars between Britain and the United States, these two societies have in common a long anti-intellectual tradition. Richard Hofstadter has written a fundamental and exhaustive work on anti-intellectualism in American society, to which there is scarcely anything to be added. He tackles here the question of the populist tradition in American culture, which glorifies immediate success, vis-à-vis the ineffectiveness of the 'eggheads'.[22] Little, however, has been published on British anti-intellectualism.[23]

Comparison between the status of 'public intellectuals' in Britain and France, to take up the terminology used by Stefan Collini, shows the many advantages that the French enjoy, and Parisians in particular.[24] As shown by the British historian Denis William Brogan at the end of a study on France: 'We British don't take our intellectuals so seriously.'[25]

Ever since the Dreyfus affair, British literati have viewed with mistrust the term 'intellectual', imported from the French, and tended to use it ironically, even as an insult. We should however remember that in the second half of the nineteenth century, the great liberal thinker John Stuart Mill, seeking to encourage the development of democracy in his country, proposed granting a double vote to educated citizens.[26] The idea did not remain a dead letter, as until 1950 graduates of certain English universities had the privilege of electing additional members of parliament.

The British Isles certainly did not lack critical intellectuals who castigated the governments of the day and challenged the foundations of the established order. From George Bernard Shaw, H. G. Wells and the Bloomsbury Group in the early part of the

---

22   Richard Hofstadter, *Anti-Intellectualism in American Life*, New York: Vintage, 1963.

23   See for example Jeremy Jennings, 'L'anti-intellectualisme britannique et l'image de l'intellectuel français', *Mil neuf cent – Revue d'histoire intellectuelle*, 15, 1997, pp. 109–25.

24   Stefan Collini, *Public Moralists: Political Thought and Intellectual Life in Britain, 1850–1930*, Oxford: Clarendon Press, 1991.

25   Quoted in H. L. Wesseling, *Certain Ideas of France: Essays on French History and Civilization*, Westport: Greenwood Press, 2002, p. 65.

26   John Stuart Mill, 'Considerations on Representative Government', in *Three Essays*, Oxford: Oxford University Press, 1975, p. 285.

nineteenth century, via writers and poets such as Christopher Isherwood and W. H. Auden, attracted by communism in the 1930s, through to Bertrand Russell and Harold Pinter, Great Britain has known men of letters not very different from the prototype of the Parisian intellectual. Besides, eminent historians such as E. P. Thompson or Eric Hobsbawm adopted a version of Marxism, and critical positions in politics, that were far more coherent than those of their Paris counterparts, thus assuming the role of committed intellectuals in the most typical sense of this expression.

At the same time, Great Britain has also been marked by a long anti-intellectual tradition with multiple origins. Some researchers explain the deep suspicion towards men of letters by the development of Protestantism, which was more ambivalent than Catholicism vis-à-vis a clerical hierarchy claiming to exercise mediation between God and the earthly community.[27] The greater autonomy of Protestant believers reduced their dependence on the clergy, and this tradition of suspicion was transposed into the secular sphere. Added to this was the fact that political modernity, initially liberal and then democratic, was established in Britain without the aid of universal abstractions, and was accompanied by an ambivalence towards ideological professionals. Ever since Edmund Burke, who at the end of the eighteenth century imputed the revolutionary earthquake of 1789 to the work of French philosophers, there has been a lively critical stance towards abstract principles, supposedly the result of the meditations of radical intellectuals. The famous British empiricism, whose scientific achievements past and present were viewed as the reward of collective work, rejected the deification of the intellectual as inventor of formulas designed to explain the workings of the world.

A view of this kind was not the monopoly of the conservative pole of British public life. A strongly anti-intellectual tradition

---

27   See André J. Bélanger, *The Ethics of Catholicism and the Consecration of the Intellectual*, Montreal: McGill-Queen's University Press, 1997.

was also widespread on the British left. The labour movement here, as distinct from its origins in France, sprung directly from the conflict between capital and labour; it was never taken in hand by intellectuals, but created and animated on the initiative of the trade unions, who at a particular moment decided to found a political party. It is unthinkable that this party, the Labour Party, would have accepted as its leader a former philosophy teacher, as was the case in France with Jean Jaurès, who headed the Section français de l'Internationale ouvrière (SFIO) established in 1905. Later on, in the interwar period, the SFIO chose as its leader a high-flying civil servant and literary critic, Léon Blum, maintaining the contrast with Britain.

This particular configuration of the public sphere may well explain why the British left intellectual always displayed a certain modesty in great contrast with the French cultural world. George Orwell, a great figure of the left, listed in order of importance the main reasons that impelled him and his colleagues to take up the pen: first and foremost, 'pure egoism' (in other words: the self-interest to appear intelligent, to win celebrity, to settle accounts); then 'aesthetic enthusiasm' (the satisfaction and sense of beauty and pleasure of a finished work); then the 'historical impulse' (the desire to bring facts to light and transmit them to generations to come). It is only after these reasons that Orwell finally mentions the 'political objective' (the aspiration to advance the world in a certain direction).[28] The order in which these motivations are listed, which does not cast particular glory on writers, shows the sincerity of the author of *Animal Farm* and *1984*. It would be hard to find, at least before the 1970s, any such scale of values in the French cultural tradition, where even the most anti-intellectual thinkers were not accustomed, in Paris, to presenting themselves as subjects moved by personal or professional motivations. In French discourse, where the Dreyfus affair long remained

---

28   George Orwell, 'Why I Write' (1946), in *Orwell and Politics*, London: Penguin, 2001, p. 460.

an absolute point of reference, the models of social and political functioning of intellectuals were always subject to categorical moral imperatives, leaving scarcely any room for 'pure egoism' as a major reason for intellectual production.[29]

In his way, the famously 'anti-intellectual' Paul Johnson also illustrates the singular place that the 'intellectual' occupies in British public opinion. For a long time Johnson was a very prominent left intellectual. He edited the *New Statesman*, a weekly of high quality and radical orientation, and established himself as a prolific and talented commentator and writer. In the mid-1970s, like many Western intellectuals, he began to slide towards the conservative pole of the political spectrum. He became a close adviser to Margaret Thatcher and purported to see the trade unions as a totalitarian threat to British freedom. Having completed his intellectual metamorphosis, he published in 1988 a successful book titled *Intellectuals*, soon translated into several languages including French, in which he attacked a number of major intellectual figures, including Rousseau, Shelley, Marx, Ibsen, Tolstoy, Hemingway, Brecht, Sartre and Russell.[30]

The figures whom Paul Johnson accused, and whose 'true face' he claimed to show in his book, were not only celebrated intellectuals. They all belonged to the specific category of thinkers who sought to improve society and committed what Johnson clearly considered as a crime: utopianism. In the lineage of Edmund Burke and Karl Popper, Johnson starts from the principle that a single human mind is incapable of judging and assessing historical processes. It is preferable to rely on hegemonic

---

29   Clearly Parisians have no monopoly in idealistic elaboration of the self-portrait of the intellectual as a subject motivated by moral purity. Edward W. Said, *Representations of the Intellectual*, New York: Vintage, 1996, is the latest example to date of naïve presentation of the 'authentic' intellectual as spiritual exile in perpetual struggle for the defence of the oppressed, and never for himself.

30   Paul Johnson, *Intellectuals: From Marx and Tolstoy to Sartre and Chomsky*, New York: Harper, 2007 [1988].

institutions, safe and stable state apparatuses, customs and beliefs anchored in long experience. The great misfortune that has befallen the modern world, according to Johnson, came from these humanist intellectuals, for the most part of the left, who were not satisfied with the achievements of Western liberalism and accordingly invented dangerous abstract formulas that led to effusions of blood and large-scale massacre. The extermination of peasants by Stalin in the USSR, the genocide under Pol Pot in Cambodia, were characteristic products of this utopian delirium, for which these great Western 'pen-pushers' were in part responsible.

As evidence of the conservative drift observable in the late twentieth century well beyond the English-speaking world, Paul Johnson's diatribe is scarcely an original contribution.[31] If it deserves a certain attention, it is not on account of the vitriolic portrait he draws of intellectuals, described in passing as sexual deviants, perverts and debauchees heedless of any morality,[32] but rather because Johnson made a new move: equating anti-intellectualism and anti-totalitarianism, he rejected for himself the label of 'intellectual'. And this is what radically differentiates him from those of his Parisian counterparts who, undertaking at the same time a remarkably similar ideological turn and passing en masse 'from Mao collar to Rotary Club',[33] continued to flatter themselves with the glorious title inherited from Zola, Sartre and others.

*   *   *

31   In France, a trendy essayist, Pascal Bruckner, had already published a similar argument in *Le Sanglot de l'homme blanc. Tiers-Monde, culpabilité, haine de soi*, Paris: Seuil, 1986.

32   The irony of history has it that in the wake of Johnson's conservative and hypocritical preachings, the novelist Gloria Stewart revealed that she had been for eleven years the secret lover of this devoted paterfamilias, whose greatest pleasure consisted in being spanked on the buttocks. See Christopher Hitchens, 'The Rise and Fall of Paul Spanker Johnson', *Salon*, 28 May 1998.

33   See Guy Hocquenghem, *Lettre ouvert à ceux qui sont passés du col Mao au Rotary*, Marseille: Agone, 2014 [1986].

Do the striking transformations of the ideological climate at the end of the twentieth century herald the end of the intellectuals, or simply a significant shift in their ideological orientations? In other words, are the place and status of intellectuals still the same as a century ago, and only their values changed? Are the classic 'means of production' of intellectuals still the source of the ways they express themselves in our intellectual world?

To deal with these questions, if only partially, I have chosen to return to the intellectual's moment of birth. It may seem that a figure who is born is capable of dying out completely one day or another. I have therefore chosen to begin with some critical remarks on the modes of engagement of intellectuals at the end of the nineteenth century. The critic al and rather sceptical gaze with which I examine intellectuals does not just come from my particular approach to history, but may also have its origin in my particular position in the intellectual field. I go on to pay particular attention to various forms of discourse that touch on intellectuals, both positively and negatively, over a long time frame.

Marxism has been a major factor in my intellectual and political development, even if I no longer define myself as a Marxist today. This is why I have taken the time to discuss the viewpoints of several Marxist thinkers on the role of intellectuals in relation to the workers' movement. And since, like many people on the left, I have been all too quick to pin the label 'fascism' on a variety of historical phenomena, sometimes mutually contradictory ones, I felt obliged to add an analysis of the presence of fascism in French intellectual milieus in the interwar years.

The terrible attack against the editors of *Charlie Hebdo* on 7 January 2015 took place while I was still writing this book. The rise of terrorism in France, and the reactions it has aroused, have only sharpened existing ideological tendencies. For this reason, I decided to devote the second part of this work to recent developments on the French political scene that attest to an important ideological shift: while the modern Parisian intellectual was born in the battle against Judeophobia, the twilight of the intellectual in the early twenty-first century is happening under the sign of a rise in Islamophobia.[34]

---

34   For several reasons I prefer to use most often the terms 'Judeophobia' or 'hatred of Jews' rather than 'anti-Semitism'. There has never been a Semitic race, only Semitic languages, which European Jews never used in everyday life. Wilhelm Marr, a secular racist responsible for the application and diffusion of the term 'anti-Semitism', cherished an irrational hatred towards Jews. He was clearly not resorting to any scientific terminology. The term 'Judeophobia' was current well before 'anti-Semitism'. Léon Pinsker, a Zionist thinker and predecessor of Theodore Herzl, used it as early as 1882.

PART ONE:

Intellectuals in the Torment of the Century

The Dreyfus Affairs: Human Rights or Author's Rights?

Nothing is worse than these gangs of semi-intellectuals. A semi-culture destroys instinct without replacing it with a conscience. All these aristocrats of thought insist on maintaining that they do not think like the common herd.

Maurice Barrès, 'La protestation
des intellectuels', 1 February 1898

The sociology of intellectuals is certainly the weakest point in all sociology, and for good reason: in this case, intellectuals are both judge and judged.

Pierre Bourdieu, 'Les intellectuels dans
le champ de la lutte des classes', 1985

Having grown up and been educated in Israel, I heard about the Dreyfus affair at an early age. In every pedagogic presentation on anti-Semitism in history, the 'affair' was used as irrefutable proof of the eternal hatred of Jews, with the conclusion that this persecution could only cease when Jews were gathered in their homeland. Some years later, having begun to examine the history of Zionism more systematically, my view of

Judeophobia in nineteenth-century France became rather more complex.

The tragic figure of Bernard Lazare captured my attention at the very start of my research. This Parisian intellectual who originally detested the Jewish immigrants from Eastern Europe became both the first Dreyfusard and the first French Zionist. But he was also one of the very first to be disappointed by the turn that the victory of the political Dreyfusards took, and by the way that political Zionism developed. I originally intended to write a new biography of this unusual libertarian, a close friend of Charles Péguy and Georges Sorel, but in the end I decided to confine this to a short article.[1]

Despite having been drawn throughout my life to revolutionary romanticism, my interest in social history took the upper hand, and deciphering the 'mystery' of the ways in which intellectuals intervened in the public sphere seemed to me more urgent than continuing to write biographies of radical figures. The Dreyfus affair is often regarded as the ideal type of intellectual mobilization. Yet this mythologizing of the 'affair' raises two problems. Firstly, the mobilization of intellectuals in the Dreyfus affair was neither so pure nor so unanimous as is generally maintained; and secondly, study of the majority of other 'affairs' involving intellectuals, whether in France or in other countries (the First World War, the rise of fascism, McCarthyism, etc.), shows that it would be wrong to see the Dreyfusards as the absolute embodiment of the intellectual.

Besides, study of writings devoted to the Dreyfus affair, and more particularly those that propose an overall synthesis of it, gives the impression that this was one and the same continuous historical event, starting in 1894 with the arrest of an officer suspected of treason, and ending with the official recognition of his innocence in 1906. This narrative, like every good plot,

---

1   Shlomo Sand, 'Bernard Lazare, the First French Zionist', in *The Words and the Land*, Los Angeles: Semiotext(e), 2011, pp. 181–201.

contains a beginning, a middle and an end, with all the ingredients of a great dramatic construction. In the wake of a biased trial, held in an atmosphere of collective hysteria, an accused man was wrongly convicted and deported to a distant prison. Discovery of the truth triggered the entry onto the stage of an enlightened 'cavalry', in the manner of a Hollywood western, and the liberation of the victim.[2]

In this chapter, I shall formulate a number of questions that deal with the character of this cavalry; on its constitution and on the causes that led it to intervene in this judicial drama.

Two affairs?

Should the Dreyfus affair really be viewed as a single narrative? Is it not necessary to unpack and rearrange the chain of events into at least two affairs, in order to clarify the nature of the public outburst that made a conventional military trial into a historical event with global repercussions? The first affair was the trial of Dreyfus at the end of 1894: a judicial farce accompanied by a strong wave of Judeophobia. The second affair began three years later, in January 1898, with the publication of Émile Zola's 'J'accuse' and the petitions of support that followed this. The three years that elapsed between these two events appear as blank pages, or rather black ones, in the history book of the Parisian agora. Presentation of the affair as one and the same event is the fruit of a republican imaginary that sought to inculcate a memory in conformity with its system of values.

It would clearly be absurd to deny the existence of a link of some kind between the two events. The second could not have happened without the first, at least not in the forms of development that it underwent. Without the second, the first would not have become a major event in the history of France, but remained

---

2   Bertrand Joly's recent *Histoire politique de l'affaire Dreyfus*, Paris: Fayard, 2014, brings important qualifications to the traditional narrative.

confined to an episode, albeit important, in a different national history. Yet the two events marked the birth of two absolutely distinct historical phenomena.

The first affair played a role in the creation of political Zionism, and it is not just a matter of chance that in 1895 Theodore Herzl wrote *Der Judenstaat* (The Jewish State) in Paris. This does not mean that Herzl wrote his manifesto because of the Dreyfus trial, nor that Western Europe was the birthplace of Zionism. The non-fortuitous element in the writing of this essay in Paris is bound up with the fact that it required a strong wave of Judeophobia in the City of Light for a decisive epistemological break to be produced in the worldview of intellectuals of Jewish origin in Central and Eastern Europe. A majority of the intelligentsia in Eastern Europe looked to Paris as a beacon in the history of progress and Enlightenment. Those who began to lean towards Zionism drew a double conclusion: first of all, that the anti-Semitic Dreyfus affair (the first affair) prefigured their 'tomorrows'; and second, that the persecution of an officer of Jewish origin, even one perfectly French by language, culture and personal identity, proved that Jews the world over, and not only those in Eastern Europe, belonged to a distinct and eternal 'ethnos'. From this historical moment, the project of inventing a Jewish nation 'existing' for close to four thousand years took shape.

Among 'Israelites', on the other hand, as French citizens of Jewish ancestry defined themselves at this time, even in the wake of the trial and the wave of Judeophobia very few saw themselves as part of the same people as the Yiddish speakers in Eastern Europe. They scarcely expressed any solidarity towards the latter, and there was even a detectable hostility on the part of Parisian Israelites towards immigrants who had fled to France from the pogroms of the Russian Empire. Very few of these French Israelites rallied to Zionism.[3]

---

3   For a different approach, see Annie Kriegel, 'Aux origines du sionisme: l'affaire Dreyfus', in *Les Juifs et le monde moderne*, Paris: Seuil, 1977, pp. 167–79.

It was the second Dreyfus affair, in 1898, that founded the modes of intervention of intellectuals in modern political life, and made Zola's 'J'accuse' the intellectual manifesto par excellence in Western democracy's culture of protest. And if this was the first time in history that secularists of Jewish origin founded an independent political national movement, it also saw the first appearance of scholarly elites in the form of an organized and autonomous group. 'Zionism' and 'intellectuals' – an interesting coincidence! After some hesitation, both terms appeared as nouns in the early 1890s, though each only acquired its full meaning in the context of the two affairs. Is this only a coincidence? Was not the Zionist movement, at least initially, founded by an intelligentsia, and in the main a very young one?

On 14 January 1898, following the appearance of Zola's famous article, the newspaper *L'Aurore* published a number of petitions demanding that the persecuted officer be retried. The signatories included writers, artists, professors, lawyers, architects and other academics. On 23 January, Georges Clemenceau, at this time the paper's editor, referred to these signatories with the little-used term *intellectuels* – the word even being printed in capitals in his article. On 1 February in *Le Journal*, a paper with a larger circulation, Maurice Barrès replied ironically with an article titled 'The Protest of the Intellectuals!' For Barrès, national bard and cultural herald of the young generation of the 1890s, the term had a pejorative connotation. It was soon adopted by the petitioners and their supporters, to the point of rapidly entering common currency in the cultural civil war that divided Paris and then France, eventually leading to the rehabilitation of the condemned man.[4]

New concepts generally appear when the need for them makes itself felt. When phenomena previously unknown appear in a

---

4   The 'intellectual' events of the time of the Dreyfus affair are excellently described in Pascal Ory and Jean-François Sirinelli, *Les Intellectuels en France: de l'Affaire Dreyfus à nos jours*, Paris: Armand Colin, 1986, pp. 5–40.

particular historical context, the ideological vocabulary sports a new terminology, which is in turn a stimulus to developments. Yet the significant involvement of new words in historical development takes place within 'scientific handcuffs', which the passing historian habitually refers to with such serious terms as 'process', 'balance of forces', or 'social structures'.

Before attempting a slightly more 'scientific' history, it is necessary to clarify a term that is today perceived as synonymous with 'intellectuals' and has already been mentioned in the preface. 'Intelligentsia' was a word used widely in Russia from the 1860s. It referred principally to a cultural elite, made up of literati who did not belong solely to the nobility, who were dissatisfied with the existing state of affairs, and who felt a moral obligation to change this.[5] The term was subsequently applied to the educated stratum as a whole, and this was how it was introduced into Germany in the early 1890s. Despite its Latin origin, however, at the turn of the century it was still rejected by the French language as foreign. In the past, the French cultural elite had never been very receptive to expressions imported from other languages. It is also possible that 'intelligentsia' had a sense that was too collective for the taste of the individualist Parisian scholar, whereas in the term 'intellectuals', the accent placed on the autonomy of the subject counterbalanced the group effect. Whatever the reason, if the 'intelligentsia' was born in the political climate of an autocratic regime, the 'intellectual' was invented with the gradual formation of a public sphere in the capital of a liberal democracy.[6]

---

5   On the concept of 'intelligentsia' in Russia and its evolution, see Martin Malia, 'What is the intelligentsia?', *Daedalus*, vol. 89, no. 3, 1960, pp. 441–58. Alexander Gella, on the other hand, maintains that the concept is of Polish origin and dates back to the 1840s: 'An introduction to the sociology of the intelligentsia', in Aleksander Gella (ed.), *The Intelligentsia and the Intellectuals: Theory, Method and Case Study*, Beverly Hills: Sage, 1976, p. 12.

6   On the origin of the term before the storm around the Dreyfus affair, see William M. Johnston, 'The origin of the term "intellectuals" in French novels and essays of the 1890s', *Journal of European Studies*, vol. 4, no. 1, 1974, pp. 43–56; and Jean-Paul Honoré, 'Autour d'intellectuel', in Géraldi Leroy (ed.), *Les Écrivains et l'affaire Dreyfus*, Paris: PUF, 1983, pp. 149–57.

What then was new about the political engagement of writers, artists and academics, to produce this linguistic marker? What differentiated the supporters of a retrial of Dreyfus, who blamed the army general staff, from their famous forebears, from Voltaire to Victor Hugo, who had likewise intrepidly challenged the powers that be, yet without being referred to as 'intellectuals'?

The 'scientific' intellectual

We should remember first of all that the last quarter of the nineteenth century saw the prestige of science reach an apogee. Almost all knowledge claimed to be 'science'. Marxian socialism itself adopted scientific guise, just as Émile Zola did not hesitate to present himself as a 'doctor in moral sciences'.[7] The tormented romantic genius had everywhere given way to the 'scientist'. This cultural atmosphere contributed to the rise of naturalism in literature, and to the formation of what are today called the 'social sciences'. There was a certain homology between the notion of 'scientist' and the still vague term 'intellectual'. Why not gratify those who supported Émile Zola with an aura of rationality and scientific truth?

The appearance of the term 'intellectual' was also bound up with political changes in French society in the late nineteenth century. Petitions signed by writers, artists and academics were a new phenomenon, which needed a new name. There had certainly been precedents, particularly in England, where petitions had been used for political aims since the first half of the century. In France, the phenomenon appeared at the turn of the 1890s, when writers and artists signed a petition against the construction in the heart of Paris of a 'monstrous Eiffel tower', and a protest circulated against the persecution of anarchists.[8]

---

7   Anne McGovern, 'From Romantic Genius to Committed Intellectual: The Emergence of Zola's Conception of the Intellectual', *Journal of European Studies*, vol. 15, no. 3, 1985, pp. 191–207.

8   See Jean-François Sirinelli, *Intellectuels et passions françaises. Manifestes et pétitions au XXᵉ siècle*, Paris: Fayard, 1990, pp. 21–2.

But it was at the time of the second Dreyfus affair, in 1898, that the petition became the characteristic expression of a new type of collective intellectual. This practice, though it did not remain exclusively Parisian, spreading across France and crossing borders to proliferate in liberal democracies, played a fundamental political role in the French cultural world, with scarcely an equivalent in other national cultures.

It is hardly surprising that the practice of petitioning grew in France, the birthplace of political democracy. The intervention of literati in the public arena had a historical precedent in the eighteenth century, when great thinkers came together to write the *Encyclopédie*. In Paris at that time, 'men of letters' formed the habit of gathering in a number of competing salons, each with a particular field of debate. The appearance of organized parties in the late nineteenth century and the presence of an urban crowd, especially in Paris, on the occasion of almost all political crises, also served as a model, implicit but decisive, for grouping together intellectual elites in a common context specific to them. This was the time when literary and artistic modernism began to find expression, in Paris, in the form of societies with a self-defined identity, while petitions, reviews and associations led by men of letters sought to occupy the public sphere, thus supporting recourse to the neologism of 'intellectuals'.

From political change to socio-cultural change: the Second Industrial Revolution, along with the development of mass democracy, contributed to the appearance of compulsory education, to the rising influence of written communication, and to a new cultural morphology of Western society. France witnessed the proliferation of producers and distributors of symbols at a rate comparable to the accelerated development of the division of labour. The number of writers, scientists, journalists and teachers increased in every Western European country in the last quarter of the nineteenth century; in proportion, the growth in the number of intellectuals was well above the rate of demographic growth.

These producers and distributors of cultural symbols appealed to their particular status in the social scale, and their primordial role in the shaping of national consciousness, while beginning to claim for themselves a greater autonomy, both from the state and from the economic forces that dominated the market.

This relative autonomy, without being synonymous with independence for universities, newspapers, or literary and artistic institutions, did undoubtedly strengthen the capacity of a section of cultural producers and agents to set, by and for themselves, the rules governing the balance of forces in their institutions. A still more important fact is that, thanks to the decline in illiteracy and with an ever-growing number of citizens speaking and reading the national language fluently, many writers could begin to live from the sale of their books and be far less dependent on the state apparatus. They felt increasingly protected by a growing community of attentive sympathizers.

But what impelled these literati, who came from every circle and current of thought, to intervene suddenly in the public arena and forcefully challenge the political and military authorities? How did writers, poets, painters and academics become 'intellectuals', in the France – or, more precisely, the Paris – of 1898? What incited them to emerge from their comfortable ivory tower, which had only just been consolidated, in order to plunge into harsh polemics, and sometimes even street brawls?[9]

These questions are not easy to answer. At first sight, it might seem far easier to decipher the motives of intellectuals than those of other people, who do not leave so many traces behind them. The abundance of written indications, however, hides as much as it reveals. The history of intellectuals is the only history in which the actors explain themselves, in which each of them writes about

9   For information on the positions taken up by intellectuals at the time of the Dreyfus affair, see 'Comment sont-ils devenus dreyfusards ou antidreyfusards?', *Mil neuf cent – Revue d'histoire intellectuelle*, no. 11, 1993.

their fellows, whereas we have scarcely any testimonies about intellectuals on the part of any other social group.

Reasons for engagement

The most traditional explanation is to attribute the intellectual mobilization to the extreme sensitivity of producers and distributors of culture and knowledge to an ideal of 'justice'. In the image of the Hebrew prophets of antiquity, or Voltaire at the time of the Calas affair, those writers who were convinced of Dreyfus's innocence, such as Émile Zola and Anatole France, rose up against injustice. Moral duty forms part of the intellectual's self-definition and is one of its hallmarks. The idea that intellectuals are guided by a kind of human generosity, and ready to fight for universal values, follows from a particular conception of their social status. Perceived as independent figures, not in thrall to the interests of a particular social class or any government apparatus, intellectuals frequently appear as the 'just' of modern times, and the standard-bearers of morality.

This explanation, however, has a number of weak points. Starting with the fact that there were very few injustices that aroused such vigilant intervention as that of Zola in 1898. And even if we restrict ourselves to the Dreyfus affair, it is notable that intellectuals were far from being unanimously mobilized against arbitrary power and raison d'état. Many intellectuals kept their distance from the fray, and many others, probably as numerous as the champions of a retrial, took the side of the political and military institutions. Maurice Barrès, Auguste Renoir, Edgar Degas, Paul Valéry and many other prominent figures stigmatized the activity of the revisionists, which they deemed irresponsible and destabilizing for the security of the state. Examination of the numerical balance between the two camps shows that the rectification of a legal iniquity was not a more imperative value for intellectual elites than it was for other mortals. Barrès expressly formulated the nationalist and pragmatic standpoint of the anti-Dreyfusard intellectuals when he declared that, even if Dreyfus was innocent, the Dreyfusards were in any case guilty.

The same situation can be found in relation to the First World War, the first real historical occasion for the total mobilization of intellectuals, in the global public arena and not just that of Paris. The great majority of scholarly elites lent their support to their respective side in the war. In no way universal, they championed the 'specific' moral justifications of their own country. The modern scholar, before proving critical or remonstrant, is above all a national intellectual.

The second argument put forward to explain the mobilization of intellectuals in support of Dreyfus puts more weight on their professional ethic. By the very fact of their profession and the supposedly scientific and rational character of their activity, intellectuals would have a natural propensity to seek the 'truth' and to promote its triumph, outside their laboratories and universities as well as within. As a result, when the truth about Dreyfus became known, many intellectuals launched into battle to reveal this fully and apply reason in civil life. According to this version, intellectuals appear as the representatives of pure reason who, in contrast to their anonymous contemporaries, do not let themselves be carried away in the instinctive movement of irrational crowds. The discovery of the truth, a result of their orientation towards universality, is based in a morality that is itself universal (rather than particular), generating a new kind of engagement that was characteristic of the Dreyfusards. Émile Durkheim, who joined the fray after some hesitation, a few months after the publication of 'J'accuse', sought to define the nature of his intervention on the basis of the new 'scientific' principles of sociology that he represented:

> If, therefore, in recent times, a certain number of artists, and especially scholars, believed they had to refuse to concur in a judgment whose legality appeared to them suspect, it was not because, in their capacity as chemists or philologists, as

philosophers or historians, they attributed to themselves some sort of special privilege and a sort of eminent right of control over the thing being judged. It is because, being men, they intend to exercise all their human rights and retain before them a matter which is amenable to reason alone.[10]

The only problem is that the great 'scientific sociologist' ignored the 'professional' orientations of Dreyfus's first defenders. Some of these were symbolist poets who tended to cultivate a strange mysticism rather than any kind of scientific research. The first revisionists, in late 1897 and early 1898, were actually such 'irresponsible' writers as Bernard Lazare and Stéphane Mallarmé, or ones only a little more 'responsible' such as Charles Péguy and Marcel Proust, rather than professors of logic or chemists working in a laboratory. Although he saw himself as a disciple of the physiologist Claude Bernard and a 'dissector' of human nature, Émile Zola would find it difficult to adhere to the guiding principles of science, despite his personal honesty and fundamental morality. Besides, the publicists and essayists in 'social science' – historians and sociologists – who later joined the Dreyfusard camp would hardly be accepted as 'scientists' today.[11]

The historian Gérard Noiriel supplemented Durkheim's reflections with an interesting explanation. According to him, the birth of the Third Republic in the 1870s and the advent of mass democracy brought about a caesura between the 'scientist' and politics, as a result of the professionalization of both 'scientists' and politicians. The intervention of 'scientists' in the name of

---

10   Émile Durkheim, 'Individualism and the Intellectuals' (1898), in Robert N. Bellah (ed.), *Emile Durkheim on Morality and Society*, Chicago: University of Chicago Press, 1973, p. 50.

11   It is also worth remembering here that the first protest in France against colonial repression, at the time of the Rif War of 1925, saw surrealist poets as well as communist writers. The counter-petition, on the other hand, was signed by members of the Académie de médecine, the rector of the Académie de Paris, the dean of the Faculté de droit, the administrator of the Collège de France and several professors. See Jean-François Sirinelli, *Intellectuels et passions françaises*, pp. 62–8.

truth could thus be seen as an aspiration for a new connection with major political questions, after the model of their illustrious forebears of the eighteenth-century Enlightenment. The problem is that neither in Paris nor in other capitals, neither in the late nineteenth century nor later, did the great majority of scientists seek to become intellectuals involved in politics.[12] In fact, only a minority of them entered the public arena, attracted by the battles under way, even if they sometimes managed to draw with them rather wider circles.

Perhaps the Spanish philosopher and essayist José Ortega y Gasset had a more precise view of the situation when he wrote in *The Revolt of the Masses* that around 1890, intellectual power in Europe was captured by a third generation of scientists whose characteristic was a growing specialization. The professionalization of new scholars led to their enclosing themselves in a narrow domain, thus leading to a new kind of cultural lack: 'The specialist "knows" his own minimal corner of the universe quite well. But he is radically ignorant of all the rest.'[13] Which, Ortega deplores, does not stop the specialist scientist from taking up pretentious positions in domains about which he knows nothing:

> He is not learned, for he is formally ignorant of all that does not enter into his speciality; but neither is he ignorant, because he is 'a scientist', and 'knows' very well his own tiny portion of the universe. We shall have to say that he is a learned ignoramus, which is a very serious matter, as it implies that he is a person who is ignorant, not in the fashion of the ignorant man, but with all the petulance of one who is learned in his own special line.[14]

---

12   Gérard Noiriel, *Dire la vérité à le pouvoir. L'avenir des intellectuels en France*, Marseille: Agone, 2010, pp. 269 and 273.

13   José Ortega y Gasset, *The Revolt of the Masses*, Notre Dame, IN: Notre Dame University Press, 1985, p. 98.

14   Ibid., pp. 98–9.

Despite his conservative elitism, or perhaps because of it, Ortega y Gasset does not spare the modern scientist, whom he unhesitatingly associates with other mortals subject to the mass political culture that was rapidly expanding in modern democracy.

To understand the intervention of intellectuals in the Dreyfus affair, a third explanation focuses on political and ideological factors. Knowing that literati have always been sensitive to ideological and political battles, and that they experience more than other people the need to dispose of a public space of debate, the attack that the Judeophobic far right launched against the foundations of the republic aroused a sense of danger, particularly among left and liberal intellectuals, which had the result of inspiring them to mobilize to rescue parliamentary democracy.[15]

At first sight, this argument seems completely logical. Yet it has the inconvenient fact that in other political cultures, faced with serious danger in the course of the advent of pluralist liberalism, no massive mobilization of democratic intellectuals is observable. Neither the rise of fascism in Italy nor the advance of Nazism in Germany led to the establishment of a front of intellectuals to try and bar the route to dictatorship. Only a few famous figures showed themselves individually, and the marginal resistance that emerged chiefly mobilized those who had already been earmarked as promised victims, either political or 'ethnic'. This is also true for the period of McCarthyism in the United States: no intellectual 'cavalry' appeared to repel the wave of patriotic hysteria. Chance had it that Joseph McCarthy finally attacked the heads of the armed forces, which had the effect of

---

15   On the causes of French intellectuals' engagement in politics, from the standpoint of the actors themselves, see David L. Schalk, *The Spectrum of Political Engagement: Mounier, Benda, Nizan, Brasillach, Sartre*, Princeton: Princeton University Press, 1979. Stimulating approaches to the relationship of literati to the political world can be found in Ian MacLean, Alan Montefiore and Peter Winch (eds), *The Political Responsibility of Intellectuals*, Cambridge: Cambridge University Press, 1990.

reluctantly bringing in the real cavalry, who were thus driven to expel from the American public sphere the threat to fundamental liberties.[16]

By the end of the 'Dreyfus storms' we are concerned with here, liberal democracy had in fact been strengthened and the wave of Judeophobia repelled, but the last explanation advanced above sins by anachronism and a teleological approach. The anti-Semitic flare-up reached its peak in 1895, and not at the end of 1897. Violent Judeophobic reactions, of an intensity equal to those of late 1894, did indeed reappear in 1898, in the wake of the Dreyfusard campaign, but the first wave of anti-Jewish hatred failed to arouse a particular riposte on the part of Parisian intellectuals, whether of the left or fervent republicans. Its only effect, as we saw above, was to contribute to the nationalist arousal of an intelligentsia in a different geographical space: that of the Zionists who met at Basel in 1897.

During the first Dreyfus affair, Judeophobia did not particularly worry the socialist left or democratic circles. Likewise, the challenge to republican principles was not central to the public affray of early 1898. The cleavage between Dreyfusards and anti-Dreyfusards was expressed within political families more than between the traditional left and right. There was from the start an anti-Dreyfusard or, at the least, non-Dreyfusard left, just as an anti-Dreyfusard right. Though contrary to a widespread belief, opposition to a retrial did not come from the far left.

As I shall seek to explain below, although new ideological cleavages appeared in the course of the Dreyfus affair, these were perhaps less a consequence of this than preliminary to it. It is

---

16   In 1957, ten years after the start of the witch-hunt in the film industry, the scriptwriter Dalton Trumbo, who had been placed on the blacklist, wrote to William Faulkner, Ernest Hemingway, William Saroyan, John Steinbeck and Tennessee Williams to solicit their help against the persecution. Despite the fact that by this time McCarthyism was on the decline, Trumbo did not receive any response. See his moving letter in David Platt (ed.), *Celluloid Power: Social Film Criticism from 'The Birth of a Nation' to 'Judgment at Nuremberg'*, Metuchen: The Scarecrow Press, 1992, pp. 494–5.

important to remember that the public confrontation that began in 1898 was one of those historical events that reconfigured the lines of ideological and political demarcation between right and left. The boundaries occupied by each of these evolved in the course of the 'affair', and it can be argued that the establishment of the historic bloc known as the 'left' in the twentieth century dates from this time. The hard core of the anti-republican right, which pre-existed the Dreyfus affair, also played a central role, but its borders also shifted as a result of the event.

The intellectuals and their field

Given the insufficiencies of psychological, political and ideological explanations, the historian Christophe Charle developed an original argument in the late 1970s. In a fascinating article focusing on the literary world, he sought to apply to the history of the Dreyfus affairs certain formulae of Pierre Bourdieu.[17] With the help of concepts drawn basically from the sociology of culture and economics ('fields', 'domination', 'social, symbolic, and cultural capital', etc.), he set out to revisit the social logic that underlies the conventional narrative constructed and maintained by republican memory.

According to Charle, the cleavages in the literary and artistic fields preceded the division of the political field, which in fact they actually produced. To understand the mobilization of writers at the time of the 'affair', we must thus first examine the constitution of the fields in question before the start of the events. In the 1890s, he explains, the literary field could be schematically divided into three groups. The first, dominant group was made up of writers, critics and 'parvenu' publicists, for the most part members of the Académie française and assured of a regular income. This

---

17　Christophe Charle, 'Champ littéraire et champ du pouvoir: les écrivains et l'affaire Dreyfus', *Annales*, vol. 22, no. 2, 1977, pp. 240–64; see also Christophe Charle, *The Birth of the Intellectuals: 1880–1900*, Cambridge: Polity, 2015.

particularly included the 'Parnassians', and practitioners of the psychological novel such as Pierre Loti, Édouard Rod, Paul Bourget, François Coppée and Ferdinand Brunetière. Against these there was a dominated fraction of avant-garde writers, rather marginal, which included the symbolists, naturalists and avant-garde playwrights, such as Stéphane Mallarmé, Francis Vielé-Griffin, Saint-Georges de Bouhélier and Firmin Gémier. These were creators of a counterculture, champions of art for art's sake, who, despite a situation of economic instability, refused to compromise with the tastes of the broad public or the prestigious institutions, and continued to publish their works in little magazines designed for their fellow thinkers. Finally, a third group, the largest one, was made up of writers and dramatists who, like Émile Zola, Octave Mirbeau, J.-K. Huysmans and Léon Daudet, wrote for a broad public, on whom they depended for their income.

The pattern described by Christophe Charle is certainly well founded. The military trial of Dreyfus, at the end of 1897, first led to an outcry on the literary and political margins. If in the political field this included only the 'Allemanist' current of the socialist movement, anti-parliamentary and little representative, along with a few independent figures such as the Alsatian Auguste Scheurer-Kestner, vice president of the Senate, and Joseph Reinach, of Jewish origin, there was on the other hand a rapid and lasting unrest in the literary field. A majority of the literary avant-garde, especially its younger representatives, mobilized in favour of a retrial well before the publication of Zola's 'J'accuse'. From Bernard Lazare, a symbolist and the first Dreyfusard, to André Gide, Charles Péguy, Marcel Proust and Léon Blum, then a young literary critic,[18] almost the entire

---

18   It is quite significant that the official representatives of the Jewish community kept a low profile and abstained from taking a position. Less well known, on the other hand, was the massive engagement of young intellectuals of Jewish origin. This fact, which was in no way accidental, has remained marginal to the collective memory of French republicanism. See on this subject Léon Blum's testimony in a fascinating series of articles published in 1935: *Souvenirs sur l'Affaire*, Paris: Gallimard, 1981.

literary avant-garde took the part of the persecuted officer. The dominant group, conversely, with the exception of Anatole France, reacted by taking the side of the army and its general staff, as well as the existing political order. From Paul Bourget to Maurice Barrès, many renowned writers unhesitatingly joined the ranks of the Ligue de la patrie française, a right-wing nationalist movement founded in 1898.

To understand these divergent stands on the part of those active in the affair, Charle uses Pierre Bourdieu's conceptual apparatus to show that they were conditioned by their positioning in the literary or artistic field: an inferior rank in these fields led towards the Dreyfusard camp, while a well-established position in the dominant circle predisposed people to join the anti-Dreyfusards. In a more significant way, then, this was not fundamentally an ideological or moral battle, but rather a struggle for symbolic power. The dominated group in the 'literary field' challenged the political authorities in order to oppose the latter's ally, in other words, the dominant group in the cultural field. Its chief objective therefore was to obtain the 'prestige' capital that it lacked, and in this way shift the entire balance of forces between the groups of writers and artists.

While Charle's analysis adds much to our understanding of the question, it is unable to explain the attitude of the intermediate group. The majority of the naturalist school and most writers for the mainstream theatre did not take up a position. And those who did get involved were in no way a united body. They were divided almost equally between convinced Dreyfusards such as Émile Zola and Octave Mirbeau on the one hand, and anti-Dreyfusards such as Léon Daudet and Jules Verne on the other. This division poses an analytical problem, since it was this intermediate group, with the strongest influence on the public, which gave the 'affair' its vital impulse and so contributed to an atmosphere close to civil war.

In the same way, Christophe Charle's article has difficulty in explaining the positions taken in the academic field. He can certainly show that the older professional circles dominated by notables were inclined to support the military establishment, while the professors who joined the Dreyfusard camp were from the new establishments and disciplines such as sociology, but the paucity of data available on this specific field obliges him to keep his conclusions hesitant.

In order to better understand the logic of intervention of intellectuals during the 'affair', Christophe Charle's argument has therefore to be qualified and completed on a number of points.[19] In many cases, individuals, even leading ones, do not act according to the social logic supposedly dictated by the cultural field. On other occasions, evidence from a sufficient number of cases is lacking to enable unambiguous conclusions to be drawn. However, while there is no obligation to subscribe to all of Pierre Bourdieu's theses, it has now become impossible to write a history of intellectuals without at least referring to this.

Historians have been well able to restore the histories of kings, armies, peasants and workers, but they have failed to deal with intellectuals, their own kind. There have been biographies of writers, stories of the world of poetry, works on professors and scholars, yet until now these have not proceeded to analyse the foundations of the social positioning of the cultural agents in question and the sum total of interests that animate them. In fact, if literati evolve in an 'intellectual world', their desires and acts in the field of cultural creation are not uniquely guided by the intellect. Competition for prestige, for the increase of symbolic capital and for the proceeds of copyright are major elements that intellectuals are faced with, in a social world marked by a balance of forces that has so far been only little investigated in historiographical debates.

A few Marxist thinkers, including Karl Kautsky and Antonio Gramsci, sought to place the intellectual in a distinct social

---

19   Charle did this himself in several of his later works, particular *The Birth of the Intellectuals* and *Le Siècle de la presse (1830–1939)*, Paris: Seuil, 2004.

hierarchy, as I shall discuss in the third chapter of this book. With only a few exceptions, however, the majority of followers of Marx have integrated intellectuals into broad social classes, bourgeoisie or proletariat, and not dwelled on the autonomous social mechanism in which the producers of culture are located, and where they act following different principles from those structuring the balance of forces in other social strata. Despite always being in the dominated situation within the dominant class, intellectuals form within this class a group with specific interests, which Marxist intellectuals, given their own positioning at the top (or near the top) of the workers' movement, were unable or unwilling to see. It was hard for those 'theorists' who represented the working class to recognize that accumulation of symbolic capital also confers a domination over people. It was conservative and liberal sociologists such as Edward Shils or Shmuel Eisenstadt, with no complexes about the existence of a fixed world of social and cultural hierarchies, who were far more aware of the specific power of the intellectual in the mechanism of social forces. But their works in this domain lacked a specifically cultural dimension, and were not backed up by empirical research.[20]

For a long time intellectuals stood on their heads; they now have to be put back on their feet – feet whose very existence there has been difficulty in recognizing . . . The descent of the 'man of letters' into the public arena has always been conditioned by considerations of status within the literary, artistic or academic field. Émile Zola, Anatole France, Maurice Barrès and Jules Verne acted in terms of a social logic, and there can be no doubt that the arguments of Pierre Bourdieu and Christophe Charle offer answers that are far more interesting than those previously

---

20   See Edward Shils, *The Intellectuals and the Powers, and Other Essays*, Chicago: University of Chicago Press, 1972; and Shmuel Noah Eisenstadt, *Intellectuals and Tradition*, New York: Humanities Press, 1972. The question of intellectuals has also been tackled by a sociologist less conservative than these two, Lewis A. Coser, author of a pioneering and wide-ranging book: *Men of Ideas: A Sociologist's View*, New York: Simon & Schuster, 1965.

given as to the reasons for the intervention of modern intellectuals in politics.

Ideological motivations?

To exclude ideological motivations from the cultural context of the social agent, as Christophe Charle tends to do, inhibits understanding of these agents' activity as much as does the customary failure to take the social and institutional environment of intellectual production into account. Even if the main function of ideology is to legitimize the activity of social actors, what might be called its more 'weighty' parts are immersed in the normative systems of political culture. Values percolate into interests, just as interests express values, and (need we point out?) interests cannot simply be summed up as the constant attempt to accumulate power.

Positioning in the literary field, recognition in the world of the arts, research subsidies in the academic world, have their effect on the 'social' consciousness of intellectuals, the forms of their action and even the contents of their creations. But these influences merge together with others: the weight of education, experience stored up before entering the intellectual field, as well as other events outside of professional life. Whether a cultural agent comes from an urban bourgeois milieu or a family of typical farmers (very few intellectuals come from the lower classes, workers or peasants), whether they are citizen or subject, man or woman, from 'native soil' or from a somewhat 'foreign' origin, in other words, whether they were connected to the dominant or the dominated in previous contexts of their existence – all this continues to have an influence on their conception of the world and their sensibility, as much as do power struggles in the arena of cultural production.

To research the origins of the formation of opinions in relation to a political event is clearly not an easy exercise. We may even maintain that this kind of debate is one of the most complicated in the sociology of knowledge. A first step towards clarifying the problem, however, may be taken by dismantling the hasty generalizations that are resorted to in the criticism of ideology. Our concepts in the domain of political culture are generally too broad and not adjusted to the complexity of motivations that animate people, as I shall illustrate with three examples drawn from the 'Dreyfus affairs'.

Conventional history describes how anti-Semites became anti-Dreyfusards, and how convinced republicans joined the supporters of a retrial. Yet this dichotomy is debatable. Bernard Lazare, André Gide and Jean Jaurès were among many Dreyfusards who expressed a fairly strong Judeophobia, before and sometimes even after the captain's military trial. Conversely, although the majority of supporters of Dreyfus considered that they were thereby defending the republic, such different people as Maurice Barrès, the legendary Communard Henri Rochefort, and many other republicans along with them, became violently anti-Dreyfusard without seeing their position as contradicting republican principles. It was only towards the end of the Dreyfus affairs that radical nationalism was channelled into the ranks of Action Française, the royalist movement that would dominate the far right until the end of the Second World War.

Introducing anti-Semitism here generally means including different ideological phenomena. Hatred of Jews covers a large spread of ideas and positions, from a project maintaining that expulsion of the 'foreigner' will resolve all the ills of society and thereby justifying the persecution of Jews (the democratization of the late nineteenth century precisely had the effect of strengthening this instrument of hatred for electoral purposes), through to a xenophobic view that does not necessarily translate into political demands for discrimination and an attack on rights, but which is deeply anchored in age-old Christian culture. The borders between these ideas and the rejection of such sentiments are never clear and precise; in periods of crisis, however, relationships and intentions undergo changes, which are translated by differentiated political expressions. If we avoid lumping all kinds of anti-Semitism together, in the way that conventional political historiography has too often done, it is possible to distinguish how, at the time of the 'affair', anti-Jewish ideologies tipped the balance both with the supporters of a retrial and with its opponents.[21]

The same also holds for the concept of 'republicanism', the bearer of a spectrum of sensibilities that the 'affair' redistributed. Two examples are worth mentioning here: it was possible to be a republican and a democrat, and yet believe that raison d'état and the sacred role of the army were supreme values that could even justify the infringement of legal procedures – even trampling on the rights of the individual in an exceptional case. A state of emergency suspends human rights and political pluralism – who knew this better than the revolutionaries of 1793, the first democrats in history! There could also be another kind of republicans, who rejected the primacy of raison d'état and gave precedence to the rights of the individual, as laid down in the Declaration of the Rights of Man and the Citizen. For this republicanism, as long as the social order is preserved, criticism may be legitimately directed at the apparatuses responsible for political order.

In the same way, given the rise of working-class claims, many Dreyfusards may have considered the subordination of army and church to the republican order as a necessary measure for rebinding the ideological ties that contribute to maintaining the continuity of social order. Some of the first Dreyfusards, young people in particular, certainly dreamed that the triumph of justice would open the way to a social transformation that would challenge the

---

21   Many Dreyfusards, and not the least of them, were contaminated by one form or another of Judeophobia; some even proclaimed this publicly. Urbain Gohier, one of the editors of *L'Aurore*, was among the most virulent of these. Fortunately, in his case a sense of justice, combined with anti-militarism, prevailed over hatred of Jews. On the fervent Dreyfusards who became Judeophobic collaborators during the Second World War, see Simon Epstein, *Les Dreyfusards sous l'occupation*, Paris: Albin Michel, 2001.

existing class hierarchy. But the expansion and rising power of the revisionist camp set clear limits to the boundaries of confrontation; and these limits were a condition for the Dreyfusard victory. This explains in particular how Émile Zola, who expressed a ferocious hatred for the Communards in 1871, could be a courageous Dreyfusard in 1898, just as the journalist Georges Clemenceau was a stubborn defender of Dreyfus in 1898 before going on to violently repress workers' strikes as head of government in 1908.[22]

Anti-Semitism and republicanism appear in France as two key factors in conceptions of the nation. The vision of the Jew as a dubious and disloyal figure is chiefly widespread among those who see the nation as an ethnic group with ancestral origins, which foreigners cannot join or belong to in an organic way. The republican Maurice Barrès and the monarchist Charles Maurras shared the same view of the nation, refusing to consider anyone as French if they were not of French 'stock', natural members of the body of eternal France.

The revolutionary tradition of the republic, however, rejected the popular conception of a 'race-people', which was also refuted by the question of Alsace-Lorraine. Consistent patriots who demanded the restoration of the two 'stolen' provinces could not base themselves on ethnocentric claims, but only on the principle of self-determination by democratic vote. Hence, among other things, the victory of Zola over Barrès, and the defeat of ethno-biological and ethno-religious nationalism in the history of the French Republic until the German invasion of 1940.

At the moment of the 'trial of the Jew', who was also an exemplary patriotic officer, cracks appeared in existing ideologies, and new ideas extracted from these were among a range of factors, including the weight of social positioning and calculations of

---

22   On the positions of Zola and other famous writers on the Paris Commune, see Paul Lidsky, *Les Écrivains contre la Commune*, Paris: Maspero, 1970. On Clemenceau, see Jacques Julliard, *Clemenceau briseur de grèves*, Paris: Julliard, 1965.

power, in the constitution of new political camps. These new ideas were clearly brought into conformity with the interests of each cultural group, yet they still expressed changes of norms that went beyond narrow strategic advantage. Only an analysis that both deconstructs globalizing worldviews into a series of particular values, and brings in the social cartography of the various cultural fields, can help us better understand the factors that came into play in the second Dreyfus affair.

This analysis holds good not just for the intellectual arena. The expansion of new ideas affects all strata of society, and within each of them the reception and production of new ideas takes a specific turn: the accredited producers of culture do not actually have a monopoly over cultural creation. The intellectual world draws its specific character from the fact that, in the general division of labour, it gains its livelihood by formulating and distributing symbols and ideas. The sorcerer in the nomadic tribe, the priest in the world of antiquity, the church and the court jester in the Middle Ages, and the salon circles of the eighteenth century, gathered the lessons of human experience and, after cultivating them, bequeathed them to subsequent generations, generally with the authorization of the ruling political and economic elites. In the age of the advent of modern democracy, when the sovereign is far more dependent on the new urban masses than its predecessor was on social groups, the weight of the shapers of ideology among intellectuals as a whole notably increased, just as their degree of autonomy rose in the late nineteenth century. The public forum in which the nature of the hegemonic ideology is determined became one of the pillars that state power relied on, in parallel with the centres of economic decision.

This subject leads us to a final set of questions with a view to clarifying the motivations that spurred intellectuals to mobilize in 1898, and we need to examine a further aspect in order to better understand the logic of their intervention. In fact, the customary argument that it was the revisionist intellectuals who brought the Dreyfus affair into the public domain is incomplete. It is true that at the end of 1897 or the start of 1898, weighty intellectual elites mobilized in defence of the accused and against the arbitrary use of state power: poets, essayists, writers, professors, scientists, painters and students, mostly Parisians, demanded a retrial and launched a campaign. This narrative, however, by focusing on well-known intellectuals, passes over another 'intellectual' precursor.

I pointed out at the start of this chapter that, in order to understand the reasons that led the intellectual 'cavalry' to mobilize, it is necessary to divide the Dreyfus affair into two parts. Yet the two affairs have to be combined again in order to demonstrate the confrontation on a different level. In fact, beyond the presence of two main events, history does not tolerate either blank pages or black holes; there is an invisible connection between 1894 and 1898.

Before the Dreyfusards launched their public campaign, other intellectuals had already transformed a routine military trial into a public affair fraught with consequences. They are less habitually classed as intellectuals, yet it was their pens that gave rise to the first Dreyfus affair. With the manipulative help of modern communications and, what was new for the time, a package of poisonous anti-Semitic incitements wrapped up in anti-German nationalism, journalists made a petty matter of espionage into a key media event. Édouard Drumont led the way with his paper *La Libre Parole*, which enjoyed a wide circulation; *La Croix* and other organs competed with this, with a considerable measure of success. Moderate and 'respectable' papers, such as *Le Temps* and *Le Figaro*, gave a serious reception to Drumont's book *La France juive*, and made a major contribution to its sales.

L'Aurore, we should emphasize once again, was at this time an untypical newspaper in terms of its boldness and orientation, the pioneer of a new critical journalism, though this still remained an island in a sea of purveyors of scandalous information, bathed in conservative and conformist ideologies. From 1894 to the end of 1897, a very specific category of literati, in other words journalists and publicists, shaped and oriented public opinion with great help from popular and vulgar stereotypes, without arousing either real opposition or discontent.[23]

To what extent did the engagement of other intellectuals – writers, artists, professors – who, in relation to journalists, saw themselves in the superior position of an elite, constitute a kind of confrontation or competition, not in the literary or academic field, but rather in a broader cultural field? The public sphere, established and expanded concomitantly with liberal democracy in the late nineteenth century, was traditionally controlled by two established bodies, journalists and politicians. When intellectual elites intervened in the public arena, they used meetings, salons and reviews for their offensive, but above all the daily press, the very media instrument that had served as a vector of Judeophobia in 1894. Although the confrontation of 1898 did not take place on this terrain, a significant fringe of the Parisian intellectual elite won a surprising victory over the cohort of journalists.

This victory was made possible above all thanks to the alliance established between the Dreyfusard intellectuals and the rising force within the political elites: basically radicals and socialists. The action of Georges Clemenceau, a politician on leave turned journalist, sealed this new alliance. This new historic bloc, witness and privileged actor of democratization, de-clericalization and the 'nationalization' of the masses in the late nineteenth century, formed itself into a configuration ready to exercise political power. The result of this confrontation, in other words the victory

---

23 See Thomas Ferenczi, *L'Invention du journalisme en France. Naissance de la presse moderne à la fin du XIXe siècle*, Paris: Plon, 1993. Even after the publication of 'J'accuse', the great majority of the press remained anti-Dreyfusard, or at best indifferent to the fate of the accused. See Janine Ponty, 'La presse quotidienne et l'affaire Dreyfus en 1898–1899: essai de typologie', *Revue d'histoire moderne et contemporaine*, vol. 21, no. 2, 1974, pp. 193–220.

of the Dreyfusards, of the republican centre left and of their own culture, reinforced in the following years the status of the 'elite' intellectuals in relation to the world of the press. This was in a certain sense the victory of the creators of 'in-depth' ideological symbols over those who wield and distribute them. In Paris, following the best political tradition, this new balance of forces represented a kind of revolution. In other liberal cultures, a similar balance had been arrived at in more genteel battles, less dramatic and ideologized, and concluding with less convincing victories of the 'great' intellectuals.

Is it necessary to add that the social structuring of the intellectual mechanism established at the end of the nineteenth century is no longer the same a century later, and not only in Paris?[24] The tremendous development of the means of production, reproduction and distribution of modern culture has brought about a change in the balance of forces between the different categories of intellectuals (though not yet in France between the centre and the margins). The organizers of media designed for the masses have achieved strongly dominant positions, not only in terms of the main modes of distribution of knowledge, but also in terms of the formation process of hegemonic ideologies, or rather 'post-ideological' sensibilities, as they are often called today. I shall return to this fundamental point in the fifth chapter.

---

24   On the different stages of development of the intellectual 'means of production' and distribution, see Régis Debray, *Teachers, Writers, Celebrities: The Intellectuals of Modern France*, London: Verso, 1981, pp. 39–126. Debray divides French intellectual history into three main periods: from 1880 to the late 1920s, when universities ruled the intellectual space; from the 1930s to the 1960s, when cultural tone and taste were set by publishing houses and reviews; and the 1970s and after, when the mass media became the main field of intellectual combat. This division is still worth considering.

CHAPTER 2

From Voltaire to Bourdieu: Who Are the 'True Intellectuals'?

All shuffle there; all cough in ink;
All wear the carpet with their shoes;
All think what other people think;
All know the man their neighbour knows.
W. B. Yeats, 'The Scholars', 1915

In France if you're part of the intellectual elite and you cough,
there's a front-page story in Le Monde. *That's one of the reasons*
why French intellectual culture is so farcical – it's like Hollywood.
Noam Chomsky, *Understanding Power*, 2002

In the prologue to this book, I mentioned my father, a manual worker and an active communist. If there was one thing that was striking in his general view of the world, it was certainly an odd duality in his relationship to intellectuals. On the one hand, he expressed in our conversations a deep contempt for the literati who, according to him, happily served the ruling political and economic classes, but on the other hand, he could not conceal his admiration for them, to the point of hoping that his son would join their ranks. I remember the evening when he came back from a parents' meeting at my high school after being informed of my expulsion. I pretended to be asleep, afraid of his reaction. Just outside my door I heard him express his deep disappointment: 'So he'll never be a professor.'

Several years after he died, I became a professor who published books and was politically engaged on the public stage. To a large extent, however, I admit that I have inherited from my father this ambivalent feeling towards intellectuals. My point of view on their role and status has never been stable, and I have found them awkward to deal with in 'scientific' terms. An intensive reading of Pierre Bourdieu's sociology of culture certainly helped me to resolve some of these contradictions. Yet in my view, this brilliant thinker did not manage to formulate a completely coherent position across his long career. The tension in his work between 'cold' analysis and 'hot' commitment constantly gave rise to changing and unexpected forms of discourse, independently of Bourdieu's general political positions, and the origin of these is not always easy to identify.

On top of the fact that the term 'intellectual' as a noun is a purely French product, the writings of the most eminent philosophers, writers and sociologists of the last two centuries abundantly illustrate how Parisian scholars have regularly worked to cultivate and embellish their image. In the previous chapter, I stressed that the word 'intellectual' only began to appear in texts in the late nineteenth century, and that in France, the history of intellectuals as a social stratum marked by particular political reflexes began with the Dreyfus affair. We can easily recognize, however, that the Dreyfusard intellectual had venerable ancestors going back to the eighteenth century, the *philosophes* or *gens de lettres* of the Age of Enlightenment. Intellectual France saw itself ever since as a 'light unto the nations', and it still suffers from the decline of this golden age.

In France, the discourse of intellectuals about themselves may be divided into two main traditions: one favourable, if not admiring, the other critical and even hostile. These two approaches have coexisted, sometimes in a conflict, sometimes in mutual ignorance, but they have always accorded the intellectual a theoretical attention that has scarcely any equivalent in other national cultures.

What brought about this discourse of intellectuals about themselves? And more particularly, what has rendered this appreciation positive or negative? To answer this question, I believe we have to consider the fundamental ambiguity of a discourse that is *about* intellectuals, is produced *by* intellectuals, and is in the main designed *for* intellectuals. By reason of this ambiguity, its more or less conciliatory character towards intellectuals would seem to depend, first of all, on the social position of the author, and secondly, on his or her positioning in relation to the dominant ideology in the intellectual field (two phenomena that are linked, but not completely identical).

To support this hypothesis, I shall draw in this chapter on the writings of a number of thinkers from the main fields of French culture, with a contrasting pair for each era, whose writings refer directly and explicitly to the image of intellectuals or their ancestor, the 'philosophes' or 'men of letters'. Though there is a large share of arbitrariness in the choice of major actors for this reconstituted dialogue, they may nonetheless be seen as sufficiently characteristic of intellectuals in modern French culture.

'Men of letters' and philosophes

To begin this set of portraits, I have chosen the two most memorable philosophes of the eighteenth century: Voltaire and Rousseau. The respective authors of *Candide* and *The Social Contract* represent two completely different tendencies within the intellectual ambience of the Age of Enlightenment. Voltaire is the prototype of the liberal who is not a democrat, the champion of the moderate liberalism that was dominant in the French cultural space in the first half of the eighteenth century. As for

Rousseau, he may be defined as the first democrat, at a time when the democratic idea was still the hallmark of a tiny minority.

It is not hard to see Voltaire as the representative par excellence of Enlightenment optimism, in the middle of the eighteenth century. The philosophe received at the courts of kings, a master of words who sees them as the source of salvation, who detests prejudice and narrow-mindedness, has left us a fascinating description of those people who were not yet referred to as 'intellectuals'. In his *Dictionnaire philosophique*, published in 1764, we find, under the entries 'Gens de lettres' and 'Philosophe', a kind of collective self-portrait of the generation of the Enlightenment philosophes.[1]

Who may be called a man of letters? Voltaire gives a clear and precise answer:

> This name is certainly not given to a man who, with little knowledge, only cultivates one genre. The man who, having only read novels, only writes novels; he who, without any literature, may happen to have composed a few plays for the theatre; who, lacking any science, has produced some sermons, are not to be counted among men of letters ... The true men of letters are capable of entering different terrains, if they cannot cultivate them all.[2]

In order to deserve the envied title, refined taste and philosophical inspiration are also needed. At some points, Voltaire equates the 'man of letters' with the 'philosophe', but elsewhere he only attributes the latter term to those men of letters who display an exceptional wisdom. The mission of the 'philosophe' is clear and complex: it is incumbent on him to advocate a high morality

---

1   *Oeuvres complètes de Voltaire*, Paris: Garnier, 1878, vol. 3, pp. 250–2, 575–7 and IV, pp. 196–206.
2   Ibid., vol. 3, p. 251.

and, along with this, to use all his intelligence to seek the truth, to refine the manners of the people, without forgetting at the same time to dispense instruction to kings and princes.

The necessity of activity in several fields, the concentration of multiple qualities, a particular mixture of aestheticism, ethics and politics – all this defined the men of the philosophical salons of the mid-eighteenth century. Those endowed with these characteristics, Voltaire claimed, even surpassed the scholars of previous generations. Yet there is one common denominator between the eighteenth-century philosophe and the earlier man of letters: 'We have always seen philosophes persecuted by fanatics', he writes. Capable as he is of thinking against the stream, the philosophe does not necessarily have to belong to honoured institutions. For Voltaire, the original thinker is a spiritual pioneer and freebooter, a frequent target for the prejudices of his contemporaries, who for the most part are mediocre or uneducated: 'The philosophe is a lover of wisdom and truth: to be wise is to avoid the mad and the bad. The philosophe, therefore, can only live with philosophes.'[3]

Despite the progress and relative openness that characterized the new era, philosophes were still treated harshly, rather like how the biblical Jews treated their prophets.[4] We should not see this assertion as the root of Voltaire's obsessive Judeophobia. He is rather seeking to describe the classical philosophe as an intellectual continuer of earlier non-conformists, and the comparison with ancient prophets proves highly significant, as we shall go on to see, when it is a question of understanding the evolution of the self-image of the modern intellectual in later years.

In turning to define the man of letters, Voltaire was not content with the criteria cited above. He sought to add another significant element: 'They generally have more independence of mind than other men; and those who are born without fortune readily

---

3   Ibid., vol 3, p. 205.
4   Ibid., vol. 4, p. 576.

find in the foundations of Louis XIV what is needed for them to consolidate this independence.'⁵ This comment would seem to correspond with a lesson Voltaire drew from his own life: he himself spent a large part of his existence seeking solutions for his financial problems, which continued to grow in proportion to the increase in his needs (which is what led him to accept the generous offer of Frederick II of Prussia in 1750). The praise he showers on Louis XIV for having transformed aristocratic patronage into royal patronage was clearly in accord with his liberal monarchist convictions, and perhaps also expressed the satisfaction of men of letters who had recently acquired greater autonomy in comparison with what had been their former level of personal dependence. This process of 'statization', which would assume decisive importance in the history of intellectuals in modern France, undoubtedly began at this time to tighten the link between intellectual elites and the central power.

But did this new royal patronage resolve all the problems of the man of letters? In a final article in the *Dictionnaire philosophique*, which we may suppose was written only later, Voltaire ignores his previous assertion and loudly laments the degraded and precarious condition of the 'philosophe' with a low income in comparison with the assured situation of the average bourgeois.⁶ We may even think for a moment that Voltaire viewed the man of letters, in other words himself, as forming part of that marginal intelligentsia so well described by the historian Robert Darnton in his book *The Literary Underground of the Old Regime*.⁷ And yet, despite his complaints, truth obliges us to say that if Voltaire often had heavy debts to deal with, he never lived in an economically marginal situation, let alone one of poverty.

It is Jean-Jacques Rousseau, Voltaire's great rival, who embodied these marginal men of letters and frequently experienced the

---

5   Ibid., vol. 3, p. 252.

6   Ibid., vol. 4, pp. 576–7.

7   Robert Darnton, *The Literary Underground of the Old Regime*, Cambridge, MA: Harvard University Press, 1985.

precarious status of the writer who lacked privileges; some of these would become revolutionaries later in the century. In the patterns of the mid-eighteenth century, Rousseau's thought belonged to a completely different register than that of Voltaire. Rousseau was distinguished from other philosophes not only by the democratic indications that are frequent in his writings, but also by his exceptional sensitivity towards the classes that he rubbed shoulders with thanks to his rapid social mobility. A native of Geneva, he never managed – perhaps because he did not want it – to fit in with the cultural elites of the Paris salons, whom he continued to despise throughout his life. We could even interpret his second major treatise, the *Discourse on Inequality*, as a theoretical response to the intellectual snobbery that flourished in Paris at this time. The hypothesis might even be cautiously raised that this philosophical 'democratism' saw the light 'against' the capital.

In this essay, and in contrast to a widespread opinion in the eighteenth century, Rousseau emphasizes that it is liberty and not reason that distinguishes man from animals. His representation of primitive man in this text is a kind of theoretical paradigm that Rousseau uses in order to criticize the social division of labour brought about by modernization, which he argues is expressed in a growing intellectualization. The division of labour, and the flexibility to which it gives rise, have made possible the prototype of the modern thinker; this 'sublime' product of human progress can present either a model or a moral degradation in relation to the fundamental values of the common people. Rousseau asserts this in peremptory fashion:

It is reason that engenders self-respect, and reflection that confirms it; it is reason which turns man's mind back upon itself, and divides him from everything that could disturb or afflict him. It is philosophy that isolates him, and bids him say, at sight of the misfortunes of others: 'Perish if you will, I am secure.' Nothing but such general evils as threaten the whole community can disturb the tranquil sleep of the philosopher, or tear him from his bed. A murder may with impunity be committed under his window; he has only to put his hands to his ears and argue a little with himself, to prevent nature, which is shocked within him, from identifying itself with the unfortunate sufferer. Uncivilized man has not this admirable talent; and for want of reason and wisdom, is always foolishly ready to obey the first promptings of humanity.[8]

This unqualified assault on the intellectual philosopher is completely expressed in terms of moral preaching, which is precisely what gives it its interest. As with Voltaire, the thinker is distinguished first and foremost by his moral positions, but, contrary to his liberal rival, the democrat Rousseau displays no sign of identification with the image of the philosopher he describes. We do not find in this extract the least element of a self-portrait on the part of the author. The thinker appears here as a distant other, embodying everything that horrified the tormented Rousseau. He sees the philosopher as a courtier, assiduously frequenting royal palaces and princely courts and spending his time humiliating himself before the powerful.

But how far is it possible to go in criticizing an existing example without putting forward an alternative model? Was Rousseau, who often did not like himself, truly lacking in any positive self-regard? We can find a different image of the man of letters by turning to his second major work, *The Social Contract*.

Despite his fundamentally egalitarian conception, Rousseau finds the need to resort to the mythological figure of the lawgiver, who appears as a miraculous intellectual:

To discover the rules of society that are best suited to nations, there would need to exist a superior intelligence, who could

---

8   Jean-Jacques Rousseau, *The Social Contract and Discourses*, London: Dent, 1923, p. 199.

understand the passions of men without feeling any of them ... The lawgiver is the engineer who invents the machine ... The lawgiver is, in every respect, an extraordinary man in the state. Extraordinary not only because of his genius, but equally because of his office, which is neither that of the government nor that of the sovereign.[9]

Would it be wrong to say that in his celebrated proposals of constitutional laws for Poland and Corsica, Rousseau saw himself to a certain extent in the role of Solon of Athens or the Geneva reformer Jean Calvin? Under a constitutional form, the first modern critic of intellectuals seems to express here a concealed aspiration, perhaps an unconscious one, for spiritual power. At all events, it is clear that in *The Social Contract* the vocation of the lawgiver, this supreme intellectual, is not to take part in the social life of the organized citizens; he is in no case destined to play an active role in what will become the concrete political field of a democratic society. According to Rousseau, in the reformed world of tomorrow, spiritual power must be an integral part of political power.

Scientists and revolutionary writers

Less than a century later, and in the light of the historical experience and lessons drawn from the 'Great Revolution', one French thinker battled throughout his life with an awkward set of questions: how to create a spiritual power of a new type? At the same time, another thinker lamented the catastrophe that, during the revolutionary fracture, had enabled philosophers and men of letters to conquer the country's circles of power in the name of the 'mind'.

Auguste Comte and Alexis de Tocqueville were among the most original thinkers of the nineteenth century, and each is

9   Jean-Jacques Rousseau, *The Social Contract*, Book 2, Harmondsworth: Penguin, 1968, pp. 84–5.

considered in his way a precursor of modern sociology. A quick look at their biographies could lead to the conclusion that the career of the former ended in resounding defeat, while the political trajectory of the latter was crowned with success. Comte tried in vain to join the academic institution that was still in the process of formation; see for example his request to François Guizot to obtain a chair for him at the Collège de France. Tocqueville, on the other hand, was for a long period a parliamentary deputy, and for a short time held the post of foreign minister. In the Parisian intellectual sphere, however, Comte's name acquired a growing reputation; eminent scholars from the Académie des sciences attended his lectures, and on the eve of his death he had already given his name to a school of thought. Tocqueville saw his literary star fade after the success of his first book, to the point that after his death his work underwent a long eclipse, remaining tangential to the French cultural sphere for nearly a century.

Despite his marginal position in the institution, Comte displayed great self-confidence and always saw himself as the representative of a new science in the process of achieving a position of superiority in the field of cultural production (which was far from being the case). Tocqueville, on the other hand, saw his own writings as defeatist reactions to the maelstrom of historical events. Whereas Comte waxed enthusiastic at the rapid progress of industry, Tocqueville worried about its social and political consequences. Comte embodied the philosophical optimism of the nineteenth century, expressed politically in a form of cautious republicanism that, given the spirit of the time, could be as Bonapartist as it was democratic. Tocqueville was the representative of a pessimistic and aristocratic sensibility, disposed if somewhat reluctantly to accept a kind of democratic liberalism and cultural pluralism that, according to him, would never manage to take root in modern France.

Auguste Comte struggled for a long while with the problem

of the deficit of stable spiritual power in the post-revolutionary world in which he found himself. The decline of the church in the eighteenth century, then the convulsions to its status under the Revolution, created from his point of view a dangerous vacuum, a constant factor of instability and social agitation. Philosophy had now to take as its mission the establishment of programmatic foundations on which a solid spiritual authority could be constructed alongside the earthly power. In his early writings of the 1820s, such as *Philosophical Reflections on the Sciences and Scientists*, Comte already systematically deployed theoretical guidelines that would evolve very little in the course of his copious work. Initially following in the steps of Saint-Simon, his abhorred mentor, he saw the new scientists as the vessels of spiritual power. As distinct from other classes, the latter now possessed two fundamental elements required for moral governance: practical competence and theoretical authority.[10]

It is interesting to note that, in another of his writings, Comte had recourse to a term little used, the *intelligences*, which he preferred to that of *savants*, before subsequently introducing a new concept, the 'contemplative class'.[11] This was entrusted with a double social and historical function: on the one hand, to collect and distribute knowledge, and on the other, to conduct its pedagogic mission by an intensive education devoted to values.[12] According to the pioneer sociologist, the development of civilization, the advance of industrialism, the increased division of labour and the aggravation of class conflict led to the necessity of establishing a spiritual and intellectual authority, which had been lacking in the Western world since the

---

10   Auguste Comte, 'Plan of the Scientific Operations Necessary for Reorganizing Society', in Roland Fletcher (ed.), *The Crisis of Industrial Civilization: The Early Essays of Auguste Comte*, London: Heinemann Educational, 1974, p. 131.

11   Auguste Comte, *Cours de philosophie positive*, vol. 6, Paris: Bachelier, 1842, p. 706, and 'Considerations on the spiritual power', in ibid., pp. 235–6.

12   Ibid., p. 236.

Revolution of 1789. A worldly power that lacked ideological legitimacy could in fact only have a limited life expectancy.

The revolution of 1848, and in particular the working-class insurrection that followed, spurred Comte to recognize the central place of the new proletariat in the worldly order, and from this point on it is possible to detect in him a certain political tilt to the left. At the same time, however, he felt an urgent need to establish the kernel of the future spiritual power, which led him to found the Société Positiviste that same year. In the charter he wrote for this 'spiritual society', he gives its aim as completing and perfecting the last revolution by reformulating ideas and moral codes for it.[13] It was incumbent on this new authority to establish and organize itself not on a national basis, but in a broad pan-European context. It was logical, Comte held, that France should stand as the spiritual centre of this intellectual construction, and that the putative father of this project should reluctantly assume its direction. Comte insisted: 'To better assure the unity of composition indispensable to the Positivist Society, I shall remain sole judge of the intellectual and moral suitability of all those who request to join it.'[14]

The precursor of sociology, more than any other thinker, thus expressed clearly, incisively and candidly the irrepressible intellectual aspiration to establish a spiritual power, which 'clerks' seemed to have lost with the decline in the authority of the church.

We do not know whether Tocqueville had the opportunity to read the first sociologist's appeal in 1848, being absorbed as he then was in political activity. If he was aware of it, it would very likely have horrified him. Tocqueville would have found both disturbing and antagonizing the analogy that Comte makes at the start of his charter between the Jacobin club at the time of

---

13   Auguste Comte, 'Le fondateur de la société positiviste', in *Du pouvoir spirituel*, Paris: Livre de poche, 1978, p. 340.
14   Ibid., p. 344.

the Revolution and his new Positivist Society. The prophet-like aspiration of intellectuals to reform the world always appeared to Tocqueville as a dangerous phenomenon in the history of contemporary France.

The course of the 1848 Revolution and its ultimate fate pressed Tocqueville to write *The Ancien Régime and the Revolution*, a brilliant work that contains a fascinating chapter entitled 'How Around the Middle of the Eighteenth Century Men of Letters Became the Leading Political Figures in the Country and the Consequences of This'. Tocqueville never felt sympathy for the writers of the Enlightenment, not hiding his opinion even when it was unfashionable. The reason he disliked them was precisely what subsequently brought these men of letters the label of 'intellectuals'; in other words, their relationship to modern politics and their way of involving themselves in it.

In conformity with his method, Tocqueville tackled the question of French literati by proposing a comparison with their British and German counterparts. He believed that, contrary to the prevailing situation in England, they had sadly remained at a distance from any public function and any intervention in current political matters. This lack of independent political and institutional activity had prevented French literati from experiencing the complexity of the state function from close up. In contrast to their German equivalents, however, who were in a comparable socio-political situation, the French did not agree to keep to the domain of pure philosophy, and set out to foster generalizing political theories: 'They all thought that it was right to replace the complex and traditional customs which guided the society of their time with simple and elementary rules borrowed from reason and natural law.'[15]

Tocqueville drew the basis on which he criticized the French Revolution from Edmund Burke, and went on to develop from

---

15   Alexis de Tocqueville, *The Ancien Régime and the Revolution*, London: Penguin, 2008, p. 141.

it the first sketch of a sociology of intellectuals. He held that abstract and literary political thought was born from the social and political positioning of eighteenth-century literati:

> The very condition of these writers predisposed them to favour general and abstract theories of government and to trust them blindly. In the almost total removal of their lives from the practical world, no direct experience came to modify the passions of their temperament. Nothing warned them about obstacles which existing conditions could bring to even the most desirable reforms.[16]

This abstract position, which failed to take account of the complexity of political life, was erected into an educational model for the people, which is where the 'philosophes' held a share of responsibility for the misfortunes that came with the age of revolutions:

> The whole nation read these writers and ended up by adopting the instincts, the turn of mind, the inclinations and even the eccentricities characteristic of writers. The result was that, when it finally had to act, the nation brought all the habits of literature into politics . . . A frightening spectacle! For what is a good quality in a writer is a failing in a politician.[17]

Only Tocqueville could have defined the Revolution as a literary act, and had the word existed at the time, he would certainly have called it an 'intellectual' one. Literati create their work starting from a uniform and a priori project; but if politicians proceed in such a way, they transform history into a fearsome practice, precisely what happened at the time of the French Revolution. Literati lacking any sense of historical reality and its complexity

---

16   Ibid., p. 142.
17   Ibid., p. 148.

became the leaders of their generation. One need only read the writings of these revolutionaries to understand the essence of this phenomenon.

What Tocqueville actually tells us is that these men of letters took power at the time of the Revolution, and he seems to have been the first to perceive that modern revolutions have been led and guided by cultural elites who metamorphosed into political elites. Recent decades have seen the development of a whole brand of political sociology that has broadened and developed this 'Tocquevillian' argument, if with far less virtuosity and far more dogmatism than its nineteenth-century originator in their quest to preserve the existing order.

Tocqueville, as we saw, wrote this book in the wake of the 1848 Revolution. Was it only Danton, Robespierre and Saint-Just that he had in mind, or did he also associate such contemporary 'intelligences' as Alphonse de Lamartine, Alexandre Ledru-Rollin and Louis Blanc? It is hard to give a definite verdict. What is clear in any case is that the mode of approach and action of writers and historians in the French political field through the mid-nineteenth century always appeared to Tocqueville as a generator of misfortune. Yet it would be wrong to deduce from this that Tocqueville recommended literati to disengage from all political action: his declarations and his personal mode of intervention in the political sphere make clear his underlying model of a different kind of political man of letters. Following the British example, Tocqueville thought the French man of letters should act as the modest and efficient servant of the public, bowing to the principles of an empirical and pragmatic policy. This clearly implies getting away from the deceptive image of the indignant prophet coming to proclaim eternal truth to the world. It is an idea that we have seen an increasing number of conservative intellectuals enthusiastically adopt.

Traitors and Watchdogs

Two books that appeared in the interwar period discuss the role and status of the modern intellectual: Julien Benda's famous essay *La Trahison des clercs*, published in 1927, and Paul Nizan's *Les Chiens de garde* in 1932, which in many respects can be seen as a direct response to the former.

Both authors gave a central place in their work to the relationship of intellectuals to politics; both preferred the word *clerc* to *intellectuel*. By using *clerc*, Benda and Nizan each stressed the close connection between the former status of the clergy and that of the modern intellectual. However, while for Benda the 'clerk' is the object of a spiritual idealization despite the deceptive title of his essay, Nizan delivers a biting, almost disgusted critique of the institutional intellectual.

Julien Benda, who grew up in an established and well-to-do family, never had to worry about making a living. In the mid-1920s his status was that of a well-known writer and critic, and his secular and moderate republicanism was the norm in the elite cultural circles of his time. The activity of the intellectual, as he defines it, should not be directed at practical goals, but rather seek pleasure and satisfaction in the arts, science, or metaphysical speculation. In sum, the intellectual is not someone whose activity consists in winning material advantages; he should rather be able to declare: 'My kingdom is not of this world.'[18]

Yet this assertion could lead to the wrong conclusion that Benda opposed on principle any intervention by intellectuals in politics. He repeatedly stresses his rejection of partisan mobilization, and his entire discourse is marked by a hostility to taking positions in the public sphere. The continuation of his text, however, reveals a more ambiguous and far more problematic relationship. It is not true, Benda maintains, that by descending

---

18   Julien Benda, *The Treason of the Intellectuals*, New Brunswick: Transaction Publishers, 2006, p. 191.

into the public arena the modern clerk derogates from conducting his mission. By their interventions in the past, great figures such as Spinoza, Voltaire or Zola 'were carrying out their function as "clerks" in the fullest and noblest manner. They were the officiants of abstract justice and were sullied with no passion for a worldly object'.[19]

It is worth remembering that at the turn of the century Julien Benda had been a young Dreyfusard; that in the 1930s, only a short while after publishing *Le Trahison des clercs*, he supported the political left; and that in the late 1940s and early 1950s he would even appear as a fellow traveller of communism, like so many others. In the late 1920s, however, a strong commitment to the left, or quite simply to politics in general, was not yet perceived as a respectable option on the part of a prestigious man of letters. (Only the surrealists at this time, who were marginal to the literary field, tried to arouse a nonconformist intellectual mobilization.) And this is why, throughout his essay, Benda emphasized the difference between the Dreyfusard intellectuals at the end of the nineteenth century and the men of letters of the 1920s: those of the previous generation, he insisted, had fought for 'universal justice', whereas those of his generation were serving a narrow and egoistic politics.

It would seem to follow, according to Benda, that one should glorify and admire the French men of letters who propagandized for the 'Union sacrée' which secured socialist support during the First World War. By their intervention, they not only defended their homeland, but also the supreme universal values of which France was the historical birthplace: fighting for France meant fighting for justice and enlightenment. Benda accordingly judged that opposition to the war and appeals to pacifism, particularly those of Romain Rolland between 1914 and 1918, amounted to an irresponsible and blameworthy attitude. The author of *Jean-Christophe* had betrayed his mission as a true man of letters and

---

19   Ibid., p. 50.

deserved public rebuke. And yet those intellectuals who really did commit treason towards the highest universal values during the war, according to Benda, were the ones across the Rhine:

> It must be admitted that the German 'clerks' led the way in this adhesion of the modern 'clerk' to patriotic fanaticism. The French 'clerks' were, and long remained, animated with the most perfect spirit of justice towards foreign cultures (think of the cosmopolitanism of the Romantics!) . . . The nationalist 'clerk' is essentially a German invention . . . most of the moral and political attitudes adopted by the 'clerks' of Europe in the past fifty years are of German origin.[20]

The great treason of the 'clerks' was rooted in a specific historical phenomenon characteristic of the modern age: the 'passion for politics'. This idea, which he repeatedly returns to, is the foundation of Benda's theoretical construction. In fact, he distinguishes two different 'political passions': one that grew up with the idea of the nation, and one that originated with the concept of class. As opposed to the glorious tradition that ran from Socrates to Renan in the late nineteenth century, waging a constant battle in favour of universal norms and a spiritual humanism, the great 'traitors' – from Fichte to Marx, Barrès to Sorel – worshipped the particular and the worldly, and by doing so they denatured their role as citizen and betrayed their spiritual vocation: 'This prodigious decline of morality, this sort of (very Germanic) intellectual sadism, is usually and quite openly accompanied by a huge contempt for the true "clerk".'[21]

According to Benda, therefore, there are 'authentic intellectuals', always in confrontation with counterfeit and treacherous ones. He puts forward various explanations in his essay, both social and political, for the historical appearance of these false

---

20   Ibid., p. 57.
21   Ibid., p. 175.

'clerks'. And he terms the period in which he is writing the 'age of politics': politics displays a force of attraction greater than that of any other domain. The reasons for the intolerable politicization of intellectuals are chiefly bound up with their socioeconomic situation. In a previous age, the man of letters possessed a stable income that assured him an independence, whereas in the new age he finds himself in a state of economic dependence, forcing him to be constantly concerned for his subsistence.

The intellectuals' new faith arises largely from the socioeconomic conditions to which they were subject, and the real problem is not the treason of the 'clerks' but rather their disappearance, and the inability to grant intellectuals a worthy existence. It is the responsibility of the modern state (but can it really do this?) to ensure a status for individuals dispensed from civic obligations and whose sole function is to preserve theoretical and universal values.[22] This is the last line of his argument: without being aware of it, Benda renews the great statist dream of Voltaire.

Yet Benda's book expresses a fundamental paradox: whereas he sees himself as one of the last 'authentic' intellectuals (he does not mention even one other among his contemporaries), he actually appears not only as the representative par excellence of the hegemonic republican nationalism (moderate and careful to reject political extremes), but also as the expression of a relationship between the intellectual and the state apparatus that is highly particular to France.

It is precisely this relationship that led Paul Nizan, a graduate of the École normale supérieure and member of the Communist Party, to rail against those whom he called the 'watchdogs' of the modern state and big capital. Nizan did not shy from maintaining unequivocally, in the face of his intellectual colleagues: 'Through a series of intricate manoeuvres, carried out under of the watchful eyes of our forefathers, the secular clergy was promoted to the position formerly held by its ecclesiastical

---

22   Ibid., p. 144.

counterpart. But this new clergy has discharged exactly the same functions as its predecessor; that is, it has borne the chief responsibility for all the forms of moral suasion, all the spiritual propaganda, which the State might require.'[23]

Like Benda, Nizan abstains from using the term 'intellectual', preferring 'clerk', 'philosopher', or even 'sociologist'. In fact, his attacks essentially target those thinkers convinced that they deal with abstract questions and argue for universal values, whereas in reality they have directly placed themselves at the service of the modern state apparatus and the ruling bourgeois class: 'It is especially noteworthy that, generally speaking, our professional thinkers are salaried employees of the State, that the weightiest opinions in this country are produced in exchange for public monies and are backed up by government sanctions.'[24]

Paul Nizan explicitly sets out to undermine the myth of the modern 'clerisy', who see and present themselves as a universal class seemingly apart from any material interest. The historical process shows that the thinkers who make up this class aspire to produce their ideas in complete tranquillity, just as the industrialists, ardent champions of social peace, dream of being able to manufacture their goods likewise.

According to Nizan, Benda's refusal to admit political reality and his open condemnation of realism are the mark of a hypocritical sophistication, as to confine oneself in neutrality in the face of today's testing political struggles actually leads to the explicit adoption of a political position: 'The desire to be a scholar, and nothing but a scholar, is less a choice by Eternal

---

23   Paul Nizan, *The Watchdogs: Philosophers and the Established Order,* New York: Monthly Review Press, 1971, p. 103. On Nizan's relationship to intellectuals in general, and particularly to Benda, see Guy Palayret, 'Une figure en trompe-l'œil: l'image de l'intellectuel dans les textes critiques de Paul Nizan', in Danièle Bonnaud-Lamotte and Jean-Luc Rispail (eds), *Intellectuels des années trente. Entre le rêve et l'action,* Paris: Éditions du CNRS, 1989, pp. 123–35.

24   Ibid., p. 101.

Man than the decision of the partisan. To abstain is to make a choice, to express a preference.'[25]

Nizan accordingly ridicules those philosophers and sociologists who present themselves as apolitical, but he lambasts still more the institutional intellectuals who had supported the war a few years earlier – the same 'clerks' whom Benda had identified with and paid homage to. Nizan does not hide his hostility towards these:

> These learned clerks simply followed the crowd and obeyed the orders of the generals and politicians. These men, most of whom were not subject to mobilization, meekly went along with the forces of ignorance and exhorted those who had been mobilized to give up their lives. Every one of their students who died in battle was a martyr to their philosophy. They pointed with pride to the dead men as so many proofs of their virtue. These dead men were their dead. These victories were their victories. M. Bergson saw the victory of the French as his victory. It was the victory of Émile Boutroux and Émile Durkheim as well. To M. Brunschvicg the battle of the Marne was nothing less than a resounding confirmation of the rightness of his philosophy.[26]

And, while Benda had stigmatized political commitment as a betrayal of the clerks' status and mission, Nizan ended his book with an appeal to men of letters to dare to betray their station by joining another class: 'It is no longer a question of doing something *for* the workers, but *with* them, in response to *their* demands. The philosopher of tomorrow must be one voice among many – and not the voice of the Mind.'[27]

Nizan's rejection of the spiritual function of the intellectual relates to a wider tendency in his Marxist philosophy, which

---

25   Ibid., p. 43.
26   Ibid., p. 37.
27   Ibid., pp. 136–7.

aimed to suppress the traditional forms of the modern division of labour. Yet this approach does not reject the possibility that the intellectual who betrays his caste may exercise for the time being a specific role in accordance with his skills. Like his predecessors who criticized the dominant intellectual, from Rousseau to Tocqueville, Nizan also offers an alternative model. According to him, the intellectual should rein in his pretensions and seek to be useful to the men living around him. He 'will have no alternative but to serve as the "technician" of their demands. His sole function will be to give expression to the unconscious urges and vague revolutionary impulses now stirring in men's brains.'[28]

The authentic and the opiomane

The term 'technician' appears at the end of Nizan's book, and it is interesting to note that it also figures, though with a rather different meaning, as a starting-point for Jean-Paul Sartre's analysis of the status of the modern man of letters, 'A Plea for Intellectuals', based on a series of lectures that the philosopher gave in Japan in 1965.[29]

At first sight, Sartre's approach seems to continue the radical tradition that Nizan, a friend of his youth, had expressed in *The Watchdogs*, but a careful examination reveals a totally different view of intellectuals. In contrast to the interwar years, the 'Sartre years' that followed the Liberation were marked, in the Parisian intellectual field, not only by a significant presence of the republican political left, but also by an unprecedented advance of Marxism, which had remained marginal before the war. It is no exaggeration to speak of a hegemony of radical Marxism in the

---

28   Ibid., p. 137. To fill out this portrait of the intellectual according to Nizan, see his article 'André Gide', in *Paul Nizan, intellectuel communiste*, vol. 1, Paris: Maspero, 1979, pp. 122–37.

29   'A Plea for Intellectuals', in *Between Existentialism and Marxism*, London: Verso, 1974. These lectures continue and complete positions formulated after the war in *What Is Literature*, London: Methuen, 1978.

1950s and '60s, which certainly was not without its effect on Sartre, then the most famous philosophical 'fellow traveller' of Marxism, and whose discourse on intellectuals was sympathetic if not relatively enthusiastic.

Sartre refers to the genealogy of the 'intellectual': originally the clerics of the church who possessed knowledge by dint of being able to read and write. Their modern heirs are the technicians, specialists in practical knowledge, who appeared with the development of the bourgeois class. At the very start of his lectures, however, Sartre warns his Japanese audience from confusing different things: 'Such technicians of practical knowledge do not yet, as a group, qualify as intellectuals, but it will be from their midst – and nowhere else – that intellectuals will be recruited.'[30]

Sartre focuses on the question of the trajectory that transforms the technician of practical knowledge into a critical intellectual. His response is both simple and direct: technicians, who possess a practical knowledge, are led by their work to carry out an activity with a universal character; in other words, to look for truth. Given that the ends of science and its paths of development are universal par essence, every technician is therefore a potential intellectual. Ordinary technicians constantly experience a contradiction between the universalism of their professional domain, the quest for truth, and the particularism of the ideology and extra-scientific objectives to which they are subject. As soon as the technician's conscience is aroused, and he applies scientific principles to their social environment, 'in a certain sense, [he] becomes *a guardian of fundamental ends* (the emancipation, universalization, and hence humanization of man)'.[31] By way of this process, they effectively become critical intellectuals.

Whereas Durkheim, in his plea for the intervention of men of letters in the Dreyfus affairs, had emphasized the fundamental

---

30   Jean-Paul Sartre, *Between Existentialism and Marxism*, p. 232.
31   Ibid., p. 266.

rationalism of the scientists which conferred on them a primacy in relation to the moral and political field, Sartre substitutes the universalism that, according to him, justifies the symbolic capital and prestige that intellectuals enjoy. Universal scientific logic leads sincere technicians to a dialectical thought, which resolves the fundamental contradiction in which they find themselves and gives them the ability to join the party of the rising working class, as fellow traveller or organic intellectual. And, paradoxical as it may seem, Sartre agrees with Julien Benda on the notion of the 'true intellectual', though in his view, intellectual authenticity must be by its very essence radical, whereas the 'false intellectual' will always prove hesitant at the decisive moment and do everything to avoid confrontation.[32]

Sartre may well have rejected, quite deliberately, any claim and aspiration to a spiritual power as formulated by Auguste Comte, and he constantly addressed marks of ritual acknowledgement to the working class and Marxism. And yet, if the Prussian bureaucracy figured as a universal class in Hegel's political philosophy, and the nineteenth-century proletariat was for Marx the torchbearer of the general interest, we may implicitly deduce from Sartre's philosophy, without exaggeration, that modern intellectuals form the new universal class. Truth is universal, the technicians of practical knowledge deal with truth, and by virtue of this they contain in themselves the potential to become universal intellectuals.

Sartre was nevertheless confronted with a dilemma: neither himself nor his fellow committed intellectuals of the 1950s and '60s had originally been technicians of practical knowledge, and at the end of the day the majority of 'modern prophets' were *not* scientists. How was it possible to overcome this contradiction and explain that a professional writer could become a universal intellectual?

Sartre's third and final lecture in Japan seeks to answer these questions. But his answer, constrained and scarcely satisfactory,

---

32   Ibid., pp. 253–4.

makes the claim that, as against the technician of practical knowledge, the writer is from the start, in his very essence, an intellectual. The very nature of his work makes the writer an intellectual,
as the particular lived experience (*vécu*) that he creates by the act
of literary writing is always accompanied by a universal dimension: 'In this sense, the writer is not an intellectual *accidentally*,
like others, but *essentially*'.[33]

Writers and philosophers who appeared as prophets at the
centre of the public stage were always a great irritant to Raymond
Aron. The liberal sociologist maintained that 'the political ambitions of successful French novelists collide with the literary ambitions of French statesmen, who dream of writing novels just as
the others dream of becoming Ministers'.[34]

In these words, Sartre's most consistent and most determined
rival in the 1950s described the relationship of Parisian intellectuals to politics. Aron had published his famous critical essay on
the intellectualism of Sartre, the revolutionary *opiomane*, ten
years before Sartre's lectures in Japan. This critique received scant
attention in the cultural arena of the 1950s. As distinct from the
hegemonic position held by liberal sociologists in the English-
speaking world, Raymond Aron was for many years relatively
isolated in Parisian cultural circles, despite enjoying a brilliant
academic career.

The starting point of the 'committed spectator', as Raymond
Aron liked to define himself, was not just anti-Sartrean, but more
generally opposed to the currents of thought that Voltaire, Comte
and Benda each embodied in their respective way. Aron's judgement is unequivocal: they displayed 'the same mixture of half-
baked knowledge, of traditional prejudices, of preferences which
are more aesthetic than rational, as in those of shopkeepers or
industrialists'.[35]

---

33   Ibid., p. 284.
34   Raymond Aron, *The Opium of the Intellectuals*, New Brunswick: Transaction
Publishers, 2001, p. 219.
35   Ibid., p. 213.

Though Aron always sought to present himself as a 'cold' academic sociologist, his critique of intellectuals in this fascinating book is more global and venomous. The first question he raises is why it is precisely in France – and we might add, particularly in Paris, the intellectuals' paradise – that 'clerks' see themselves as rebels and revolutionaries.

Aron's answer, unsurprisingly, is identical to that of Tocqueville a century earlier: the literati interested in politics express the bitterness and frustration of being kept at a distance from political action, and feel that their preaching is not taken into consideration.[36] The fact of being cut off from the sphere of political decision generates a messianic intellectualism and the insistent need to speak in the name of humanity as a whole. Parisian intellectuals, with their particular nostalgia for great ideas, consequently choose to intervene against every crime committed on earth, actually seeking to imitate the spiritual power that the Catholic church used to possess.

The intellectuals' religion of messianic humanity, though born in France, is not exclusively French. Similar secular beliefs are widespread in Europe, Asia and Africa. According to Aron, the revolutions of the twentieth century were led by intellectuals. 'In Russia, it is intellectuals who grant the supreme investiture. Communism is the first intellectuals' religion to have succeeded.'[37] The Soviet Revolution swept away capitalists, bankers, elected representatives; in other words, all those who in a parliamentary democracy bar the intellectuals' access to the summits of power. Therefore, communist power is by definition an intellectual power. According to Aron, both Lenin and Stalin were typical of the revolutionary intellectual transformed into political leader. By placing these assertions in the context of the well-known hostility that Raymond Aron maintained towards the USSR, we can understand why his critique

36   Ibid., p. 219.
37   Ibid., pp. 278–9.

of intellectuals, his own colleagues, was so radical and intransigent.

From Sartre to Stalin, the conservative sociologist has no pity for the modern intellectual. The tone of Aron's book is harsh, his underlying premises pejorative. Aron was careful not to include all clerks under the same judgement, and like his predecessors who criticized the self-sufficiency of intellectuals, he in turn very openly praises the positive intellectual. In the 1950s, this atypical liberal thinker followed Tocqueville in referring to British literati as 'moderate and reformist', an example to follow.[38] The role of the intellectual, without being marginal, should be circumscribed and limited; he should seek to behave as a kind of agent of the public, able to evaluate the leading institutions, and particularly to adapt to a politics of the possible.

Aron asserts his particular repugnance for the share of hypocrisy contained in the dominant discourse of the left, and cannot restrain an acrimonious reprimand:

> But why do the intellectuals not admit to themselves that they are less interested in the standard of living of the working class than in the refinements of art and life? Why do they cling to democratic jargon when in fact they are trying to defend authentically aristocratic values against the invasion of mass-produced human beings and mass-produced commodities?[39]

Raymond Aron was sometimes decidedly more 'materialist' in his sociological approach than his Marxist rivals, practitioners of historical materialism, a fact that itself attests to the hegemony of Marxism at this time. But in the end it fell to another French sociologist to apply himself systematically to demolishing the illusions of intellectuals and breaking down the Chinese walls they had erected by their mastery of the pen.

---

38   Ibid., p. 234.
39   Ibid., p. 228.

Dominant and dominated

In an interview given in 1978, Pierre Bourdieu summed up his work so far on the cultural field by declaring: 'If you like, I brought back into play what was out of play: intellectuals always agree among themselves to leave out of play their own game and their own stakes.'[40]

Faced with the leftist intellectuals of the 1960s and '70s, who were intoxicated with their 'role as a revolutionary avant-garde', the author of *Distinction* presented a cold and clear analysis that aimed to define the position of the intellectual field in relation to the political arena, as well as reveal the balance of forces within this field. Though Bourdieu was already a famous sociologist, in these decades he abstained from any public intellectual activity. He did not join Sartre or Foucault, and had not yet 'descended' to demonstrate and protest in the street.[41]

Bourdieu's work did accomplish a great deal towards shifting the field of research on the 'upper' cultural stratum, both stimulating and accelerating a non-normative approach to the notion of the modern priest and prophet. Bourdieu gave a definition of intellectuals that was quite unambiguous and would hardly change in future years: 'as holders of cultural capital, intellectuals are a (dominated) fraction of the dominant class and . . . a number of the stances they take up, in politics for example, derive from the ambiguity of their dominated-dominant position'.[42]

From Bourdieu's point of view, scientists, academics, writers, essayists and journalists are intellectuals. All these professions should be the object of research, and no one should flinch from

---

40   Pierre Bourdieu, 'The Sociologist in Question', in *Sociology in Question*, London: Sage Publications, 1993, p. 37.

41   We may recall here that Sartre and Foucault only became committed intellectuals at a mature age, after having built up a stable and well-assured symbolic capital (the young Foucault's brief and inactive membership of the Communist Party, from 1950 to 1953, corresponded to the air of the time and was not significant).

42   Pierre Bourdieu, 'How Can Free-Floating Intellectuals Be Set Free?', in *Sociology in Question*, p. 43.

applying critical sociology to sociologists or to him- or herself. Bourdieu personally admitted on many occasions that he did not feel at ease in the role of intellectual, considering that this was a privileged, even aristocratic, social status canonized by modern society. Taking his distance in this way led to his being accused of theoretical anti-intellectualism by a number of his colleagues, an accusation that he always rejected. However, as against the tradition running from Voltaire to Sartre, Bourdieu declared without hesitation: 'In fact, it is very common for intellectuals to use the competence (in the quasi-legal sense of the word) that is socially conferred on them as a pretext for speaking with authority far beyond the limits of their technical competence, especially in the area of politics.'[43]

From this starting point, we can understand why Bourdieu explicitly rejected Sartre's universal model, and even expressed reservations about Foucault's prototype of the 'specific intellectual', which I shall discuss below (chapter 5). In his conclusions, he rejected any idea of intellectual superiority in areas where the agent of 'high culture' has to intervene as citizen, just as he never lost sight of the fact that the dominated intellectual continues to belong to the dominant, from a political and economic point of view. We could thus say, with a little exaggeration, that Bourdieu's ambition was to do for symbolic capital what Marx had done a century earlier for financial capital.

In the 1980s, however, after the deaths of Sartre and Foucault, with the decline in fashion of the radical left in Parisian intellectual circles and, above all, in the wake of important changes that took place in Bourdieu's own intellectual positioning (he reached a peak of celebrity with his election to the Collège de France in 1981), his discourse on the sociology of culture underwent a change of tone. His turn towards a normative and positive position was expressed in a short obituary on Michel Foucault of 1984:

---

43 Ibid., p. 45.

[Intellectuals] are not representatives of universality, still less a 'universal class', but it does happen that, for historical reasons, they are often *interested in universality* . . . it is urgent today to create an international of artists and scientists able to propose or impose reflections and recommendations on the political and economic powers that be. I will just say – and I believe Michel Foucault would have agreed – that the only possible basis for a power that is specifically intellectual and intellectually legitimate, lies in the most complete autonomy in relation to all existing powers.[44]

We shall never know whether Foucault would have agreed with this formulation of Bourdieu's. And to claim that Auguste Comte, the first Parisian sociologist, found his final heir in Bourdieu, perhaps the last great Parisian sociologist, would be an insidious approximation: certainly such a comparison would have met with an angry response from Bourdieu. The fact remains, however, that from then on in his writings there are more explicit declarations demanding a greater weight for those whom Bourdieu had qualified as 'dominated' while belonging to the dominant class.

The changes that took place in Eastern Europe in the late 1980s, and the role played at this time by various intellectuals, shifted Bourdieu's position. In his public expressions, he now set out to give an increasingly important place to the idea of an international of intellectuals.[45] Bourdieu's fullest expression in this subject was in a lecture entitled 'The Corporatism of the Universal', delivered in Japan in 1989, in which he sought to lay down the theoretical and strategic foundations for a renewal of intervention by the 'producers of culture' in the public arena.[46]

---

44   Pierre Bourdieu, 'Intellectuals and Established Powers', in *Political Interventions*, London: Verso, 2008, pp. 131–2.

45   See for example Pierre Bourdieu, 'History Dawns in the East', in *Liber* (supplement to *Times Literary Supplement*, no. 4524), 15 December 1989.

46   Pierre Bourdieu, 'The Corporatism of the Universal: The role of intellectuals in the modern world', *Poetics Today*, vol. 12, no. 4, 1991, pp. 655–69.

Whereas Sartre had given his famous lectures at a time when the political engagement of intellectuals was at a peak, Bourdieu formulated his ideas at the start of a period of stagnation in which 'great intellectuals' had begun to disappear from the public stage. This explains their mobilizing character, and the attempt to create new instruments of intervention: 'The first objective of intellectuals should be to work collectively in defence of their specific interests and of the means necessary for protecting their own autonomy.'[47] Specific mechanisms and instances must thus be created that will enable intellectuals to intervene in politics in a collective fashion, under the aegis of their own authority.

In the past, the 'clerks' who became fellow travellers or even organic intellectuals of political parties had always given priority to universal battles over the promotion of their own interests, forgetting in the process that 'one defends the universal by defending the defenders of the universal'.[48] What must now be vigorously defended, Bourdieu explains, is the republic of scientists, writers and artists. But defended against whom? Against journalists, essayists and 'bad sociologists' who, if we are to believe the 'good' sociologist, are like foreign invading forces in the intellectual field. The autonomy of this field is thus threatened by a Trojan horse, installed with the support of 'public opinion' and market forces.

In the 1980s, Bourdieu belonged to the dominant pole of the international academic field, and the Socialist government entrusted him with a mission to reform the educational system. However, he always thought poorly of his relative inferiority in the Parisian media field, which probably explains this new discourse, whose aim was no longer to reveal the objectives and rules of the game of intellectuals, but rather to defend the autonomy of one category of these. From now on, the defence mechanisms had to be directed not so much

---

47   Ibid., p. 660.
48   Ibid., p. 661.

against political power as against others 'dominated within the dominant class'.

The activity of literati should not be reduced to defence of their own interests. Bourdieu has in mind the good of society as a whole, which has to face up to a new danger: the advent of the technocrats – this new state nobility – has displaced intellectuals from the public arena. Faced with this disturbing process, Bourdieu set out in search of a strategic tool capable of bringing them back to the foreground of the democratic stage. The prototype for this could no longer be the old Sartrean model, nor the more modest formula of the 'specific intellectual' as defined by Foucault. It was necessary to draw on an older past: the model would now be that of the collective intellectual of the eighteenth century that focused the attention of all educated people of that time. 'I am thinking, for instance, of the "philosophes" of the *Encyclopédie*',[49] he confides, and goes on to propose the creation of a network of encyclopaedists on an international scale, fortunately without indicating how and by whom these would be appointed. He found it also necessary to add, moreover: 'It is not a question of taking power, but of taking counter-power, a bit of counter-power. When power appeals to science, science must equip itself with a counter-power.'[50]

This final project of Pierre Bourdieu can close the circle of images opened by Voltaire. It would certainly have been possible to add other couples to this list, but the aim of this chapter is not to claim that intellectuals' social positioning or the place of their discourse in relation to the dominant ideology in the cultural field directly determines, always and in every case, all the theories and assertions they are led to formulate. It has tried to point out that the self-portrait of the intellectual, their self-esteem or their

---

49   Ibid., p. 667.
50   'D'abord defender les intellectuels . . .', conversation with Didier Eribon, *Le Nouvel Observateur*, 12–18 September 1986, p. 82.

disdain for their colleagues, form a tangle that is no less complex than in the case of restaurant waiters, taxi drivers, company directors or salaried employees. My intention is simply to emphasize that any analysis of an ideological discourse on intellectuals must take into account their level of charismatic authority in their own eyes, and their way of locating themselves in the cultural and ideological world in which they intervene. The place from where they express themselves is in fact always marked by a balance of forces, which most often finds expression in their discourse.

It goes without saying that this rule equally applies to the author of the present book. Coherence demands that a chapter dealing with the discourse of intellectuals and proposing the hypothesis that their positioning in relation to the dominant ideology has its repercussions on the salient lines of discourse, inevitably turns into a critical discourse on intellectuals. The point of view presented in these pages, accordingly, belongs to the negative tendency of the critical tradition, which means that within the intellectual field it occupies a position of inferiority.

CHAPTER 3

Marx and His Descendants: Symbolic Capital or Political Capital?

Just as, therefore, at an earlier period, a section of the nobility went over to the bourgeoisie, so now a portion of the bourgeoisie goes over to the proletariat, and in particular, a portion of the bourgeois ideologists, who have raised themselves to the level of comprehending theoretically the historical movement as a whole.

Karl Marx and Friedrich Engels,
The Communist Manifesto, 1848

The first task of Marxism is to conceal the class interest of educated society in the age of development of large-scale industry – the class interest of those privileged mercenaries, the intellectual workers in the capitalist state.

Jan Wacław Machajski, *The Intellectual Worker,* 1905

When I became involved in political activism, I was still a manual worker, and this probably contributed to my subsequent attitude towards 'intellectual workers', which was hesitant and suspicious. At that time a young leftist, I inclined towards what Marxists contemptuously call 'workerism'. For this reason, I immediately preferred the idea of the 'spontaneity of the masses' developed by

Rosa Luxemburg to that of the 'revolutionary vanguard' as found in Lenin, Trotsky or Mao. Within the radical organization I had joined, I was one of the few manual workers among a majority of teachers, professors and especially students. All of these without exception, however, worshipped the proletariat, or else the revolutionary peasantry of the Third World.

I still remember an anecdote that one of the older militants in the group told me. When he visited Paris in the 1960s, he was invited to a meeting of the group's fraternal party there. The hall was gradually filling up when suddenly a man appeared whom everyone present clustered around. My Israeli friend, assuming that this was the group's leader, asked the people around him who he was. Their immediate reply was: 'It's the worker!'

The passage from the *Communist Manifesto* that I used as an epigraph to this chapter has not enjoyed much attention on the part of Marx's commentators, nor indeed in subsequent Marxist writing. The terms 'intelligentsia' and 'intellectual' were not yet in use as nouns when the *Manifesto* was written; it was the term 'ideologist', which appeared in France soon after the Revolution, that was used to define the 'revolutionary bourgeois' literati. Marx and Engels sought in this way to resolve the problem of their own identity – rather hastily, but in an unsurprising manner – as associates of a historical movement in which the proletariat was to be the principal actor.

While the revolutions of 1848, which broke out only a few weeks after the publication of the *Manifesto*, highlighted the role of typical literati – Lamartine and Ledru-Rollin in Paris, the members of the Vorparlament in Frankfurt and the radical students in Vienna – the contemporary 'bearers of ideology' (liberal, democrat or socialist) could not yet find a label for their political action and cultural positioning in class terms. The great universal aspirations that had blossomed in 1848 rapidly collapsed into national egoism and economic particularism, but the upsurge of abstract universalism was not yet in a position to generate among educated elites a particular consciousness that expressed a hierarchy and interests distinct from those of the 'major' classes.

We do not find in the writings of Marx and Engels any thorough discussion of the division of labour between those who 'know' and those who do not, between 'knowledge workers' and manual workers. Francis Bacon's motto '*Ipsa scientia potestas est*' (knowledge itself is power) seems to have been totally absent from their field of vision when they occupied themselves with the establishment and form of the workers' association. In describing the political actors who belonged to revolutionary committees during the French Revolution, and the state apparatus to which this gave rise, they used the terms 'bourgeois' or 'petty bourgeois'. The founders of scientific socialism made no reference to a distinct category made up of those new groups who, before entering politics, had not only built up goods, but also a cultural capital that they were able to make effective use of in the power struggles for control of the state.

The question of relations between representatives and represented, and that of the transparency and validity of any political representation, are totally absent from Marx and Engels's sustained and dense reflections, and this is in no way the result of chance. Who knew better than they did that the nobles who joined the bourgeoisie became bourgeois themselves, all too familiar with the secrets of the market economy? They very likely assumed that the bourgeois who went over to the proletariat would thereby become part of a future socialist civilization without classes. It is hard to believe, however, that they failed to realize that this transition would not transform learned scholars into socialist production workers. If they did have any awareness of this problem, it was repressed into obscure corners of the world of Marxist thought. The 'thinking portion' of the workers' movement never became the object of sociological critique by the founders of historical materialism.

It was not until the end of the nineteenth century, when the Second Industrial Revolution saw the emergence of new forms of division of labour and a growth in the educated strata, that Marx's theoretical descendants, with considerable hesitation, began to approach the question of the 'capitalists of knowledge'. The 1890s saw the publication of some surprising texts from thinkers who defined themselves as Marxists, and who began to question the meaning of 'ideologists going over' to the camp of revolution. Yet historians have paid little attention to this Marxist debate on the positioning of the educated in relation to the workers' movement.[1] The majority of historians who have seriously considered the history of socialism were socialists themselves and, as professional intellectuals, any critical discourse that might make them a distinct object of research, rather than an 'organic' part of the great revolutionary class, did not enjoy their sympathy or give rise to favourable theoretical developments.

There is also another reason for the lack of historiographical interest in this late nineteenth-century debate. It was precisely at this time, with the rise of workers' parties throughout Europe, that the great debate between revolutionaries and reformists broke out in the socialist movement. The unfortunate effect of this polemic was to drag the best socialist minds into bitter and interminable clashes, which again drove any theoretical clarification of the problematic of intellectuals to the margins of historical knowledge.

The corporatist intelligentsia

Every specialist in the history of socialism knows that Karl Kautsky, the theorist of the great German Social Democratic Party, held a key place in the debate between reformist revisionism and orthodox Marxism. It is less well known, however, that Kautsky was also the first 'debater' in a fascinating discussion

---

1   Régis Debray is something of an exception, though he formulates a point of view very different from the present analysis. See Régis Debray, *Le Scribe*, Paris: Grasset, 1980, pp. 161–209.

about the status of the intelligentsia in the new process of modernization. Kautsky, the 'pope' of Second International Marxism, was in fact the first thinker to have tackled this subject, long before such academic sociologists as Émile Durkheim, Max Weber or Karl Mannheim, and to have made the literati an object of systematic research.

Kautsky, a prolific Marxist thinker in the German cultural sphere, inaugurated this debate before Parisian Marxists, and it was not accidental that he gave it a more radical turn both theoretically and politically, to the point of challenging the relationship between the producers of 'high culture' and socialism. Any new clarification of the subject, I believe, must begin with an analysis of the nature and the fate reserved for this forgotten discourse in the history of Marxist ideology.

1895 saw the simultaneous publication in the Stuttgart-based *Neue Zeit* and the Parisian *Le Devenir social*, the two most important Marxist periodicals of the time, of Karl Kautsky's essay entitled: 'Die Intelligenz und die Sozialdemokratie'. As a noun, the word 'intellectual' was totally unknown in Germany, and its use in France still remained unusual, which is why Kautsky resorted to the term *Intelligenz*, knowing that it had been widespread in Russia since the 1860s in the form of 'intelligentsia'. The editors of *Le Devenir social* preferred to replace this little-known word with 'liberal professions' in the title, though not in the body of the article.[2] This translation did not distort Kautsky's ideas, as he had not retained in his essay the moral and political sense that the term carried in Russian. We shall see that the meaning given by Kautsky to the intelligentsia in 1895 was purely an occupational one, anticipating in this its use in modern sociology.

But we should not be deceived. Kautsky was not a professional sociologist but a socialist theorist, and his motives for writing this essay were explicitly political. By way of introduction, he

---

2   Karl Kautsky, 'Le socialisme et les carrières libérales', *Le Devenir social*, May–June 1895, pp. 105–19 and 265–74.

declared: 'Of all the problems that our party has recently found along its way, the two most important are propaganda in the countryside and the conquest of the intelligentsia.'[3] The fact that the question of the intelligentsia occupied a place alongside that of the peasantry shows us its centrality in the problems of European socialism in the mid-1890s. Three years before a heated debate on the subject of the intellectuals and politics was to break out, on the occasion of the Dreyfus trial, the most prominent representative of Marxism in the Second International tackled with keen awareness the question of 'intellectuals', seeking, as distinct from both liberal and conservative spokespeople in France in 1898, to integrate this into a consideration that was both social and political.

Kautsky admits to his readers right away the two main motives that impelled his concern with the intelligentsia: first of all, this was a subject already debated on the European left, and secondly, the social stratum described by this term was undergoing a process of structural modifications that required a specific approach. On the first point, Kautsky seems to be referring to a lively discussion that had taken place in the early 1890s in left-wing students' associations, focusing on a new and unexpected concept of the 'intellectual proletariat'. The rapid growth of European universities in the last two decades of the century, and the growing political dissatisfaction among an increasing number of students, had found expression in the creation of socialist student associations. Thus, while previously radicalization led students to join individually the existing revolutionary democratic or socialist organizations, specific socialist associations now appeared whose ranks were exclusively made up of students.

The quest for a definition appropriate to the spirit of the age and the deteriorating economic situation of many students led to the emergence of the term 'intellectual proletariat'. This broad concept enabled many socialist students to continue having the

---

3   Ibid., p. 106.

sense of belonging to a cultural elite, while viewing themselves as an integral part of the rising workers' movement. Discussion on this intellectual proletariat was particularly lively in France, with Jean Jaurès taking an active part in it.[4] Recourse to this combination of words manifestly opened the way to the birth of the term 'intellectual' used as a noun.

Kautsky, in his long essay, welcomes the advance of socialist ideas among the student youth, and concludes by inviting them to continue spreading these principles, not so much in the working class but rather in their own milieu. However, apart from examining the relations between the student world and the workers' parties, the Marxist theorist understood very well that socialism was now faced with a significant new phenomenon. With the strong development of the division of labour, and the extension of higher education, an increasing number of students, on completing their studies, joined a social stratum that bore new characteristics.

Would the Marxist prediction that all intermediate social groups between the bourgeoisie and the proletariat were condemned to disappear in the face of the growing accumulation of capital be refuted by the growth of this new intelligentsia? As an orthodox Marxist, Kautsky decisively rejected such a heretical question. True, the intelligentsia was indeed an intermediate social stratum, but it was absolutely different from the classic intermediate social groups formed at the start of capitalist modernization. Though not an organic part of the working class, the new intelligentsia was a stratum of employees, and by virtue of this its relation to the means of production differed fundamentally from that of other intermediate groups. Intellectual work certainly used to enjoy many privileges, but the conditions of its production had changed; its new producers had nothing in common with parasites or exploiters.

---

4   See Jean Jaurès, 'Les étudiants socialistes', *La Petite République*, 13 May 1893.

According to Kautsky, the new members of the intelligentsia are from varied origins: they may be descendants of existing intelligentsia, children of fallen noble families, or else from a lower social class. Above all, however, it turns out that this new stratum is made up of sons of the middle class: small proprietors whose capital is endangered by new productive processes, and who are keen to guarantee their children a more secure economic future. Thus, one of the main factors in the constitution of the intelligentsia in the late nineteenth century was not necessarily a need inherent to industrial development or a consequence of the expansion of the state apparatus, but proceeded rather from the desire of a class on the decline to protect its descendants from the risk of proletarianization: hence the appearance of the strange socio-economic phenomenon of 'overproduction in the intelligentsia'.[5]

Despite the fact that the economic and demographic statistics available today refute the hypothesis of a surplus intellectual population in the late nineteenth century, it is important to mention that most publications of the time that discussed the status of the various cultural producers did make estimates of this kind.[6] The unease of intellectual youth has always been bound up with a sense of frustration resulting from the difficulty of finding employment that corresponds to the nature of their intellectual formation. In other words, the level of expectation generates dissatisfaction and protest. Moreover, the economic instability that marked the decade preceding the publication of Kautsky's text temporarily created pockets of unemployment among the literati, which had the effect of slowing down the upward mobility expected by university

5   Karl Kautsky, 'Le socialisme et les carrières libérales', p. 112.

6   See Louis Pinto, 'Les intellectuels vers 1900: une nouvelle classe moyenne', in Gérard Grunberg, Georges Lavau and Nonna Mayer (eds), *L'Univers politique des classes moyennes*, Paris: Les Presses de Sciences Po, 1983, pp. 140–55, and 'La vocation de l'universel: la formation de la représentation de l'intellectuel vers 1900', *Actes de la recherche en science sociales*, vol. 55, no. 1, November 1984, pp. 25–6.

graduates. Did such a situation contribute to producing a 'natural' impulse for the young intelligentsia to join the socialist camp?

Kautsky's response strikes a pessimistic tone. Though it would clearly be wrong to follow the strange behaviour of the British trade unions and reject all scholars on principle (after all, had not Marx written in the *Manifesto* of the possibility of 'ideologists' joining the working class?), it would be equally wrong to lose sight of the fact that 'the intelligentsia does not have general class interests, but solely professional ones'.[7] Essentially members of a kind of social hierarchy, intellectuals were incapable of joining regular trade unions; they could only affiliate to corporatist associations. By their mentality, modern intellectuals were closer to the artisans and their guilds in the latter days of feudalism than to the workers of modern industry. They were almost always immersed in situations of professional dependence, and their work conferred on them a certain number of privileges. Generally considering that these were due to their natural talent, they sought to maintain them at all cost.

Kautsky concludes with a severe verdict: 'The prevailing spirit among them is competition, the desire to get on at the expense of their colleagues. Nowhere is there so much professional jealousy, hunting for positions, servility and pride, as among artists and scholars.'[8] And for this reason, the protest of these professions is not the expression of a dissatisfaction that might find embodiment in a broad class solidarity. Their demands were always limited to social recrimination, expressing irrational phobias such as anti-Semitism or anti-feminism which socialism could not be party to.

Though Kautsky never seeks to flatter the intelligentsia, he does not want to reject them explicitly. We even find in this text an appeal inviting a section of them to join the political party of

---

7   Karl Kautsky, 'Le socialisme', p. 133.
8   Ibid., p. 114.

the working class. He believed that such a convergence could arise at two extremes in the world of cultural production: on the one hand, the lower intelligentsia who were being proletarianized, and whose conditions of existence were close to those of the working class; and on the other hand, certain superior, 'aristocratic' fringes (chiefly professors and journalists), whose intellectual activity allowed them to present the general interests of society. But Kautsky warns his readers: the adhesion of these categories to the workers' movement must take place individually and not collectively. According to him, the autonomous organization of a socialist intelligentsia was a negative phenomenon to be opposed; he cites the *Kathedersozialisten* (socialists of the chair) as an example of an illegitimate organization of independent scholars.[9]

Here we find the secret that motivated the writing of Kautsky's text: the Social Democratic Party could not tolerate the presence of competitors in the field of political representation. The working class could only be represented by a single political body, whose composition was not purely working class, but where cultural differences between classes must not be translated into an institutional partition of the movement, either within the party or, a fortiori, outside of it. The appearance in late nineteenth-century Europe of specific socialist collectives and organizations for the high intelligentsia, after the example of the German professors who undertook to formulate new socialist theories or the Fabian Society in Britain, had aroused disquiet on the part of Marxist intellectuals, who saw themselves as the exclusive and 'authorized' supporters of the working class. The popularity of socialist ideas had led to an intolerable sense of competition between the different movements that appealed to these, and aroused new reflections on the 'going over' of 'ideologists' to the side of the proletariat.

---

9   Ibid., p. 268.

The state intellectual

In France, the problem of the socialist intellectual gave rise to an ideological fracture among the Marxist supporters of the workers' movement. Contrary to Marx's predictions, according to which the defeat of France in 1870 would also be expressed by the victory of his own views over those of Proudhon, Marxism in France remained a marginal phenomenon in the field of 'high culture'. We might even say that the spread of Marxism, as an ideology bearing a global view of the world and serving as a guide for great political movements (rather than simply a tool for analysing societies) happened in the generation after that of Marx, and above all east of the Rhine. In other words, Marxism only appeared as a powerful myth capable of mobilizing masses towards revolutionary modernity in 'pre-revolutionary' societies such as Germany, Italy, Austria-Hungary, Poland, Russia or even China.

In France until 1905, there was only one socialist party among several others that claimed to be Marxist (and subsequently a communist party, founded in 1920). And yet, strange as it might appear, we should also emphasize that until the temporary eclipse of certain republican myths with the defeat of 1940, Marxism never succeeded in taking solid root in the cultural field. In the country of Voltaire and Zola, leaving aside the particular period from 1945 to 1975, it was republicanism, with either a conservative or socialist shade and often pervaded by an acute national consciousness, that always constituted what Raymond Aron called the 'opium of the intellectuals'.

Despite all this, there were a few singular Frenchmen in the 1890s who rowed against the current and took a particular interest in the thought of Marx. Intellectuals such as Georges Sorel, Paul Lafargue, Charles Bonnier and Hubert Lagardelle made valiant efforts to open the world of French thought to Marxist positions, and in this way to go beyond the idealist approach that had for so long characterized and dominated French socialism.

Yet the French intellectual world continued to ignore Marxism, which had the effect among other things of a certain dogmatism on the part of Marx's French followers.

Georges Sorel, the future author of *Reflections on Violence*, still saw himself as a Marxist at the end of 1897. He had just broken with the ideological framework of organized Marxism, but not yet become the trenchant and raging theorist of revolutionary syndicalism. His attachment to historical materialism led him to formulate, apropos the status of intellectuals in politics, a series of questions that a Marxist such as Kautsky was unable to raise in the very self-assured mental universe of German social democracy.

In 1898, exactly half a century after the writing of the *Communist Manifesto* by Marx and Engels, Sorel published an original essay entitled 'The Socialist Future of the Syndicates'.[10] The substance of this essay bears on the characteristics and future of workers' organizations, yet the place of literati is not ignored, and in fact this text could equally well have been titled: 'The Statist Future of Intellectuals'. It is interesting to note that Sorel used the word 'intellectual' just before Zola's petition of support for Dreyfus was launched in January 1898, which would give the term a wider public resonance. Thus, between the appearance of Kautsky's essay and the end of 1897, the urgent theoretical need for a specific concept to define the new stratum of literati was sharply felt.

As a faithful Marxist, Sorel used a quotation from *Capital* as an epigraph to his essay:

Large mechanized industry achieves separation between manual work and the intellectual powers of production, which

---

10   Georges Sorel, 'The Socialist Future of the Syndicates', in *From Georges Sorel: Essays in Socialism and Philosophy*, Piscataway, NJ: Transaction Publishers, 1987. Alain Menegaldo's doctoral thesis, sadly unpublished, deals with Sorel's relationship to intellectuals: *Rôle et place des intellectuels dans le mouvement ouvrier chez Georges Sorel et Édouard Berth*, Université Paris VIII, 1982.

it transforms into the power of capital over work. The skillfulness of the workers appears weak before the prodigies of science, enormous natural forces, the greatness of social work, all incorporated into the mechanical system, which constitutes the power of the master.[11]

Sorel, who had been an engineer before becoming a Marxist thinker, drew a surprising conclusion from this argument: 'The contemporary hierarchy has as its principal basis the division of labour into intellectual and manual categories.' The problem has become more acute, according to Sorel, because political democracy has reinforced this hierarchy by 'the theory of ability', and 'strives to utilize the people's superstitious respect for learning'.[12]

As a theorist of syndicalism, Sorel would later make the same criticism of Marxism, but at this time, the end of the nineteenth century, he enthusiastically supported Kautsky's conclusions on the new 'thinking class': intellectuals had narrow professional interests and not broad class ones, and their demands were most often opposed to the general interest of the working class. In parallel with this, and here his approach is different from that of Kautsky, Sorel began to focus on the modes in which intellectuals were present in the socialist movement. Whereas Kautsky sought to stigmatize the political intelligentsia who were outside the socialist movement, Sorel makes the intellectuals organized within the socialist parties the main target of his critique.

Perhaps in Germany, he maintains, intellectuals have become humble administrative servants of the workers' party. In the 'land of the Gauls', however, they are always to be found in the leading stratum of such parties. The structure of political socialism in France is very much a faithful replica of the hierarchical forms of class in society. Socialist intellectuals even potentially constitute

---

11   Georges Sorel, 'The Socialist Future of the Syndicates', p. 303.
12   Ibid., p. 76.

a kind of 'representative dictatorship of the proletariat'.[13] The literati, whether revolutionary or reformist, have made it their main objective to conquer political power; in other words, to take over collective management of the state apparatus. If their project should succeed, the producers would continue at the end of the day to be governed by a new class, which would be hardly different from the present ruling class. This is how Sorel formulates it: 'The true vocation of the intellectuals is the exploitation of politics . . . We need not try speaking to them of eliminating the traditional forms of the state: in this respect their "ideal" is reactionary, however it seems to "good people".'[14]

Sorel does not take the trouble to explain to his readers whom precisely he sees as intellectuals. He clearly does not have in mind scientists in their laboratories, and when he wrote this essay he had not yet become the vehement opponent of the whole literary intelligentsia that populated the Paris salons; he even associated himself with them by signing the second petition of support for Dreyfus. The 'negative intellectual' mentioned in his essay is, more or less, the 'philosopher-king' that Sorel detested throughout his life, the intellectual who practises a liberal profession, particularly the advocate or journalist, and converts himself into a socialist leader or activist. This kind of intellectual finds complete legitimacy in the role of authentic representative of the class of working people. Fundamentally, in Sorel's thought, the key indicator of a significant improvement in the condition of the working class, in historical terms, is not the increase in the number of its representatives in parliament but rather the actual strengthening of its power over the process of production. The real site of the workers' activity is and will remain the workshop or factory, and not the parliamentary lobby; it is over their place of work that they can really take control of their destiny and organize their own lives.

---

13 Ibid., p. 78.
14 Ibid., p. 79.

In the parliamentary forum it is always speech that governs. Manual workers find themselves in a position of permanent inferiority in the public sphere, given the strength of the political intellectual in the domain of phraseology and rhetoric. The 'verbal aristocracy' of the socialist left draws its force essentially from social struggles, but at the same time it strengthens quite 'naturally' its hierarchical position in relation to those it represents.

Whereas Kautsky and the whole of 'revolutionary' Marxism looked condescendingly at the reformist moderation of the British trade unions, the debate between reformists and revolutionaries did not interest Sorel at this stage. He never believed in a general insurrection on a 'great day', and neither did he support a steady growth in the workers' material consumption. He always attributed greater importance to action that could show concrete results, in other words the struggle of working people on their own behalf, hence the importance and priority that he gave to the unions, whose final objective was the gradual control and management of the means of production: 'The role of the intellectuals is an auxiliary role: they can serve as employees of the unions. They have no role as leaders.'[15]

When Sorel reached the conclusion in the following years that the progressive intellectual class had become hegemonic in the socialist movement, in the wake of the storms of the Dreyfus affairs, he would not be content with this distribution of functions. As a theorist and champion of revolutionary syndicalism, he reduced the role of the intellectual who marches alongside the workers' movement to the critique of existing bourgeois

---

15   Ibid., p. 93. Sorel's critique of the workers' parties would serve as a basis for the famous theory of the 'iron law' of bureaucratization of any political organization, as developed by Robert Michels in 1911: *Political Parties: A Sociological Study of the Oligarchical Tendencies of Modern Democracy*, New York: Free Press, 1966. See Jean-Luc Pouthier, 'Georges Sorel et Roberto Michels', in Jacques Julliard and Shlomo Sand (eds), *Georges Sorel en son temps*, Paris: Seuil, 1985, pp. 287–94.

society.[16] The progressive intellectual, on the other hand, the dispenser of political promises of a 'radiant future', would gradually become for Sorel an actual adversary of the workers.

The fact that it was the British workers' movement rather than German social democracy that became the model for this French Marxist was a singular occurrence in the ideological landscape of European Marxism. It is also a significant element towards understanding the subsequent rallying of several French followers of Marx to revolutionary syndicalism. On this subject, however, we should make clear that the critique of the modes of presence of intellectuals within workers' movements, while remaining marginal to the Second International, was no longer just a characteristic of the socialist intellectual sphere in France. At the same time as Sorel was attempting to apply historical materialism to intellectuals and Marxism itself, another ex-Marxist, at the other end of Europe (or rather in Asia) was undermining the theoretical foundations of Russian social democracy.

In 1898, Jan Wacław Machajski, a Polish social democrat exiled in Siberia, published his first hesitant reflections on the nature of the relationship between socialist political elites and the mass of working people.[17] For him, exactly as for Sorel, the great silence of Marxist theory on the question of the positioning of qualified intellectuals within the proletariat's movement of liberation was in no way fortuitous, but actually concealed an additional form of domination over the mass of workers. Machajski rapidly came to the following point of view:

The suppression of private capitalists will not be enough for the modern working class, the contemporary slaves, to cease being slaves, condemned to manual work throughout their lives. The consequence of this will not be that the national

---

16   See for example the introduction to *Reflections on Violence*, Boston: Dover Publications, 2004, pp. 57–63.

17   Jan Wacław Machajskii, *Le Socialisme des intellectuels*, Paris: Seuil, 1979.

surplus-value they create disappears, but rather that it passes into the hands of the democratic state, as a maintenance fund for the parasitic existence of all the plunderers, the whole bourgeois society. After the suppression of the capitalists, this will continue to be a dominant society, one of cultivated rulers and governors just as before, a world of 'white hands'.[18]

According to Machajski, political socialism in all its tendencies, from social democracy through to anarchism, was preparing the ground for forms of exploitation and domination that bureaucratic state apparatuses would put into effect in the future. Machajski died in 1926 and so did not see the reign of Stalin, but he had time to witness the beginning of his pessimistic forecasts being fulfilled, in the 'great proletarian state' founded in the wake of the Bolshevik Revolution.

A 'non-class' intelligentsia

The anti-intellectual position of Jan Machajski aroused sharp criticism from representatives of all socialist organizations in the Russian Empire, particularly from Georgi Plekhanov, the father of Russian Marxism; whereas in France, Paul Lafargue, Marx's son-in-law and the best-known representative of Marxism at this time, associated himself with the critique of intellectuals embarked upon by Georges Sorel.

In fact, Lafargue had already cautiously advanced a critical point of view on the holders of academic qualifications in the late 1880s, when the debate on the 'intellectual proletariat' began.[19] Yet he only decided to publish his contentions in a more trenchant manner after the storm bound up with the second Dreyfus affair and the entry of a socialist for the first time

---

18   Ibid., p. 122.
19   Paul Lafargue, 'Das Proletariat der Handarbeit und der Kopfarbeit', *Neue Zeit*, vol. 6, 1887, pp. 349–55, 405–11, 452–61, and vol. 7, 1888, pp. 128–40.

into a centre-left coalition government. In March 1900, on the invitation of the Group des étudiants collectivistes, Lafargue delivered a lecture in which he sharply questioned the Parisian intellectual elite that had become somewhat socialist under the effect of the post-Dreyfusard air of the time.[20]

Contrary to his orthodox image as subsequently propagated by certain Marxists, Lafargue was an original and incisive thinker who rejected any dogma, though also known for his lack of coherence. His lectures present, side by side and in a certain disorder, both original theoretical hypotheses and bitter complaints, attesting to a kind of political frustration. According to his own account, Lafargue was mobilized against intellectuals because of a new split in the socialist movement, provoked, as he saw it, by the outcome of the second Dreyfus affair, and marked by the rapprochement of intellectual elites to the positions of Alexandre Millerand and Jean Jaurès, thereby strengthening the moderate wing of French socialism at the expense of its radical tendency. The new Parisian intelligentsia's lack of interest in Marxism further inflamed the hostility of French Marxists towards the archetype of the Parisian intellectual.

To sharpen his critique of the modern man of letters, Lafargue resorts to a comparison with the most powerful intellectual corporation of the pre-modern world: the church. Contrary to the prevailing idea, he maintains, this key institution of the seigniorial age was actually liberal and open towards its members, despite the intolerance it showed towards its adversaries. The church paid serious attention to science and offered its protection to scholars, with a clear objective: 'It sought, like the clergy of ancient Egypt, to stand alone in the world in knowing and understanding.'[21]

Knowledge has always conferred power on those possessing it. In the modern world, however, Lafargue maintains that

---

20   Paul Lafargue, 'Le socialisme et les intellectuels', *Cahiers de la quinzaine*, 5 May 1900, pp. 48–92.
21   Ibid., p. 55.

knowledge has become a commodity, and as with any other consumer good, its increased diffusion lowers its value and reduces its price. The intellectual of modern times has put his competence on sale in the market, thus himself creating a situation of dependence in relation to the fluctuations this displays. And if, in the eighteenth century, there were revolutionary scholars in the image of the writers of the *Encyclopédie*, the nineteenth century saw literati become faithful servants of all the new regimes that arose. They certainly did not stop developing their science, but they placed this in the service of the existing order. It must be understood that science is not simply an instrument of liberation, it can also be transformed into a force of hindrance and constraint.

Lafargue never reneged on this criticism, and regularly lambasted various categories of intellectuals. It was a well-known fact, for example, that the majority of economists sold their science to the highest bidder. People in the literary sphere, with a few notable exceptions, produced a literature of apology for the ruling classes. But the most repulsive category among the cultural elites remained the stratum of political intellectuals, who represented a real danger for the future of the working class. It was rare for men of letters to join the socialist movement as ordinary members and rank-and-file activists; on the contrary, they always saw themselves as leaders and guides of an expanding movement. This innate tendency of scholars was constitutive of the way in which they conceived their discipline. 'There are naturalists who, because they are familiar with the world of oysters, believe that they can direct human societies.'[22]

Contrary to the leaders of his party, Lafargue was a Dreyfusard from the start, but he was disheartened by the fact that the intellectuals who signed petitions used their academic titles as a means of persuasion. He deemed misguided and deceptive Durkheim's argument that intellectuals could better decipher political reality

---

22   Ibid., p. 70.

thanks to the scientific or rational practices inherent to their activities.

Lafargue was not the only Marxist to rail against 'intellectualist' pretensions. In the wake of the first petitions of intellectuals for and against Dreyfus, Charles Bonnier, a fellow Marxist and a close friend of the socialist leader Jules Guesde, published two articles in which he questioned the legitimacy of exploiting the prestige of intellectuals in the domain of politics. His verdict on intellectuals is remarkably close to that of Lafargue:

> They do not understand either the social question or the class struggle, for the sufficient reason that, being scholars in their own specialism, and having devoted all their powers of penetration, criticism and method to a particular study, they have no more powers left to judge the events around them.[23]

A scientific intelligence in a specific and circumscribed field does not necessarily imply a more elevated social awareness, and all the less so in that all social science is faced with the fact of class conflict. Bonnier fully applies this approach in his analysis, reaching the decisive conclusion that intellectuals must associate themselves with the workers' movement in order to acquire the new socialist science.

The Marxism of the Second International, as well as both non-Marxian socialism and the new academic sociology, laid claim to being 'scientific', a label that conferred assurance and certainty. It shared with its ideological competitors the same positivism that sought to base its prestige on the aura of science, the object of much genuflection in the late nineteenth century. Unhappily for Marxists in France, however, as against the situation in Germany, Italy or Russia, the best scholars of the left preferred a 'social science' that confirmed the national democratic achievements of the Third Republic to the 'Marxist science' that focused on

---

23   Charles Bonnier, 'Prolétarisés et savants', *Le Socialiste*, 18 December 1898.

analysing the class struggle. This gave rise to an increased tension in the critical discourse of Marx's French heirs towards those new cultural agents, from Charles Péguy to Léon Blum, who were committed to a different socialism.

It is necessary to emphasize, all the same, that the orthodox Marxist opponents of Jaurès were not alone in deeming it timely to denounce intellectuals. At the turn of the century, Hubert Lagardelle, who had supported the Dreyfusard campaign as a young socialist and was subsequently to edit the important journal *Le Mouvement socialiste*, had not yet become the spokesman of revolutionary syndicalism for which he would later be well known. At the start of his ideological journey he defined himself as a follower of Marx, but this did not prevent him from passionately supporting Jaurès and severely criticizing the majority of Marxists who abstained from intervention in the second Dreyfus affair. Like Lafargue, Lagardelle was invited towards the end of 1900 to give a talk to the Groupe des étudiants collectivistes, and he also chose to devote this to the question of intellectuals. His lecture, on which he would base a long article, took the form of a systematic summary of all the positions formulated until then by Kautsky, Sorel and Lafargue.[24]

Why did such a heated debate on the status of intellectuals take place precisely in Paris? Lagardelle set out to answer this question by resorting to a 'materialist' analysis. In France, he stressed, industry had developed more slowly than in England or Germany, as well as in modalities that involved a lesser degree of working-class concentration, a greater persistence of the petty bourgeoisie and a significant growth in the educated stratum. With didactic intention, Lagardelle began his lecture, in contrast to his predecessors, by presenting a kind of profile of the modern intellectual:

---

24   Hubert Lagardelle, 'Les intellectuels devant le socialisme', *Cahiers de la quinzaine*, 18 January 1901, pp. 5–62.

What is understood above all by this expression is all those with a somewhat developed culture, who have, if you like, received a secondary or higher education, and above all those who practise the liberal professions: lawyers, judges, doctors, engineers, professors, schoolteachers, civil servants, journalists, writers, etc. It can also include artistic workers, office employees, etc. In a word, all those whose practical activity is particularly of a cerebral order; this is the sense in which the term 'intellectual' is opposed to the term 'manual'.[25]

Can these people be viewed as a new social class? To answer this question, Lagardelle took up Marx's concepts of the 'class in itself' as distinct from the 'class for itself' and applied them to the new 'clerks'. Intellectuals cannot be seen as a 'class for itself', since they lack a common socio-economic and ideological basis. Their stratification, and the tremendous competition in which they find themselves, prevent them from forming a solid and independent social 'bloc' that might aspire to win collective rights. As far as intellectuals are concerned, therefore, recourse to a class term risks leading to error. 'Sub-class would be more suitable, or rather non-class.'[26]

This social stratum, however, which cannot be termed a 'class', was very much present in political life, and its self-representation posed a problem. The high level of education that its members had acquired gave them an image of themselves superior to that of manual workers, and incited them to offer themselves as the best representatives of the general interest. This tendency had led many intellectuals to descend into the public arena and fill the ranks of political elites, on both right and left. It would be no exaggeration to maintain that the modern state was ultimately in the expert hands of intellectuals: 'They have governed on behalf

---

25   Ibid., p. 14.
26   Ibid., p. 17.

of other classes, but they have governed. The public power, in fact, belongs to the professionals of politics.'[27]

This was the reason why, with the advance of the workers' movement and its growing electoral weight, many intellectuals were drawn towards the left. According to Lagardelle, the intellectuals who joined socialist parties could be classified in five main categories: 1) higher technicians – engineers, chemists, agronomists – whose professional activity alongside manual workers made possible the development of a class consciousness close to that of workers; 2) university graduates who had not found an employment corresponding to their qualifications and who entered the socialist movement driven by immediate interest, in order to make a career there; 3) literati with a great sensitivity who viewed the world of work through an ideal of justice and social equality; 4) political chameleons, always ready to change their colours according to the ideas in fashion; 5) scholars led by their scientific knowledge to decipher the direction of history, who were certainly the most sincere group.

Lagardelle was aware that these categories did not find pure expression in reality, but he argued that such a distinction between different groups allowed a better understanding of the general relationship between intellectuals and the socialist idea. Knowing that Lagardelle and other Marxist intellectuals did not fall into the first category, it is permissible to suppose that the last category was included in order to motivate and explain their commitment alongside the workers' movement. The world of work, Lagardelle argued, was clearly in a position to generate in its ranks 'proletarian intellectuals', deserving and capable of becoming leaders of the socialist movement, but at the same time this always needed professional scholars endowed with the theoretical capacity to produce the abstract syntheses and generalizations that the ideology of the working class required at different stages of its formation.

---

27   Ibid., p. 23.

Only intellectuals were in a position to produce socialist theories, and for this reason, their role should be limited to laying down the philosophical and juridical principles that the workers' movement needed. To truly liberate itself, however, the working class had to preserve full control of its sovereignty and completely dismiss the battalions of political intellectuals, who naturally desired to appropriate the leading positions. The great problem of French socialism was that it suffered from a relative historical delay in which the influence of traditional forms of political action was such that, within its own movement, the majority of the proletariat was still dominated by an intellectual minority that alone was capable of inserting itself into the bourgeois political game. This was also the reason why workerist tendencies arose in France that rejected any kind of intervention in the political domain. Lagardelle disapproves of these tendencies, which he deems negative, sterile and ultimately prejudicial to the class of working people.

Lagardelle's lecture should be seen as the last serious contribution produced by a French Marxist at the turn of the century on the question of intellectuals. From this time on, the subject dropped off the agendas of the socialist left, and was only taken up as an important point of criticism in the milieu of revolutionary syndicalism. (By way of exception, it would later appear in the work of Paul Nizan.)[28] Heterodox Marxists such as Sorel and Lagardelle soon reached the conclusion that, while the mythology of the revolutionary proletariat developed by Marx was certainly meaningful and valuable, it should not be allowed to form a utopia for intellectuals, who cultivated it simply to promote their cultural aspirations to hegemony. The socialist

---

28   Lagardelle himself gave his position a more radical turn in a new version of his article, 'Les intellectuels et le socialisme ouvrier', *Le Mouvement socialiste*, February, March, April and May 1907, pp. 105–20, 217–3, 349–64 and 409–20. For other 'syndicalist' positions, see for example Robert Louzon, 'Les intellectuels', *La Vie ouvrière*, 20 July 1914, pp. 84–9; and Édouard Berth, *Les Méfaits des intellectuels*, Paris: Marcel Rivière, 1914.

idea should remain a myth borne by the workers themselves, since if this were not the case it would disappear in the future as a mobilizing ideological force. This theoretical logic eventually led both thinkers to break off any relationship with the socialist movement and Marxism, and Lagardelle would even sympathize openly with Italian fascism in the early 1930s and subsequently join the Vichy administration.

The organic intellectual

It is an irony of history that, while Hubert Lagardelle held a respectable diplomatic post in Mussolini's Rome, on behalf of the French Republic, another innovative Marxist held in a fascist prison was also concerned with the question of intellectuals. Antonio Gramsci, one of the founders of the Italian Communist Party and now confined to intellectual activity, devoted himself in the early 1930s to writing his *Prison Notebooks*, which contain essential reflections on the role of intellectuals.[29] It was also around this time that the French communist writer Paul Nizan published *The Watchdogs*, discussed in the previous chapter. But while Nizan's essay scarcely aroused any comments, Gramsci's *Notebooks*, published shortly after the Second World War, achieved a celebrity that very few Marxist writings were able to boast of in the second half of the twentieth century.

These two approaches to intellectuals are certainly not of the same theoretical value. *The Watchdogs* is somewhat reminiscent in its style of Paul Lafargue's caustic publications, but Nizan's obvious literary talent does not make up for a lack of theoretical

---

29   As far back as 1927, Gramsci had started to envisage 'research on the history of Italian intellectuals, their origins and groupings in relation to cultural currents' (letter of 19 March 1927, in *Letters from Prison*, vol. 1, New York: Columbia University Press, 2011, p. 79). But it is only in a later letter that we find an echo of this specific text: 'The plans for research I've made concerning Italian intellectuals cover a very wide field, since I don't believe there are any books in Italy on this subject . . . In any case, my concept of the intellectual is much broader than the usual concept of "the great intellectuals"' (letter of 7 September 1931, ibid., p. 204).

depth. In Gramsci's analyses, on the other hand, we find a freshness almost unmatched in the writings of Marxists of the time of the Third International, whether 'organized' or 'independent'. This however is not the only reason for the great popularity that Gramsci's 'intellectual' positions enjoyed on the scholarly left in the last quarter of the twentieth century. As against Nizan's critical and sarcastic viewpoint, which reduces the role of the intellectual in socialist politics to a marginal one, Gramsci's theoretical argument gives new and reinforced legitimacy to the key position of intellectuals in the political party of the modern working class. This approach obviously had a seductive effect on many intellectuals, who wished to perpetuate the socialist ideal despite successive historical setbacks.

Although Gramsci was well acquainted with the writings of both Kautsky and Sorel, it is hard to detect what he knew of the 'forgotten' debate that had taken place at the turn of the century. His theoretical starting point had been, once again, the cardinal problem of 'ideologists going over to the proletariat', but as distinct from the unsatisfactory shortcut of the *Communist Manifesto*, he developed a brilliant and sophisticated Marxist interpretation.

Though the left had been defeated with the advent of fascism, Gramsci set out to show that this tragic development in Italy did not refute the truth of the Marxist analysis: the insoluble contradiction at the basis of the capitalist economy remained unresolved and would necessarily lead to revolution. The temporary defeat of the working class did not contradict Marx's fundamental postulates, but it did bear on the 'superstructure', in other words, on cultural hegemony. The socialist movement had not been able to clarify this matter, hence, according to Gramsci, the importance of debating the question of intellectuals and their position in modern class society.

It is difficult in the confines of the present essay to analyse in detail the concepts of 'historical bloc', 'hegemony' or 'subaltern classes' that occupy the *Prison Notebooks*, and without which it is hard to trace the figure of the intellectual as seen by Gramsci. Yet an examination of the Marxist view of intellectuals would be incomplete without a presentation of these concepts. This will inevitably be brief and schematic, with a view to bringing out the broad lines, at the cost of leaving aside the specific historical analyses that figure in the *Notebooks* and make them such a fascinating work. Gramsci took as his starting point the key question already posed somewhat differently by Lagardelle at the turn of the century: 'Do intellectuals form an autonomous and independent social group, or does each social group have its own specialized category of intellectuals?' (We should remember that, in order to evade the fascist censorship, Gramsci used the word 'group' in place of 'class', knowing that in fascist Italy there were officially no classes!) His response leans unambiguously towards the second option:

> Every social group, coming into existence on the original terrain of an essential function in the world of economic production, creates together with itself, organically, one or more strata of intellectuals which give it homogeneity and an awareness of its own function not only in the economic but also in the social and political fields.[30]

The Italian Marxist understood very well that no social class in history has been able to maintain itself stably in power on a purely economic basis or solely by force. It is Napoleon who is supposed to have said, very accurately: 'One can do everything with bayonets except sit on them.' To stabilize its power in the long term, any dominant group needs a system of cultural and juridical norms to be shared by society as a whole; only such a system makes possible the creation and perpetuation of the dominant relations of production. It is precisely because of this

---

30   Antonio Gramsci, *Selections from the Prison Notebooks* (Notebook 12), London: Lawrence & Wishart, 1971, p. 5. For the Italian thinker, 'All men are intellectuals . . . but not all men have in society the function of intellectuals' (ibid., p. 9).

historical need that every class society sees the appearance of intellectuals, who create the required ideological consensus by organizing culture, education and the legal system. Alongside this central stratum, the cornerstone of any stable hierarchical structure, there are always other people of high culture, experts carrying out technical economic functions, as well as a supplementary category whose members fill the apparatuses of state power.

Intellectuals maintain heterogeneous relations with the rulers of the world of material production; they are not its direct employees, as bodyguards are for example. Their relations are mediated by a complex balance of forces in the political and cultural superstructures, which leaves them various degrees of autonomy. Important and real as it is, this autonomy has its limits, and despite the image of independent creators that intellectuals traditionally have of themselves, there is always a form of hidden dependence.

Contradictions sometimes emerge between this or that stratum of intellectuals and the dominant economic class; these oppositions, however, no matter how intense, always end up with compromises that contribute to consolidating the hegemonic consensus. At the end of the day, the illusory consciousness of intellectual independence has always served the ruling class very well: the 'independent' intellectual appears as bearer of the universal interest, and by this fact alone manages to better conceal both the specific interests of the rulers and their own. This is one of the ways in which the cultural hegemony so essential for the maintenance of the social order is created.

Hegemony, according to Gramsci, effectively means domination founded on a kind of acceptance. The dominated accept the rules of the social game, being convinced that these serve them and form part of an immutable natural order. It is important therefore that the intellectual, who forms a connecting link in the creation of hegemony, should always appear as a free and independent producer of culture. Gramsci emphasizes that the 'independence' intellectuals believe they enjoy has played an important role throughout history in the prevalence of the philosophical idealism characteristic of many cultures. Philosophical texts always give the impression that it is ideas that orient and guide the world, and a conception of this kind has always been the intellectuals' preference. In modern times, this imaginary portrait of the independent man of letters was the foundation of social utopianism.

Like Lafargue before him, Gramsci saw the church as the most important intellectual body in the pre-capitalist world:

> The most typical of these categories of intellectuals is that of the ecclesiastics, who for a long time (for a whole phase of history, which is partly characterized by this very monopoly) held a monopoly of a number of important services: religious ideology, that is the philosophy and science of the age, together with schools, education, morality, justice, charity, good works etc. The category of ecclesiastics can be considered the category of intellectuals organically bound to the landed aristocracy.[31]

The members of the *noblesse de robe*, who colonized the state apparatus in the age of absolutism, formed another type of intellectual. The growth of big capital was accompanied by the emergence of new categories of 'organic' intellectuals. These literati, creators of new cultural and juridical norms, served as mediators and prepared the ground for the constitution of the historical bloc that the bourgeoisie headed and that became hegemonic in the modern age.

The 'organic' intellectual, in Gramsci's terms, is thus the agent of culture who supports the rising revolutionary class and procures it the intellectual and cultural coherence that it needs in order to win power and impose its new systems of values. The

---

31   Ibid., p. 7.

'traditional' intellectual, on the other hand, is the agent of the organic culture of yesterday: those who supported the ruling class of the previous period, now on the decline and condemned to disappear. It is important to note, however, that the 'traditional' intellectuals representing the old order are still perceived by the masses as the torchbearers of cultural continuity and tradition, and at the same time, as free from any class interest. Their image of autonomy precisely contributes to the fact that their life continues beyond the period of domination of the class that they supported and served. Their cultural and political weight can still influence present and future reality. Hence the persistent influence, for example, of priests, rabbis or imams in otherwise secularized societies.

Throughout this presentation, and leaving aside the purely historical debate, it is clear that what Gramsci has in mind is the nature of the organic intellectuals who support the workers' movement. Given that modern political parties are for Gramsci the actual intellectual bodies of modern times, the organic intellectual of the working class is actually embodied in its political party. At the end of the day, Gramsci sees this party as the ruling body, a successor to the utopian figure of the 'prince' as magnificently described by Niccolò Machiavelli.[32]

In order for the workers to succeed in becoming the ruling class, they have to be able to establish around them a historical bloc that unites all the dominated and exploited strata of society. The mission of revolutionary culture is to build bridges between interests that are parallel but not identical. To this end, the workers need a political party that fulfils the classic function of the organic intellectuals of the past. The 'organic' party can serve as mediator, coordinating and promoting, in a long political and cultural process, the 'intellectual and moral reform' that

---

32   Ibid., pp. 125ff. Here (p. 127) Gramsci criticizes Sorel who, as we saw, rejected the party – in other words the political stratum – believing only in the union.

will lead to the advent of a classless society. This approach also makes clear the status of the educated within the party. A select leading stratum emerges among the possessors of high cultural capital, able to fashion and transmit the foundations of the new culture.

This analysis, which justifies the primacy of the party over the union, and the superiority of organization over the spontaneity of the masses, is designed at the same time to legitimize the hegemony of the communist intellectual in the hierarchy of the party. In contrast to Marx, Gramsci was well aware that his personal commitment in favour of the revolution was not enough to make him a member of the working class like any other; which explains, among other things, the place given in his work to the notion of the organic intellectual. The party that is not afraid of its intellectuals is an integral part of the historical movement that will lead to the victory of the working class.

This analysis, while undoubtedly penetrating, leaves aside an awkward fact that Gramsci himself mentions in his historical account: not all social classes in the past had organic intellectuals. Gramsci was well aware, for example, that neither slaves in the Mediterranean world, nor serfs and villeins in feudal Europe, despite their 'central place in the relations of production' and their spontaneous revolts, became a hegemonic class, just as they did not find intellectuals who placed themselves in their service. Gramsci's model of a ruling class in history is not all those that held a key place in the relations of production, but rather classes whose control (or embryonic control) of the means of production aroused the parallel formation of a body of intellectuals that supported them.

In the world of capitalist production, the workers have been and remain a dominated class, and nowhere have they achieved control of the modern labour process in technical or managerial terms. The expansion of Taylorism, a synonym for assembly-line work (which Gramsci welcomed), further reduced the possibilities of the workers effectively controlling their means of labour.

The centrality of the working class in modern industry might be seen as closer to the modes of existence of slaves or peasants in pre-modern societies than to the dominant status of slave-owners, nobles or bourgeois. Perhaps we should see this as one of the reasons for which the imprisoned Marxist thinker, a champion in his youth of workers' councils and revolutionary spontaneity, reached the pessimistic conclusion that the working class could only become hegemonic via the intermediary of the party that represents it.

The revolutionary intellectual in the party, the figure of the modern 'prince', was thus endowed with an unprecedented status by one of the founders of the Italian Communist Party. Yet Gramsci's writings leave unanswered the question: who is it that grants whom a margin of autonomy (if indeed there is to be one) at the moment of victory? Is this subject the working class, or rather the party as 'organic intellectual'? The history of 'state socialism', as realized in the Soviet Union, gave a cruel response to this question at the very time that Gramsci was writing his *Prison Notebooks*.

The Soviet Revolution, and the establishment of the most enormous state apparatus of the twentieth century, sealed the fate of a serious materialist debate on the question of the balance of political forces between workers and intellectuals in the communist movement. The discourse of Stalinist communism may well have always been somewhat marked by rhetorical anti-intellectualism, but the muddying of the difference in social and cultural positioning between representatives and represented within the 'historical movement of the working class' was not just peculiar to Gramsci; it was common to all supporters of the Third International. The absence of a Marxist perspective on the situation that the balance of forces had created between the represented workers and the party that represents them, and that was inscribed in actual class relations, was one of the factors that made possible the veneration of the 'first socialist state' and the celebration of the cult of its leader that was characteristic of triumphant totalitarian Stalinism.[33]

Even a less Stalinist Marxism, in the liberal Western world after the Second World War, did not formulate a fundamentally different conception. The consolidation of parliamentary democracy in the course of the twentieth century ultimately maintained the working class in the role of a secondary actor in socialist politics. It certainly exerted its full quantitative weight to have the principle of democracy adopted, but the structures of pluralist liberal representation have always been the exclusive preserve of possessors of a definite cultural capital. The workers, deskilled by Taylorism since the 1920s and thus further stripped of their intellectual capacities, were condemned to remain a mute voice, called on from time to time to have their political interests furthered in parliament. Political Marxism preferred not to turn its attention to this question, and the fact that it continued to express itself in terms of a class terminology did not prevent it, just like other currents of socialism, from viewing the modern worker above all as a citizen, the cornerstone of representative democracy. This means that the mythological worker, the historical agent of the future in the Marxist vision, has effectively become a useful electoral asset, thanks to whom many achievements of the welfare state were obtained while perpetuating all the mechanisms of political power based on the social division of labour, a division that has even been amplified with the modernization of production.

The writings of Machajski were not part of the Soviet educational syllabus alongside those of Lenin and Plekhanov, nor were they made available by the many publishing houses of the communist movement and its friends across the world. They were cast into the dustbin of history (to use Trotsky's arrogant

---

33   On the status of intellectuals in the world of 'actually existing socialism', see the fascinating essay by two Hungarian researchers, George Konrad and Ivan Szelenyi, *The Intellectuals on the Road to Class Power*, Brighton: Harvester Press, 1979.

expression) until they were rediscovered and published in the West during the 1980s. The critical approaches towards intellectuals of Sorel, Lafargue or Lagardelle were also erased from the collective memory of Marxism, and sometimes made use of by its adversaries. More than a century and a half after the publication of the *Communist Manifesto*, it is still possible to maintain that, if a considerable number of 'bourgeois ideologists' became critics of capitalism, few of them perceived, or were prepared to recognize, that knowledge capital, just like all capital, has been used by those who possess it as a means of domination over others.[34]

---

34   A substantial debate on Marxism and the intellectuals is also offered by Alvin W. Gouldner, *The Future of Intellectuals and the Rise of the New Class*, New York: Seabury Press, 1979.

CHAPTER 4

The Discreet Charm of Fascism:
Flirtation or Love Story?

*I conducted myself in full awareness, in the prime of my life,
according to the idea that I hold of the duties of the intellectual.
The intellectual, the clerk, the artist, is not a citizen like any
other. He has duties and rights that are higher than other
people's.*

Pierre Drieu La Rochelle,
'Moi, l'intellectuel', *Exorde*, 1945

*I thank the French intellectuals, writers, artists, musicians and
academics who have been kind enough to present an appeal for
clemency on my behalf . . . This list includes the greatest minds of
our race, and my debt to them is immense.*

Robert Brasillach, letter of 3 February 1945

Early in 1983, I finished writing my doctoral thesis on Georges
Sorel, which I presented to the École des hautes études en sciences
sociales (EHESS). The historian Pierre Vidal-Naquet, who was
one of the jury members, contacted me a short time after to tell
me that the editor of *Esprit* had asked him to write a critique of
Zeev Sternhell's book *Ni droite ni gauche*, which had recently

been published.[1] He had replied to them that, on the basis of my thesis, he believed this was a task that I was best placed to perform.

Despite being very touched by the compliment, I was quite hesitant in responding to this request. I feared somewhat for the future, out of the intellectual caution that is characteristic of freshly qualified academics. I wanted to teach at Tel Aviv, and (needlessly) believed that writing too harsh a critique of Sternhell's approach to fascism would compromise my chances of being employed by an Israeli university. In the end, I agreed to write the piece. It was published and provoked a virulent reaction on the part of Sternhell, which was certainly understandable given his point of view. I replied to this in rather moderate terms, and Vidal-Naquet immediately took up my defence.[2]

In my critique, I had demolished Sternhell's central thesis that fascism had been born and had prospered in France, already before the First World War, and was only subsequently adopted in Italy. Raymond Aron would shortly make a similar point: 'His book is the most totally ahistorical that could be conceived. The author never puts things in their context. He gives such a vague definition of fascism that this could be applied to anything.'[3]

Just as too many historians from a right-wing political background have tended to exaggerate the scope of left revolutionary currents, so researchers from the left have analysed rightist currents in terms of a simplistic and insufficiently nuanced ideological approach. Naturally we are all anti-fascists, but for many years we have used the term 'fascist' far too readily, basically in order to tarnish our adversaries. In this case, the lack of a tried-and-tested conceptual apparatus is indeed Sternhell's major fault. His haste to see a large number of French intellectuals and

---

1   Zeev Sternhell, *Neither Right nor Left: Fascist Ideology in France*, Princeton, NJ: Princeton University Press, 1995.

2   *Esprit*, August–September 1983, pp. 149–60 and December 1983, pp. 189–95.

3   *Le Monde*, 18 October 1983.

politicians as genuine fascists strikes me as lacking any foundation. I want therefore in this chapter to explore various other approaches, at least some of which seem to me quite original.

Contrary to Italy and Germany, France had won a decisive military victory at the end of the First World War, and the majority of its citizens did not feel any humiliation or frustration in national terms. Interwar France, in contrast to its two continental neighbours but like its neighbour across the Channel, was a 'satiated' colonial power, and not a hotbed of thwarted imperialist aspirations. A great social revolution had taken place at the end of the eighteenth century, generating a dynamic political mobility for potential elites, along with the first expressions of a uniform state nationalism. Neither Germany nor Italy had experienced a successful revolution in the course of their respective national unifications; these were effected 'from above' by conservative monarchical dynasties, in both cases very similarly.

This particularly explains why fascism did not strike deep roots in twentieth-century France (or Great Britain), and why no original ideology developed that would support and justify it. Nor did national socialism have more success, despite the long tradition of Judeophobia that was deeply anchored in certain strata of French Catholic culture. The country of Robespierre and Danton did not need a 'national revolution' of a new type, contrary to what the Vichy regime purported to believe, and everything goes to show that 'revolutionary' figures of the kind of Mussolini and Hitler could not have obtained any real success.

From the start of twentieth century, however, the French Republic had to reckon with a popular monarchist right wing whose temperament was anti-democratic, anti-parliamentary and Judeophobic, and which succeeded in focusing conservative and nationalist discontent. However, there is a frequent tendency to lose sight of the fact that, despite the serious political and economic crises of the interwar years, France remained a liberal democracy until its military defeat in 1940. Parliamentary government was not defeated by the rise of autonomous domestic forces. Rather, anti-liberal and anti-parliamentary currents took advantage of the historical opportunity provided by the changed balance of forces consequent on the French army's defeat. Active collaboration with the occupiers was certainly widespread, but it should be stressed that the establishment of a 'new' regime at Vichy was preceded by the German conquest of Paris. The Vichy regime represented less of a 'national revolution' than a traditional conformist conservatism: anti-communist, anti-republican and Judeophobic. This is the essential point that should not be forgotten.

One preliminary remark is necessary. The use here of the terms 'fascism' and 'Nazism' is neither rhetorical nor fortuitous. Despite the strong resemblance between Italian fascism and German Nazism in a number of fields (the statized character of social life, the mode of resolution of the conflict between capital and labour, the aestheticization of politics), there is nonetheless a profound difference between the two regimes, which does not justify or support a long historiographical tradition that frequently seeks to combine them in a single globalizing terminology. In the domain of identity and national memory, which indisputably play a key role in the ideology and myths elaborated by the two movements and regimes, the resemblance between them is minor.

The national ideology of Italian fascism, directly inherited from the Risorgimento, was certainly arrogant and aggressive, but this was an inclusive political nationalism, whose limits both past and present were marked by cultural and territorial criteria. Its affinity with the French Jacobin tradition was evident, and radically differentiated it in terms of ideology and mentality from the nationalism founded on origins that characterized Nazism in Germany. The Nazis cultivated an exclusivist ethno-biological national consciousness; and this fundamental difference was expressed in a particular historical practice that sealed the fate of millions of victims: Jews, Poles, Roma, homosexuals, Soviet soldiers of Slavic origin. Many historians, especially though not only Germans, continue to use the term 'fascism' as a generic name to embrace all far-right movements of the twen-tieth century; but this rhetoric prevents a serious perception of the specific project of the Third Reich, and especially of its quite particular identity policy.[4]

The emphasis on what differentiates the two movements and the regimes they established makes it possible to cast a further light on the respective powers of attraction that Italian fascism and German Nazism exerted on French political culture between the wars. In fact, though neither fascism nor Nazism were indig-enous movements in France, certain particular versions of these totalitarian nationalist radicalisms managed to attract the sympa-thy of marginal political circles, as well as of some singular intel-lectual groups.

The intention here is not to expand on the nature and action of the currents and movements in France that identified with or supported fascism and Nazism; this is the subject of a copious literature, and I do not possess any new data that might signifi-cantly alter the consensus now reached by research.[5] The aim of this chapter is rather to clarify certain questions concerning the modes of reception of fascism and Nazism in the French intel-lectual field, which do not yet seem to have received the full attention required. Although these imported ideological prod-ucts occupied a relatively marginal place in the French mental universe, it is well worth understanding what made for their temporary success.[6]

---

4   It was left-wing writers before the Second World War who were initially responsible for the assimilation of the very different identities of fascism and Nazism, but the archetypical attempt to submerge Nazism in a 'universal fascism' was that of the German 'liberal' Ernst Nolte: *Three Faces of Fascism: Action Française, Italian Fascism, National Socialism*, New York: Holt, 1966.

5   Much has already been written on fascism in France, from the early and reliable article by Raoul Girardet, 'Notes sur l'esprit d'un fascisme français, 1934–1939', *Revue française de science politique*, July 1955, pp. 529–46, to Pierre Milza's more recent overview, *Fascisme français: passé et présent*, Paris: Flammarion, 2000.

6   Although there are several biographies of fascist and Nazi intellectuals, there are few attempts at an overview. See in particular Alastair Hamilton, *The Appeal of*

Fascists and 'nonconformists'

Intellectual interest in the versions of the radical right that were victorious in two of France's neighbours may be divided into two very distinct periods: first, the decade 1925–35, when curiosity, attention or even understanding for the dictatorial regime in Italy did not yet express a clear choice of affiliation to a political camp antithetical to the liberal and democratic world; and then the decade 1935–45, in which this identification was unambiguous, and intellectuals who placed themselves with the radical opposition embodied by the revolutionary right fell either into fascism or even Nazism.

Mussolini's arrival in power in 1922 did not make any special mark on Parisian cultural producers. The confused and contradictory messages of the new Italian government, supported by a conservative-liberal coalition, aroused neither notable enthusiasm nor attraction.[7] We should mention here, however, that until the mid-1920s Soviet communism also failed to receive much admiration from French intellectuals. It was only in 1925, when *fascismo* had consolidated its base and openly became a 'strong-arm' dictatorship, that the first attempt to imitate it appeared in France: Georges Valois's Faisceau, born in a split from Action Française (a right-wing monarchist and Judeophobic movement), won a certain popular support for a brief period. The financial crisis that happened under the government of the Cartel des Gauches, in 1924, led to an increase in sympathy for anti-parliamentary expressions, combined with a virulent anti-capitalist and anti-Bolshevik

---

Fascism: A Study of Intellectuals and Fascism, 1919–1945, New York: Avon, 1973. Jeannine Verdès-Leroux, *Refus et violences. Politique et littérature à l'extrême droite, des années trente aux retombées de la Libération*, Paris: Gallimard, 1966, deals largely with the relationship of writers to fascism, and its approach and conclusions are very different from the positions expressed here.

7   For an idea of the reception of Italian fascism in France, see Pierre Milza, *Le Fascisme italien et la presse française, 1920–1940*, Bruxelles: Complexe, 1987.

discourse.[8] To what extent did this movement arouse the curiosity of Parisian literati?

Georges Valois himself, along with his young and talented assistant Philippe Lamour, devoted the greater part of his time in these years to the Faisceau, though it is hard to see them at this stage of their lives as typical intellectuals. Very few men of letters, however, ventured to join this new political movement. Whereas in Italy at this time eminent intellectuals gave enthusiastic support to the Duce's triumphant movement, the Faisceau only drew relatively limited attention in France. There were indeed a few writers, essayists and artists, such as Hubert Bourgin, Pierre Benoit, Abel Bonnard, Philippe Barrès, Georges Suarez and the painter Forain, who expressed support and even contributed to *Le Nouveau Siècle*, the movement's organ. But these had not yet won recognition in the 1920s, and they failed to spread any sympathy for this imported fascism in the cultural field. The fact that the young Hubert Beuve-Méry, later a founder and editor of *Le Monde*, was active in the Faisceau's youth movement, or that Paul Nizan, then a student at the École normale supérieure, appeared one day in the new party's blue uniform, does not add up to a significant audience for the Faisceau among the young intelligentsia.[9] The rapid disappearance of the movement, two years after its foundation, tends to confirm that the first fascist attempt in France lacked any firm appeal, and failed to leave a consistent sediment propitious to a future development.

In the 1920s, fascism was still perceived as a local and purely Italian phenomenon. In France, the historical birthplace of

8   See Yves Guchet, *Georges Valois. L'Action française, le Faisceau, la République syndicale*, Paris: L'Harmattan, 2003, pp. 145–201; Allen Douglas, 'Violence and fascism: the case of the Faisceau', *Journal of Contemporary History*, vol. 19, no. 4, 1984, pp. 689–712; Samuel Kalman, 'Georges Valois et le Faisceau: un mariage de convenance', in Olivier Dard (ed.), *Georges Valois: itinéraire et réception*, Berne: Peter Lang, 2011, pp. 37–54.

9   Annie Cohen-Solal, *Paul Nizan, communiste impossible*, Paris: Grasset, 1979, pp. 45–6.

Bonapartism, where the *boulangiste* episode[10] was still present in many minds, no need was felt to import an ideological and political product from a Latin sister nation always viewed with a certain condescension. However, in the years that followed the birth of the Faisceau, first fascists, and then pro-Nazis, would claim that the ideas of national totalitarianism had initially arisen in France, and had prospered in Italy and Germany only subsequently. This kind of boasting, which was quite rightly not taken seriously in the intellectual world, failed to convince French citizens that fascism was the natural alternative to a 'degenerate' parliamentary democracy.[11]

The Faisceau, which proclaimed itself republican, put forward a view of the world more modern and dynamic than Action Française.[12] Its nationalism, while extreme and noisy, was less ethnocentric than that of its parent body. The movement seems to have been too much to the left for the taste of the traditionalist intelligentsia, who preferred to cultivate nostalgia for a mythological past, monarchist and Catholic. And above all, Action Française, xenophobic, ethno-religious and claiming to stand for French purity, was more in tune with those many intellectuals who saw themselves as perfect Gallo-Catholics. The Faisceau, on the other hand, was seen as philo-Semitic; like Italian fascism, it had activists of Jewish origin in its ranks, whom Valois saw as welcome representatives of modern dynamism. This was a long way from any import of Nazi racism, which was unknown in Paris at this time.[13]

---

10   General Georges Boulanger built his popularity in 1886–87 on an unlikely coalition including among others Bonapartists and Blanquists. He fled the country in 1889 after plotting a coup d'état. *Translator's note.*

11   Zeev Sternhell is one of the few to have been convinced by this 'indigenous' and vain self-portrait of the French fascists.

12   We should point out that significant fascists such as Georges Valois, Pierre Drieu La Rochelle and Marcel Déat saw themselves as fully republican and continuers of the French Revolution. See Shlomo Sand, 'Les représentations de la Révolution dans l'imaginaire historique du fascisme français', *Mil neuf cent – Revue d'histoire intellectuelle*, vol. 9, no. 1, 1991, pp. 29–47.

13   It is worth mentioning here that the Parti Socialiste National (PSN) of Gustave Hervé, the first abortive attempt at a French proto-fascism in 1919, was also philo-Semitic and even pro-Zionist. See Gilles Heuré, *Gustave Hervé, itinéraire d'un provocateur: de l'antiparlementarisme au pétainisme*, Paris: La Découverte, 1997, pp. 305–7.

The turbulent and rebellious modernist avant-garde, which might have been seduced in the 1920s by an extremist anti-parliamentary movement, as was the case with Italian Futurism, was mainly channelled into anti-militarist and anti-bourgeois protest; the same year that the Faisceau was founded, its more politicized part began to move towards communism. Surrealism, despite its deeply anchored irrationalism and its characteristic verbal violence, was always able, with a few minor exceptions, to dissociate itself from any form of national egoism, the ideological cornerstone of all movements of the far right. The presence of the founder of Italian Futurism, Filippo Marinetti, at a meeting held in the Vélodrome d'Hiver in November 1926 to mobilize support for the formation of a Latin fascist bloc, failed to arouse any particular interest in Parisian cultural and artistic milieus, and was even perceived as simply a manipulation on the part of the Italian foreign ministry.[14]

The intervention of literati in politics was not seen as 'good form' in the 1920s, as witnessed in the publication in 1927 of Julien Benda's *La Trahison des clercs*, discussed in a previous chapter. But the temptation for intellectuals to remain in their ivory tower, which was very marked in the wake of the Great War, steadily evaporated after the economic crisis of 1929, and still more with the collapse of the Weimar Republic in 1933. In the 1930s, growing sections of the cultural elites became involved in a new kind of politicization. Many writers, poets and essayists, as well as some academics, rapidly became politically engaged. Celebrities from the world of literature and science, from André Gide to Romain Rolland, André Malraux to Roger Martin du Gard, the philosopher Alain and the scientist Paul Langevin, led a large cohort of writers and artists into a consistent anti-fascism in the lineage of the left republican tradition. Discontent about the bourgeois economic order, which seemed in the process of collapsing, also permitted the

---

14   Yves Guchet, *Georges Valois*, p. 180.

emergence of a cultural atmosphere favourable to support for the USSR and communism. In the early 1930s, new voices that had previously been marginal in the intellectual field began to make themselves heard.

Some educated young people, from a variety of ideological backgrounds and each with their own political views, chiefly but not exclusively on the right, undertook to challenge the habitual cleavage between right and left. Around small but dynamic magazines, and with a few parallel attempts to create more visible groups, the principles of liberalism and democracy were put on trial. The unprecedented aspect of this phenomenon was that this critique had no hesitation in including fascism as a legitimate option in the spectrum of solutions offered to escape from the economic and cultural crisis that the industrial world was undergoing. Should we see in this adventure the premises of a French intellectual fascism?

These young intellectuals, active in such periodicals as *Esprit*, *Ordre nouveau*, *La Revue du siècle* or *Réaction*, have been described in subsequent historical research as '1930s nonconformists'.[15] This challenge to the existing social order was undertaken on a basis that is hard to classify in terms of traditional political parameters. The attempt to describe all those who took part in it as fascists, on the grounds that they rejected both parliamentary liberalism and Soviet communism, expresses a certain dose of ill intention and a lack of analytical sensitivity.[16] All the same, to deny that many French fascists of the 1930s came from these same circles would suggest a tendentious or hypocritical blindness.

---

15   The most exhaustive work on this subject is Jean-Louis Loubet del Bayle, *Les Nonconformistes des années 30*, Paris: Seuil, 1969. See also Jean Touchard, 'L'esprit des années 1930: une tentative de renouvellement de la pensée politique française', in *Tendances politiques dans la vie française depuis 1789*, Paris: Hachette 1930, pp. 89–118; and Pierre Andreu, *Révoltes de l'esprit*, Paris: Kimé, 1990.

16   Zeel Sternhell, as mentioned above, presents an example of this approach, seeing all those 'neither right nor left' as embryonic fervent fascists. See my critical article on this unsatisfactory conceptual apparatus: Shlomo Sand, 'L'idéologie fasciste en France', *Esprit*, August–September 1983, pp. 149–60.

The term '1930s nonconformists' can itself lead to error. Firstly, because of the timeframe it defines, and secondly, because it covers intellectual currents that are different and even opposed. To be exact, this 'nonconformism' should be confined to the first half of the decade. During these years, it was still possible to view various aspects of fascist corporatism sympathetically, preferring this to the Stalinist five-year plans without thereby becoming a fervent fascist. At this time, the critique of bourgeois individualism, the rejection of rationalism and the idea of progress inherited from the Enlightenment, the disgust with the materialism bound up with the market economy, and finally, the refusal to see the working class as the exclusive revolutionary subject that would liberate humanity, were not yet identified as incontestable markers of the totalitarian nationalism 'above class' that was being established on the other side of the Alps.

The writings of young intellectuals such as Alexandre Marc, Arnaud Dandieu, Robert Aron, Denis de Rougemont, Georges Izard, André Ulmann, Emmanuel Mounier and many others, including some of Jewish origin, regularly question the traditional division between right and left, note their unease with the immobilism of the republican idea and the failure of parliamentarianism, and sometimes even express sympathy for the ideas of fascism. At the same time, however, it is not hard to identify in their writings a rejection of the dictatorial aspects of the Italian regime, an express disagreement about the repression of political opponents, and above all, a critique of its radical nationalism. Strange as it might appear, the 'nonconformism' of the early 1930s could be seen as a laboratory for testing modern theories of economic management, with Catholic intellectuals tilting towards the left, as well as a practical and conformist path towards joining the fascist camp.

Contrary to what a certain Marxist–Leninist doctrine has transmitted to a good number of historians coming from the left, it turns out that philosophical views that are close or even similar can give rise to political positions that are opposed and contradictory. From this shared cultural malaise, and these same theoretical questions, both frenetic collaborators with the German Occupation and determined anti-Nazis would emerge, some of the latter being among the first to join the Resistance. André Philip, for example, a theorist of neo-socialist planning in the early 1930s, rallied courageously against the Occupation, while the Belgian Henri de Man, the most prominent theorist of planning, became a prominent collaborator.[17]

In a certain sense, the participation of such figures as Emmanuel Mounier, editor of *Esprit*, Robert Aron, a founder of Ordre Nouveau, and Jean de Fabrègues of Jeune Droite in the congress on corporatism held in Rome in 1935 can be seen as one of the last acts of 'revolt' against the existing order, protest against the 'capitalist muddle' and promotion of corporatist and 'plan-ist' solutions that did not favour the establishment in France of an authoritarian regime.

The period of hesitation in which certain French intellectuals took up a kind of intermediate position came to an end that same year. If the period of 'neither right nor left' and its dialogue among young intellectuals with different sensibilities and values was not formally ended, this ideological confusion was now being disturbed by political events. At the end of the day, it is impossible to understand the phenomenon of fascism, and its seductive power, without locating the arguments around it in a precise political context. The question was not about its left or right character; fascism was rather a response to the challenges of a particular historical period, and the catalyzer of a desire for action and a vigorous aspiration to power.

---

17   The fate of two German 'nonconformists' from this time reveals the same contradiction in a still more acute form. Otto Abetz became fully committed to Nazism and was appointed German ambassador to occupied France; whereas Harro Schulze-Boysen, who also came from the 'neither right nor left' tendency, set up an underground anti-Nazi group and led a spy network in Berlin connected with the 'Red Orchestra'. Brutally tortured and executed, it is no exaggeration to say that this lone combatant caused the German war machine more damage than any other single person in the Second World War.

A reconfiguration of camps

The conquest of Ethiopia by fascist Italy, in 1935, caused commotion in the international community and shook the foundations of the League of Nations. Following the Nazi seizure of power in Germany and the anti-parliamentary riot of 6 February 1934 in Paris, it had the effect of accelerating the recomposition of the intellectual field in France. In October 1935, *Le Temps* published the famous petition of intellectuals who rallied 'in defence of the West'. This petition, which proclaimed its 'peace-loving' character, was written and published in the name of the higher values of Western colonization. It described the invasion of Ethiopia as 'the civilizing conquest of one of the most backward countries in the world'. The signatories opposed the threat of sanctions imposed on Italy by the League of Nations, and strongly denounced 'a false juridical universalism that puts the superior and the inferior, the civilized and the barbarian, on the same footing'.[18]

The defence of the Italian invasion of Ethiopia was deemed to preserve the European balance and the unity of the West in the face of the risk of a new war. Beneath the appearance of a petition in favour of maintaining peace was an ideological charter that would clarify quite unambiguously the traditional difference between right and left. The world of the left did not always seriously believe in equality between populations: democrats and moderate socialists had often approved the 'civilizing mission' of an 'enlightened' colonialism. In the twentieth century, however, it became unacceptable to openly proclaim an innate inequality between peoples, and a fortiori, to translate this principle into a public declaration of support for the conquest of a sovereign state. Left-wing pacifists were therefore not alone in rejecting this pseudo-pacifist petition; the majority of 'nonconformists' were also unprepared to add their names to it, and some of their

---

18   This text is reproduced in Jean-François Sirinelli, *Intellectuels et passions françaises. Manifestes et pétitions au XXᵉ siècle*, Paris: Fayard, 1990, pp. 92–4.

number went as far as signing a counter-petition. The intellectual field would now split rather like it had done at the time of the second Dreyfus affair, but with different actors.

The interest of this petition, a symptomatic document, lies not only in what it says, but also in the ideological coalition that it attracted, whose composition allows us to glimpse the boundaries of the intellectual camps that would emerge a year later, in reaction to the advent of the Front Populaire and the outbreak of the war in Spain. If Italian fascism had come to power thanks to a historic alliance with the moderate right, and if Nazism had won out in Germany with the help of traditional conservative forces, the petition of intellectuals 'in defence of the West' had the air of a French caricature of these earlier historical blocs. The petition actually reflected an alliance between a conservative intelligentsia that was increasingly marginalized in the central cultural field, and currents that aimed at radical change, seduced by the strength of Italian fascism and German Nazism. To a large degree, it sketched in advance what would happen to the French intellectual world after the defeat of 1940.

The petition had received the signatures of several hundred writers, essayists and journalists, most of them Parisians. These included sixteen members of the Académie Française, prestigious writers on the moderate right, all the big intellectual names of Action Française, a number of future collaborators under the German Occupation, and of course, all those young literati who had begun to identify with fascist ideas at the time of the anti-parliamentary demonstrations of 6 February 1934. Among the latter were also representatives of the 'Jeune Droite', who are customarily classified as '1930s nonconformists'. Thierry Maulnier, Jean-Pierre Maxence and Jean de Fabrègues signed the petition, alongside Pierre Drieu La Rochelle, who had already described himself as a fascist a year before,[19] Robert Brasillach,

---

19   See his first 'theoretical' text: Pierre Drieu La Rochelle, *Socialisme fasciste*, Paris: Gallimard, 1934.

who would soon identify with Nazism, and a few others who would follow in his wake: Paul Chack, Henri Béraud, Alphonse de Châteaubriant, etc.[20]

Maulnier, Maxence and Fabrègues, three talented essayists who emerged from Action Française, had belonged to the 'nonconformist' discussion circles of the early 1930s. In the previous decade, the fascist project still did not seem sufficiently attractive in the eyes of the intelligentsia caught up in the monarchist movement, but this was no longer the case for these younger people in the 1930s. The mindset on the far right may well have remained strongly anti-German, but the advance of Nazism had the paradoxical effect of strengthening the impression that the future belonged to revolutionary-nationalist mass movements and to authoritarian regimes of a new kind. There was something intoxicating in the force that was spreading in Germany: why not try to build a strong regime in France, capable of rivalling Italy and Germany on an equal basis? In this respect, theoretical 'nonconformism' appears as a kind of crossroads, at which it became possible to formalize a radical philosophy with a modernist character without being immediately suspected of importing anti-French ideas.

The magazine *Combat*, launched early in 1936, and the weekly *L'Insurgé* that followed a year later, were as yet neither 'nonconformist' publications with no clear political identity nor organs of the traditional nationalist right. Both were situated on the periphery of Action Française, but there was a new wind blowing, combining conservatism and revolution in doses that were previously unknown, and to which a fascist discourse could explicitly be attached. In its first number, *Combat* took a position of support for Italy in its conquest of Ethiopia. True, its editor Thierry Maulnier held that only a 'minimum fascism' should be imported

---

20   Marcel Aymé, still close to the moderate left in 1934, was also a signatory. This act seems to prefigure the shift that would lead the pacifist writer to collaboration under the Occupation. See Michel Winock, *Le Siècle des intellectuels*, Paris: Seuil, 1997, pp. 265–6.

into France.[21] Faced with the Bolshevik threat and the Front Populaire government, however, these same spokesmen frenetically called for a national revolution and the advent of a strong and authoritarian regime that would enable the proud French spirit to take part in the battle against international plutocracy.

Other scribes rapidly joined with Maulnier, Maxence and Fabrègues in formulating a 'national socialism' inspired by the Italian model; these particularly included the young writers Maurice Blanchot, Claude Roy and Robert Francis, and the journalists René Vincent and Pierre Andreu. The last of these, among a number of others, was actively involved in the Parti Populaire Français (PPF) founded in Saint-Denis in 1936 by the former communist leader Jacques Doriot.[22]

It should be made clear, all the same, that the growing popularity of fascism consequent on the Nazi seizure of power, and the habitual equation today of Italian fascism with Nazism (and with Francoism in Spain from 1936), are not a sufficient basis for maintaining that the 'minimum fascism' evoked by Maulnier can be identified with German Nazism or even with its conception of the nation. Action Française, for example, could in the same breath extol Mussolini and Franco, but decry and condemn Hitler. We thus find, in one section of fascist intellectuals and for varied reasons, evident reservations towards the 'totalitarian mystique' and the political brutality of German Nazism.

While a Judeophobic writer such as Robert Brasillach contributed to *Combat* right away, others such as Thierry Maulnier and Jean de Fabrègues denounced Hitlerism and the *völkisch* racism that was one of its main characteristics. Their 'Western' and 'Christian' values led them to develop an anti-communist

---

21   See Paul Serant, *Les Dissidents de l'Action française*, Paris: Copernic, 1978, p. 221.

22   On his involvement with *Combat* and the PPF, Pierre Andreu's memoir is an interesting testimony: *Le Rouge et le blanc, 1928–1944*, Paris: La Table Ronde, 1977, pp. 122–32. My own interviews with Pierre Andreu, who in his old age rallied to the ecological left, were a great help to me in deciphering the political to-ings and fro-ings of the 1930s.

conception and defend 'European superiority', but they opposed the biological materialism of German race 'science', and the 'zoological' determinism on which its view of history was based. Thus, while Thierry Maulnier's group was not exempt from anti-Semitism, this was not its rallying cry. The same holds for the group of intellectuals who enthusiastically joined Jacques Doriot's Parti Populaire Français.

This party, following on from the Faisceau that preceded it, may be seen as the French political movement most similar to early Italian *fascismo*. Its leaders, some of whom had come from the Communist Party, did not call themselves fascists, but the young intellectuals who rallied to the new party had fewer scruples. In contrast to Valois in the 1920s, Doriot, a former leader of the Young Communists, seduced a good number of intellectuals who were seeking a more definite engagement in political life. Immediately after its foundation, the PPF attracted writers, critics, essayists and journalists from all political backgrounds: there were the ex-communists Paul Marion and Camille Fégy, the modernist philosophers Bertrand de Jouvenel and Alfred Fabre-Luce, who both came from the Radical Party, and the novelist Pierre Drieu La Rochelle. These talented figures were rapidly joined by the writers Jean Fontenoy, Paul Chack and Pierre Bonardi, the literary critic Raymond Fernandez (who took charge of the party's intellectual wing), the historian Jacques Benoist-Méchin, the future political scientist Maurice Duverger, the journalist and essayist Claude Jeantet, and some veterans from the Faisceau of the 1920s, such as Georges Suarez and the *académicien* Abel Bonnard.[23] Claude Jeantet and Bertrand de Jouvenel were contributing editors of the PPF central organ, *L'Émancipation nationale*, along with Maurice-Yvan Sicard (under the nom de plume 'Saint-Paulien'), and Pierre Drieu La Rochelle was also a regular contributor.

---

23   A list of intellectuals who joined the PPF is given in Jean-Paul Brunet, *Jacques Doriot, du communisme au fascisme*, Paris: Balland, 1986, pp. 232–4.

These literati who proudly proclaimed their nationalism saw France as a power in decline. Obsessed by the idea of decadence, which formed one of the cornerstones of their political commitment, they imagined they had found the authentic French Mussolini in the anti-communist workers' leader Doriot. They were in the main young Parisian intellectuals, in a hurry to make their reputations and thirsty for power. Most of them despised the toadying required for advance in the intellectual hierarchy, and did not feel the need to conceal their strong ambition under cover of the universalistic and enlightened discourse that was customary for the cultural left. All the young PPF intelligentsia shared a disgust for bourgeois hypocrisy and a hatred of communism. The hoped-for rebirth of a strong and virile nation stimulated them to devote the best part of their time and their writing to a new kind of protest politics.

There were different sensibilities among them. The motivations of writers with a fluent pen, such as Drieu La Rochelle or Fernandez, were not exactly the same as those of more systematic thinkers such as Jouvenel or Fabre-Luce. For some of them, the aestheticization of politics that they saw in fascism had more charm than the principles of statization of economic life and the call for a new ruling elite. For others, the planning of a rational economy, to put an end to class struggle and create a new national community, was more attractive than the demonstrative and colourful parades staged in the streets of Rome or Berlin. Yet until 1938, there was a minimal common basis that conferred on the Doriot movement a certain resemblance to the Communist Party: intellectuals worked to give it a respectable cultural identity, compatible with a reasonable dose of critical and nonconformist discourse. Rather like Gramsci, at the same point in time, they knew that the ground of culture had to be conquered before political power could be won.[24]

---

24   Jacques Benoist-Méchin would subsequently declare, not without a certain exaggeration: 'I do not hesitate to maintain that no French political party ever had such an intellectual potential' (Jacques Benoist-Méchin, *De la défaite au désastre*, vol. 1, Paris: Albin Michel, 1984, p. 54). Gabriel Leroy-Ladurie was the main organizer of the party's intellectual sector behind the scenes.

In contrast to the Communist Party, the PPF was funded by banking circles (Lazare, Worms and Rothschild), without this arousing any particular discontent among the 'revolutionary anti-bourgeois' circles that had joined and represented it.

It is true that Drieu and Jouvenel both paid certain compliments to the Hitler regime at this time, but their view of the world remained fascist in the Italian vein rather than Nazi. The cult of the leader, the deification of the total national state, the renewed enthusiasm for French imperialism and the desire to suppress class conflict were not accompanied, in their case, by a radical racial theory or a deep and perverse hatred towards those not belonging to their race. Their view of national identity was still in essence typically Jacobin, and their remarks about Jews and foreigners hardly went beyond the negative stereotypes that were widespread in French cultural circles. It is worth recalling here that one of the PPF leaders, Doriot's right-hand man, Alexandre Abramsky, never hid his Jewish origins, and it was perfectly well known to PPF members that he was in charge of the party's finances.[25]

The attraction of Nazism

The ideological mosaic of the PPF's fascist intelligentsia, however, would see its components gradually evolve. The defeat of fascism by Nazism in Austria, and the application of racial legislation in Italy in 1938, encouraged an ethnocentric radicalization on the part of Drieu and his companions, some of whom had already adopted a more incisive Judeophobia before their collective resignation from the party in the wake of

---

25 Abramsky's death in 1938 removed certain scruples and facilitated openly anti-Semitic expression in the party press. On the circumstances of Abramsky's death, see Victor Barthélemy, *Du communisme au fascisme*, Paris: Albin Michel, 1978, pp. 130–1. Bertrand de Jouvenel was also of Jewish origin, a fact well known to all his fascist friends.

the Munich agreements.[26] Not all of Drieu's fellow travellers shared in this perverse slippage (Jouvenel, for example, could not do so on account of his mother's Jewish origin), yet Nazification increased nonetheless with the decline in the PPF's influence and the hope of seeing a genuine fascist regime established in France.

Moreover, although Doriot's party could certainly not be defined as Nazi in the 1930s, it had been joined and supported by some intellectuals whose ideas were far less inhibited. Alexis Carrel is a good example of this: a famous surgeon and biologist who had received the Nobel Prize for medicine in 1912, he developed racist theories in the 1930s. This 'scientific' racism, which had its antecedents in the French intellectual world of the nineteenth century, was now also represented by other men of science, such as Ernest Fourneau, a member of the Institut, and Victor Balthasar of the Académie de médicine; both became fellow travellers of the PPF.

The Nazification that affected these fascist intellectuals well matched the heavy Judeophobic atmosphere of the late 1930s,[27] but it had already flourished earlier within another group, which emerged directly from the far right and not, like Doriot's party, from the left. The weekly *Je suis partout*, founded in the 1930s, was originally simply conservative. From 1936, after breaking away from its Fayard publisher, it acquired a tone that can be termed genuinely Nazi, even if it was still possible after this date to find some articles that expressed reservations towards the simplistic nature of Nazi propaganda (in September 1939, it was even anti-German for a short period). However, its verbal violence against the Front Populaire government, its crude racism, its rampant Judeophobia and proclaimed sympathy for

---

26   The development of Judeophobia in the work of Drieu La Rochelle is described in Charlotte Wardi, 'Drieu et les Juifs', in *Drieu La Rochelle*, Paris: L'Herne, 1982, pp. 289–98.

27   In 1938, Flammarion decided to republish Édouard Drumont's *La France juive*.

Nazi repressive methods and displays of force, were exceptional even in the French fascist milieu.[28]

The writers and journalists who took part in this literary enterprise were a different kind of intellectual: Robert Brasillach, Lucien Rebatet, Georges Blond, Alain Laubreaux and other members of the editorial team came in the main from Action Française, having left it out of dissatisfaction with the ponderous conservatism of the monarchist movement. They kept its traditional anti-Semitism, but in contrast to those who had left Action Française in the 1920s, infused this with an ever more essentialist and venomous content. Anti-Semitism had become fashionable throughout Europe at this time. The perspective of a national revolution that would cleanse France of 'foreign elements' that sullied its culture, and especially Jews from Eastern Europe who were seen as dangerous, became the leitmotif of these crude publicists, whose desire was also to see France join the camp of strong states.

And so in 1937, when René Vincent delivered a sharp critique of Louis-Ferdinand Céline's anti-Semitic provocation *Bagatelles pour un massacre*, Lucien Rebatet responded venomously to him in *Je suis partout*, enthusiastically defending Céline's Judeophobia. In April 1938, the weekly devoted a whole issue to the problem of Jews who had infiltrated into the French nation and supposedly threatened to change its character. These articles, antipodes of delicacy and tolerance, attracted a critical reply from Thierry Maulnier in the pages of *Combat* (this 'responsible' and 'normally national' fascist organ was disposed to support only a 'logical anti-Semitism' and not an exaggerated one). Maulnier's

---

28   Robert Brasillach, its editor, expressed his admiration for the dark and fascinating Nazi aesthetic on his return from a visit to Germany: 'The cult of the fatherland was expressed in daytime and night-time offices, in Walpurgis nights lit up by floodlights and torches, in tremendous music, in songs of war and peace sung by millions of men' (Robert Brasillach, *Notre avant-guerre (1939–1940)*, Paris: Le Livre de poche, 1992, p. 303). For more on *Je suis partout*, see Pierre-Marie Dioudonnat, *'Je suis partout', 1930–1944. Les maurrassiens devant la tentation fasciste*, Paris: La Table Ronde, 1973.

reservations and calls for 'moderation' led Brasillach to wonder in his memoirs whether liberal intellectuals had not mingled with revolutionary nationalists on *Combat*'s editorial board.[29]

There clearly were no liberals among the editors of *Combat*. Differences of temperament between Parisian fascists and Nazis, however, began to appear in the late 1930s, even if these are not always easy to identify and their boundaries were sometimes vague and fluctuating. Despite the strong ambient Judeophobia, to graft a racial conception onto a French national identity that was not fundamentally ethnocentric was not an easy task, in contrast to German national culture. Whereas in the late nineteenth century racist theories were still upheld only by marginal intellectual circles with no real audience, they had won a wider vulgarization and popularization by the late 1930s. *Je suis partout* did not seek to deepen the biological parameters of the 'different other' theoretically, but a tendency emerged from its pages and circles close to it that prefigured the future anti-Jewish legislation of the Vichy regime.

The connection to Nazi ideology was not reducible to the dehumanization of those designated as Jews. As regards their political and ideological adversaries, and the position of France in an imagined fascist international, the difference between enthusiastic imitators of Nazi Germany and other fascists went well beyond nuance. Their respective cultural restraints and level of verbal violence were also of a different order; Maulnier's group at *Combat*, that of Drieu in the PPF or that of Brasillach at *Je suis partout* cannot be seen as a bloc with one and the same position, as historians coming from the left have too often tended to do. (Their approach to the radical right has similarities with certain analyses of the far left produced by conservative scholars.) These differentiated sensibilities ultimately weighed significantly on the level of commitment of the respective parties in their

---

29   See Géraldi Leroy and Anne Roche, *Les Écrivains et le Front populaire*, Paris: Presses de la Fondation nationale des sciences politiques, 1986, p. 70.

collaboration with the occupying power and participation in the reactionary and anti-Semitic Vichy regime from 1940 to 1944.

The collaboration of several pacifists coming from the left may appear logical, moved as they were by their opposition to the prospect of a new world war.[30] But the main question, which has so far remained without a convincing response, is how the great majority of the nationalist camp, its royalist and fascist branches as well as its national-socialist one, could ally with an occupier that had established its headquarters in the capital and divided the country in two. Could anyone accept such a national humiliation and continue to be called a fascist? Could a 'national socialist' have any other raison d'être than to preserve the *grande patrie* in its totality and even expand its *Lebensraum*?

The explanation that is almost universally given in the scholarly literature is that the hostility of the far right towards liberal democracy, and its fears of the horrors of Bolshevism, played a decisive part in the accelerated process that transformed heated champions of French nationalism into fervently pro-German 'Europeans' from one day to the next. This explanation contains part of the truth, but it is not sufficient when we turn to examine the itinerary of the majority of those intellectuals who were gripped in the 1930s by fascism or the Nazi spirit. A purely ideological explanation is not coherent or reliable enough when we observe the trajectory of other intellectuals who, like the writer Raymond Abellio or the journalist and literary critic Claude Jamet, passed directly in 1940 from the left to the camp of active collaborators without going through progressive phases of fascization and Nazification.

Contrary to the fascists of the 1920s, with only few exceptions those intellectuals who rallied to fascism in the 1930s, or who came out as pro-Nazi before the war, welcomed the occupiers

---

30   On those members of LICA (Ligue internationale contre l'antisémitisme) in the 1930s who became virulent anti-Semites after 1940, see Simon Epstein, *Un paradoxe français. Antiracistes dans la collaboration, antisémites dans la Résistance*, Paris: Albin Michel, 2008.

and condemned any act of resistance against them. Moreover, the widespread assumption that the fascists preferred to remain in Paris and regroup under the protection of the German army, while the conservative right chose to act within the Vichy regime, is also inexact. Some fascist intellectuals from the 1930s, among whom Paul Marion and Jacques Benoist-Méchin were the most prominent, enthusiastically placed themselves in the service of the Pétainist apparatus at Vichy. In reality, activists who had succumbed to the charms of Nazism well before the war preferred to remain in Paris, with which no authentic intellectual could sever their connection, to relish the power and glory of the 'virile' conqueror from the east. Regionalist conservative intellectuals, however, who proclaimed a cult of the soil and hated modernity, placed themselves under Pétain's wing, with the evident hope of seeing Vichy replace Paris, the decadent 'Jewified' capital populated by *métèques* (literally 'aliens', but strongly pejorative in use).

Close study of the attitude of the political sphere under the Occupation leads to the conclusion that, among those who experienced French defeat not only as a moment of great peril and confusion to which one had to adapt so as to preserve what remained, but also as a historical occasion to renew French political culture, many felt personally frustrated and paralyzed under the political configuration of the Third Republic. We know that politicians greedy for power, who had broken with the traditional parties, were among those most active in the 'national revolution'.

The differences and splits within political movements were never generated by ideology alone. In Action Française, the fascist challenge that Georges Valois launched to Charles Maurras also flowed from the personal rivalry between an ambitious politician and the movement's spiritual guide, whose absolute power could not be contested. Jacques Doriot's break with the Communist Party was not originally due to a difference of ideas. The fact that the Comintern, in other words

Moscow, had preferred Maurice Thorez as party leader played a decisive role in his abjuration of communism. The case of Marcel Déat presents similar characteristics: a young and dynamic figure in the Socialist Party (SFIO), leader of the 'neo-socialist' current, he came into conflict with the party leadership and left it to found a reformist party which had scarcely any success. In the wake of national defeat, Déat headed a pro-Nazi collaborationist movement. The same held for Gaston Bergery, a promising young leader in the Radical Party who rallied to the Vichy regime, and perhaps also for René Belin, the deputy general secretary of the CGT, who was appointed minister of labour by the Vichy government.

The ambition of all these figures, in the 1930s, was to rise rapidly to the top of their respective movement, but they came up against a balance of forces within its apparatus that blocked their ascent. It is hardly surprising, therefore, that among those who had broken with their original party or organization before the war on account of too slow an advance in their political career, many were tempted to seize the opportunity of the crisis of 1940 to occupy the new sites of political power.[31]

The assertion that ideology has always been more of a means than an end in the career of most professional politicians may today seem extremely commonplace. The decline in the mobilizing power of ideologies since the late twentieth century helps us better envisage this aspect of that century's political culture. On the other hand, an attempt at a similar analysis in the intellectual field arouses a great deal of reticence. How is it possible that those whose main task is to produce ideas and values are not always guided in their choices by the force of these same ideas? We generally expect more 'spirituality' on the part of intellectuals, both in their literary preferences and in their

31   On the political dissidents of the 1930s who became fascists or pro-Nazi collaborators, see Philippe Burrin's absorbing book *La Dérive fasciste. Doriot, Déat, Bergery*, Paris: Seuil, 1986.

political choices. The thirst to acquire additional symbolic capital is perceived as a secondary matter, supposedly not pertinent in the biographies of those who have their heads wrapped in the clouds.

But to explain how a radical nationalism was transformed into pure defeatism, it is necessary to go beyond a linear history of political ideas. On the eve of the war, fascist intellectuals, and a section of those who inclined towards Nazism, such as Pierre Drieu La Rochelle, Raymond Fernandez and some others, had vigorously rejected the Munich agreements and the Italian regime's territorial claims to Nice and Savoy. The integrity and security of France mattered more than the nature of its political regime. All the more so, as one of the primordial criteria for judging the viability of a political power was its capacity to defend the country's security and strengthen its power and imperial prestige: hence the stigmatizing of parliamentary liberalism, seen as debilitating and emasculated, and the rejection of communism, suspected of treason and collusion with Moscow. The burning desire for a strong national state had been the banner of the entire far right.

This is why, in the wake of French defeat, former fascist intellectuals such as Jacques Arthuys, Georges Valois, Philippe Barrès, Georges Oudard and Jacques Debu-Bridel, with a background in the 1920s Faisceau, or like Claude Roy of the *Combat* group (he had also published in *Je suis partout*), refrained from collaboration, and in some cases even joined the armed Resistance.[32] Others, like Bertrand de Jouvenel and Thierry Maulnier, kept their distance throughout this period from the

---

32   The fascists of the 1920s were clearly more anti-German than those of the 1930s, which may explain the engagement of many of them in the Resistance. For the same reason, former leading figures in the Croix de Feu – François de la Rocque, Georges Riché, Joseph Pozzo di Borgo and Noël Ottavi – who were neither fascists nor intellectuals but belonged to the nationalist far right, also joined the Resistance. The author of spy novels Pierre Nord (André Brouillard) was also a courageous *résistant*.

political intoxication of their old friends. Both had well understood that in 1940 neither democratic liberalism nor Bolshevism
were any longer a danger to the integrity of France, which made
the strange enthusiasm for a European union under the Nazi
jackboot incomprehensible.

The 'national rebels' and national defeat

The majority of the more conformist fascist 'rebels', and above all
those who had succumbed to the Nazi fever, immediately and
scrupulously launched an assault on the centres of power, in an
intellectual field that was now wide open. Pierre Drieu La
Rochelle took the place of André Gide as editor of the *Nouvelle
Revue Française*, the editorship of the pro-Nazi *Je suis partout* fell
to Robert Brasillach, and that of the *Petit Parisien* to Claude
Jeantet. Georges Suarez was appointed editor of *Aujourd'hui*, a
magazine with wide circulation from which Henri Jeanson had
just been expelled, and Alphonse de Châteaubriant could finally
found his own political and literary weekly, *La Gerbe*. Others
were content with flattering invitations to congresses in Germany,
larger print runs for their books (after those of their rivals had
been banned from publication), or seats in the 'high places' of
culture and literature. Intellectuals such as Jacques Benoist-
Méchin and Abel Bonnard joined the apparatus of the Vichy
state and, unlike their colleagues, could thus hope not only to
write history but also to make it directly. At the end of the day,
the thirst for power and personal glory did not weigh any less
than the desire to defend the honour and prestige of the nation,
even when the two were not always compatible.

Both the sentiment of a victory won over the left, and along
with it the taste for revenge, were too intoxicating in late 1940
for these nationalist intellectuals to bother about such trivialities
as the neutralization and disintegration of the French armies.
Even the German oversight of the new French government,
whose foreign policy was subject to the advance approval of the

representative of the occupying 'brother' country, did not seem an inhibition to them. The immense satisfaction expressed in 1940 by many intellectuals was not just due to the fact that an authoritarian nationalist ideology had ended up flooring the supposedly cowardly and anti-national parliamentarianism; the social positions of the far right in the intellectual field had played a no-less-decisive part in the outcome of events.

From the socio-cultural point of view, the 'nonconformists' of the early 1930s, the fascist intellectuals of *Combat* and the PPF, and the philo-Nazis gathered around *Je suis partout*, came mainly from a younger generation keen to establish its own place in the sun. The fact that in those years a culture of the centre left had occupied the intellectual centre of gravity tended to fuel anti-thetical positions among the protesting intellectuals. In the 1920s, revolt against the upholders of the dominant culture, champions of a republican nationalism inherited from the First World War, had led to a pacifist and revolutionary universalism. The consolidation of the status of the intellectual left, which became broadly anti-fascist in the 1930s, incited young contenders to adopt antagonistic ideas by way of reaction.

Drieu, Maulnier, Jouvenel, Fernandez, Fabre-Luce, Brasillach, Rebatet and many others would certainly have succeeded in gradually inserting themselves into the intellectual system without the need to constantly challenge it by waging a kind of cultural civil war. But like earlier intellectual generations in a modern elitist culture that cultivates isolationism, they rejected integration, a synonym for them of submission; they hoped on the contrary to take the system by storm and adapt it to their ideological and aesthetic tastes.[33] The recourse to fascist rhetoric and national-socialist myth was clearly not just instrumental in nature: at least some of these actors sincerely believed in the values of the 'conservative revolution' and sought to promote

---

33   On the phenomenon of 'generations', see Jean-François Sirinelli (ed.), *Générations intellectuelles*, Cahiers de l'Institut d'histoire du temps présent, no. 6, 1987.

them, but their discourse need not be understood as a strictly ideological challenge.

Groups that were dominated in the field of cultural creation tried in the 1930s to use the changes expected in the political domain in order to advance their status. In 1940 they persuaded themselves of the correctness of their predictions, hence the sentiment of victory with which they welcomed the defeat of their country. It is important to emphasize that the conservative, traditionalist and anti-democratic right could not have seized political power at Vichy by its own strength without the intervention of a foreign army. In the same way, the fascist or pro-Nazi intellectuals could not win hegemony in the Parisian intellectual field in 1940; for this they always needed the assistance of the German ambassador Otto Abetz. And their hegemony was short-lived and very relative.

In occupied Paris, and under the Vichy regime, autonomy for cultural creation was reduced, and the space for the victorious intelligentsia to intervene turned out to be puny in comparison with the level of autonomy that cultural producers enjoyed in the ordinary political conditions of a pluralist democracy. The more 'reasonable' fascists and pro-Nazis understood this soon enough, but their initial enthusiasm had generated a momentum that they could no longer really control. Even if we should not see history as the fate of a Greek tragedy, the paths that led Drieu La Rochelle to suicide and Brasillach to execution were already traced.

The fate of these two intellectuals, while not necessarily representative, does cast an additional light on the nature of the flirtation – traumatic and short-lived – of French culture with fascism and Nazism. The talents of both were undeniable: Drieu's novels are still a pleasure to read today, and we can continue to admire Brasillach's film criticism. Equally undeniable, however, was their veneration for fascism and Nazism. In contrast to the philosopher Bertrand de Jouvenel, who tried to conceal his early attraction to fascism,[34] or Céline, who constantly denied having

---

34   See the chapter on his relationship with Doriot's party in Bertrand de

been the veritable ambassador of Judeophobia that he was both before and during the war, Drieu and Brasillach, right up to their violent deaths, were too proud to renege on their active commitment during the stormy decade from 1935 to 1945. They saw themselves as 'pure' and responsible intellectuals, and wanted to die as martyrs.[35]

Both thus ended their lives as authentic Nazis, but this does not mean that their ideological starting points were the same. Drieu, the elder of the pair, began his literary career in the 1920s under the influence of surrealism.[36] Brasillach, on the other hand, took his first steps as a literary critic with Action Française. Their gifts were soon recognized in the milieus where they intervened and wrote, but a sense of marginality never left them, and they expressed their tormented and wounded image in a language that was always protesting and provocative.

The common denominator in the biography of these two leading intellectuals of the pro-Nazi camp is that they both experienced defeat in the educational system that was the pride of the Third Republic. Drieu made a suicide attempt after failing his final examination at the École libre des sciences politiques, and kept to his last day a particularly bitter memory of this event, which had put paid to his ambition to become a diplomat. Brasillach twice failed the *agrégation*, and finished his education at the École normale supérieure without the qualification to begin an academic career.[37]

Jouvenel's autobiography, *Un voyageur dans le siècle*, Paris: Robert Laffont, 1979, pp. 297–307.

35   On the atmosphere in the last phase of the Occupation, and the situation of the collaborationist intellectuals, see Gisèle Sapiro, *La Responsabilité de l'écrivain. Littérature, droit et morale en France*, Paris: Seuil, 2011, pp. 525–627.

36   There have been many efforts to decipher this enigmatic and disturbing writer, in particular Dominique Desanti, *Drieu La Rochelle, du dandy au nazi*, Paris: Perrin, 1978; and Jacques Cantier, *Pierre Drieu La Rochelle*, Paris: Flammarion, 1992.

37   See on this subject the excellent article by Géraldi Leroy, 'Robert Brasillach contre les intellectuels', in Danièle Bonnaud-Lamotte and Jean-Luc Rispail (eds), *Intellectuel(s) des années trente*, pp. 251–7.

The hypothesis that these early and painful failures were responsible for the transformation of his brilliant talent into a moral monstrosity – Brasillach declared in 1942 that 'we have to rid ourselves of the Jews en bloc and not keep the children'[38] – is hardly a serious psychological explanation; not every frustrated intellectual, however injured their pride, became a fascist or a Nazi. Yet we could suggest with all due caution that these previous biographical episodes played their part in the fact that the two writers seeking literary legitimacy always felt an acute sense of victimhood and rejection. Their trajectory to the polar opposite of the values of the Third Republic was largely paved by the sense of their bitter failure, which they ascribed to the republic's cultural institutions.

Not all French fascists and pro-Nazis underwent similar personal trials, and it would be futile to look for these among the much larger and more significant number of uninhibited conformists like Jean Cocteau, Henry de Montherlant, Jean Giono or Marcel Aymé, who practised a moderate and 'normal' collaboration under the Occupation so as to be able to continue calmly producing their work. Yet it would not be mistaken to maintain that those cultural producers who were rejected or insufficiently recognized by their colleagues sought for a brief period to become the masters of cultural creation in Paris. Seeing the victory of Nazism as an opportunity to take their revenge and finally bring their work to a wide public, several marginalized writers accordingly embarked on active collaboration with the Occupation and established themselves in the power networks set up by the Germans.[39]

Comparable strategies can be identified among intellectuals

---

38   Quoted in Bernard Laguerre, 'Brasillach', in Jacques Julliard and Michel Winock (eds), *Dictionnaire des intellectuels français*, Paris: Seuil, 1996, p. 182.

39   The work of Gisèle Sapiro on the social and biographical context of writers and their attitude under the Occupation remains irreplaceable: *The French Writers' War, 1940–1953*, Durham: Duke University Press, 2014.

and artists who joined the Resistance. Often rebellious and sometimes frustrated, some of these saw opposition to Nazism as a way of acquiring a certain prestige in a competitive cultural field. Their system of values was certainly different from that of the collaborators, but their engagement in the Resistance was also not necessarily exempt from personal ambition. The cultural field that emerged in the wake of Liberation in 1945, dominated by intellectuals and artists who had been in the Resistance, would not only break with the cultural practices inspired by fascism and Nazism, but also with those that had prevailed before 1940.

Once the fascist menace had been eradicated, the cultural coalition that opposed it gradually fell apart, and the new debates that arose finally led to the enthusiasm for fascism and Nazism of a section of the Parisian intelligentsia being forgotten. A black stain in collective memory, a source of unease and bad conscience, the presence of fascism and Nazism in Parisian intellectual history has since generated several historical controversies and analyses that I see as mistaken. Sometimes described as a long love story, the relationship that certain French intellectual circles maintained with fascism and Nazism was actually more like a temporary flirtation. This, in my view, is what distinguishes French fascism from the ideological and intellectual traditions such as traditional Judeophobia, secular republicanism or patriotic communism, which were all deeply and lastingly anchored in the French cultural landscape.

CHAPTER 5

Twilight of the Idols: The Critical Intellectual Domesticated?

When the privileged class feel comfortable with their principles, when they have a good conscience, when the oppressed are well convinced of being inferior creatures and are even proud of their servile condition, then the artist is at ease.

> Jean-Paul Sartre, Preface to René
> Leibowitz, *L'Artiste et sa conscience*, 1950

The new technology of information greatly reduces the practical power of ideologies . . . The mass media ensure the maximum socialization of private stupidity . . . Bad information drives out good information because truth is becoming more and more expensive.

> Régis Debray, *Teachers, Writers, Celebrities:*
> *The Intellectuals of Modern France*, 1981

All through my life I have aspired to become a critical intellectual. And now, just when I have finally succeeded, the status of this strange creature of pluralist democracy is on the decline. It shows little originality to state today that the moral intellectual stands in a twilight zone. Yet it is hardly an encouraging personal experience to sense that, at the very heart of the process of writing, the value of words in forming moral sensibility and adopting political positions is steadily weakening. A growing disarray about the use of words assails the author concerned to remain true to himself, and paralysis is a particular threat.

Yet blindness towards historical processes, or ignorance of them, will not help us to take leave of the twentieth century. Despite a rather deep pessimism, I have not succumbed to fatalism; I am still one of those who think that only a critical examination and intransigent vision can lead to new paths and original perspectives. Clarifying the modes of circulation of knowledge, and deciphering the dynamic by which social consciousness emerges, is still a requirement of all thinking subjects, even if they are aware that their words risk being rapidly blown away with the air of the time.

I should point out that the debate on the retreat of intellectuals is not new; it had already begun in the middle years of the last century. In 1960, the same year as Jean-Paul Sartre's *Critique of Dialectical Reason*,[1] the American sociologist David Bell published his celebrated collection of articles *The End of Ideology*. Sartre was then at the peak of his intellectual glory, and closest to the theoretical Marxism that was blossoming among the Parisian and French intelligentsia. It is hardly surprising, then, that Bell's work had to wait thirty-seven years to be translated into French and enjoy a favourable reception there.[2] Towards the end of the century, Paris thus made up for its delay and joined the 'ideology of the end of ideologies'; in other words, the conservative intellectual tradition whose presence in the English-speaking world had always been much stronger.

---

1   Jean-Paul Sartre, *Critique of Dialectical Reason*, vol. 1, London: Verso, 2004.

2   Daniel Bell, *La Fin de l'idéologie*, Paris: PUF, 1997. See for example Henri Mendras's review in the *Revue français de science politique*, vol. 47, no. 3, 1997, pp. 497–9.

One thesis proposed by Bell directly concerned the status of the critical intellectual. He held that the radical man of letters, in the first half of the twentieth century a striking figure in the Western world, was now in a phase of decline or even disappearance. From the early eighteenth to the mid-twentieth century, Western society had needed mobilizing ideas, as it modernized and developed its liberal and democratic configuration. After the Second World War, however, the consolidation of the welfare state and a flexible political pluralism made the ideological man of letters superfluous.

According to Bell, the radical intellectual emerged and prospered so long as the general development of Western culture needed rallying ideologies to cope with changes in the form of society. The defeat of fascist ideologies in 1945, the decline of cynical Stalinism in the USSR in the late 1950s, and above all, the strengthening foundation of the welfare state in the West, weakened the tendency to reject what existed by invoking global critical theories.

For Bell, the extinction of ideologies and the disappearance of the universal radical intellectual was part of a purely conceptual process, flowing from thinkers' ideas that had no connection to their social position. The new consensus among writers and scholars arose from the fact that the consumer society had become less conflictual and more inclined to unanimity. The overall satisfaction of large strata of the population had silenced the intellectual's traditional moral conscience, which had ceased to dream of an ideal future society. As a counterpart, literati increasingly became technical experts called on to perfect the material and spiritual products of the post-industrial affluent society. It was only in the Third World, Bell claimed, that rebellious or revolutionary men of letters still existed, but they would disappear here too with the progress, prosperity and pacification of the international economy.

In 1966, Noam Chomsky, professor of linguistics, rejected this unsatisfactory explanation. In an essay on 'the responsibility of intellectuals' he accepted the hypothesis of the decline of the critical intellectual, but explained this phenomenon on the basis of a more sociological approach: the expansion of the welfare state in the 1950s gave intellectuals a respectable place in administering its imposing state apparatus.[3] In other words, state support for educational establishments, research laboratories and cultural institutions rose rapidly, and a corporatist class interest spurred wide sections of the intelligentsia to comfortably join the existing order, and thereby subscribe to the prevailing consensus. This process, which properly got under way only after the Second World War, saw a proliferation of guaranteed jobs for the expanding class of intellectuals. Despite the Cold War, the 1950s augured a radiant social future, with the welfare state a seemingly boundless historical reality that would soon extend to all human societies.

It is quite unlikely that Bell would have written about the 'end of ideologies' in the 1960s. From Berlin to Paris, London to Berkeley, cultural sites resounded with the echoes of student demonstrations that would shake the academic world, while the old totalizing ideologies whose disappearance Bell had prophesied experienced a renewal of popularity on all university campuses. Intellectual youths denounced the consumer society and seemed to totally reject the material advantages it offered. Critical intellectuals such as Herbert Marcuse, Jürgen Habermas, Louis Althusser and Michel Foucault became the new spiritual guides of the educated elites of a turbulent young generation.

And yet, from the standpoint of the early twenty-first century, Bell's prediction of the death of mobilizing ideologies and the decline of both the intellectuals that produced these and the intelligentsia that adopted them, might seem increasingly well founded, at least in the Western world. Since the mid-1970s, the great utopias have come to be seen as useless, and it is good form

---

3   Noam Chomsky, 'The Responsibility of Intellectuals', in *American Power and the New Mandarins*, New York: Vintage, 1969, p. 344.

in intellectual milieus to give thanks for the positive and comfortable values of the existing order. The student and intellectual malaise of the 1965–75 decade, which ended without any real damage, is now described as a 'crisis of growth'.

In Paris, which Raymond Aron called the paradise of revolutionary rhetoric, the majority of 'rebel' intellectuals have rediscovered the advantages of Western civilization, especially the bourgeois comfort that this offers to the established and recognized agents of culture.

The universal and the specific

In the early 1990s, the English historian Tony Judt similarly undertook to explain the decline in prestige of the critical intellectual, particularly in Paris, in connection with the welfare state, or, more precisely, with the start of its historical decline. At a time when the first social signs of the stagnation of the capitalist economy appeared, his explanation quite logically took the opposite tack to that of Noam Chomsky: 'Like the state, the major figures of French intellectual life were the natural source of authority and legitimacy; with the decline of the state-as-provider has come the fall of its intellectual *doppelgänger*.'[4]

Rational and convincing hypotheses may unfortunately prove inexact. History rather resembles the body of a frog in a laboratory, which can be dissected in various ways. Judt correctly observes that the breakthrough of the Sartrean intellectual was concomitant with the development of the welfare state, and that the weakening of the latter likewise saw a decline in the image of the prophet of universal protest. Yet Judt did not take sufficient account of the fact that the meridian of the Parisian intellectual, in the late 1950s, was the culmination of a process that long antedated the welfare state.

---

4   Tony Judt, *Past Imperfect: French Intellectuals, 1944–1956*, New York: New York University Press, 2011, pp. 296–7.

A look back at the mid-1970s, when the protest of the young intelligentsia in the Western world began to run out of steam, shows that Michel Foucault was one of the first to sense the change that was under way in the status of the intellectual as emitter of universal messages. In 1976, for example, he maintained that the intellectual as 'conscience of the world' was in the process of losing his status, if not his right to exist.[5] The political battles waged since the eighteenth century, mainly against the arbitrary power of the sovereign in the name of general rights and equality before the law, had finally given birth to the modern prophet. Power, Foucault explained, was not exclusively concentrated in the state apparatus; it lay in each structure and each level of social life.[6] The struggle against the means of domination had accordingly ceased to be universal and become partial and local. The man of letters who had appeared in the public sphere and spoken in the name of the general interest had become superfluous, as the traditional forms of representation of generality had lost their meaning.

No one can represent 'all' others, and so Foucault's new intellectual proposed to speak for himself and his kind; he was the absolute antithesis of the critical man of letters without a precise specialization. He was not a 'superior genius', but rather a scientist or technician in a laboratory. The specific intellectual becomes politicized in the course of his particular scientific or scholarly work; it is in this context that he expresses his opposition to the existing order. That is the reason why dissatisfaction with the dominant culture is stronger in research and educational establishments than within the literary and artistic *bohème*.

---

5   Michel Foucault, 'La fonction politique de l'intellectuel', *Politique Hebdo*, 29 November 1976, pp. 31–3 (reprinted in *Dits et écrits*, vol. 3, Paris: Gallimard, 1994).

6   We could cautiously suggest that, without really wishing for this, Foucault expressed the beginning of the split between power and politics that would soon be embodied in globalization. The voice of elected national governments has a lesser weight on major decisions than does the power of international financial groups and large corporations.

The 'specific intellectual', to continue with Foucault, began to show himself in the wake of the Second World War. Robert Oppenheimer appears as a typical embodiment of this 'specific intellectual', at the historical juncture between the universal and the specific. The battle that the American physicist waged against the use of the atom bomb arose directly from his scientific work, but given that the product of his work concerned humanity as a whole, this particular specificity turned into universality. Clearly, not every specific intellectual becomes a political figure, but his particular social positioning in one of the production apparatuses of 'truth' can create conditions for a local issue to transcend its original discipline and come to assume a general significance.

From Foucault's point of view, 'truth' is less the totality of facts revealed in the course of a research process than the set of rules that make it possible to distinguish 'true' from 'false' and identify the power mechanisms that institutionalize this 'truth'. The new intellectual does not wage a battle for 'truth', but stubbornly struggles to defend this 'truth' status along with his economic and political position in society. It follows from this that, contrary to the universal intellectual, the specific intellectual takes as his mission, not to change the consciousness of society, nor what people think, but rather the structure of the political, economic and institutional order designed to produce 'truth'. There can clearly be no question of separating the apparatuses of power completely from truth, given that every truth already constitutes a power, but rather of challenging the hierarchical order of ideological production.

The invention of the specific intellectual unfortunately did not function as Foucault had envisaged it during the 1970s. This brilliant Parisian thinker, probably rather more erudite than his writer-intellectual antecedents, had omitted to explain to the reader why the specific intellectual sought to substitute new apparatuses for producing 'truth' for those currently in force. Foucault categorically rejected the Freudo-Marxist conception of alienation as a motivation of change, without replacing this with an alternative theory that would have indicated another kind of contradiction capable of challenging the social status quo. In reality, Robert Oppenheimer was not the archetype of the man of science; he was rather an *exception* among thousands of other scientists who continued to produce and perfect the modern means of extermination without expressing protest or even discontent (unless occasionally about their salaries).

In the last analysis, the 'specific' students of the late twentieth and early twenty-first centuries, just like their 'specific' professors, have been rather well integrated into the organization of the dominant systems for producing 'truth'. Perhaps only women and gay students and intellectuals, on account of the intolerable processes of inferiorization to which they are subject, have succeeded in translating Foucault's messages about the dispersion of powers into specific action programmes. These particular changes, however, remain targeted and limited, and have hardly contributed to developing among the producers of knowledge a critical intellectualization able to challenge the existing social and political order.

Foucault's critique of the universal intellectual found reinforcement in the person of Jean-François Lyotard. In parallel with his radical doctrine of the end of grand narratives and the death throes of totalizing aims, Lyotard published in 1984 an essay titled 'The Tomb of the Intellectual'.[7] As a 'lucid' postmodern intellectual, Lyotard could not continue to cling to the vestiges of hope, still fundamentally universal, that persisted in Foucault's theoretical work: individual creative activity remained the only intellectual function that could oppose the existing order. Since all universalism, according to Lyotard, ends up in a totalitarian obsession, individual and specific, non-transmissible action is the only possibility of protest that remains. Only

---

7   Jean-François Lyotard, 'The Tomb of the Intellectual', in *Political Writings*, London: UCL Press, 1993.

defensive and local interventions can fend off the resounding defeats that intellectuals have regularly experienced since the Age of Enlightenment.

Three years later, it was the turn of the American historian Russell Jacoby to tackle the question of the 'disappearance' of the intellectual. In his book *The Last Intellectuals*, Jacoby depicted the higher education establishments of the late twentieth century as so many great cemeteries of independent and critical scholars.[8] Since the 1970s, the world of the university had been peopled with former leftists who were now teachers or researchers: the most original and creative of the rebel students of the 1960s had preferred to remain in the cocoon of their revolt; they reigned over the majority of humanities and social science departments, and were now setting the main research orientations. This silent 'cultural revolution' of the 'specific intellectuals', however, had in no way changed the mentality of the broader public. The guarantee of employment, the brilliant careers and growing professionalization failed to generate a new generation of 'public' intellectuals, along the lines of that which had marked Western culture, and American culture in particular, since the early 1920s. For Jacoby, the public intellectual was a producer of 'high' culture, able to address a wide educated public, and to give impetus to a political and moral state of mind by dialogue with his readers.

Previously, young intellectuals began by writing in small-circulation reviews, and these efforts to reach the reading public prepared them to move on to newspapers and magazines. Nowadays, academics do not have to make the effort to write a 'public' prose, and have often lost the ability to do so. Researchers write only for scholarly journals and seek to be as 'scientific' as possible, so as to obtain rapid promotion in the academic hierarchy. To be a professional sociologist, anthropologist or historian,

---

8   Russell Jacoby, *The Last Intellectuals: American Culture in the Age of Academe*, New York: Basic Books, 1987.

you have to be accepted and recognized by other sociologists, anthropologists and historians. Academic compartmentalization has destroyed any possibility of instilling and transmitting to new generations the more recently established intellectual traditions. Theoretical discourse is becoming ever more hermetic, esoteric and undecipherable for the non-professional reader. Academic language is like a new kind of Latin, designed above all for the promotion of its users and the maintenance of a knowledge enabling them to distinguish themselves and preserve strategic positions of power. The public arena is dying; it is invaded by second-rate dilettantes, since there are no surviving heirs to the great intellectuals of the past.

Jacoby's book leads to the conclusion that, in the age of the 'global village', the university has once again become what it was at the start of the modern age, in other words, a closed institution producing knowledge designed to serve the existing rulers and to ensure its producers this monopoly. We know, however, that the paradigms of liberalism, democracy and political liberties, such as the *Encyclopédie*, for example, arose in the eighteenth century in salons where no academic degrees were awarded.

In the 1980s, following the writings of Lyotard and Jacoby, other publications also discussed the sorry fate of universal intellectuals, who had emerged with the modern age and played a preponderant part in the formation of political sensibilities, but whose mission seemed to be exhausted in the late twentieth century. Growing circles of scholars were then seized by an intellectual melancholy; eminent experts, each in their own domain, shut themselves up in their ivory towers, abandoning the public arena to a new category of actors, and ultimately to a new kind of moral sensibility.

From utopia to anti-totalitarianism

To try and make this 'end' of the intellectuals more clear, it is useful to return to the 'beginning'. In the early nineteenth century, Henri de Saint-Simon wrote in his third letter to farmers, manufacturers, businessmen 'and other members of the industrial class',

> Gentlemen, up to now your interests have been defended only by lawyers or metaphysicians; as a result, they have been defended badly. Above all, because these *intellectuals* have no personal interest in claiming your political rights ... I shall make a double proposal. On the one hand, I invite positive intellectuals to unite and combine their forces in order to wage a general and definitive attack on prejudices and begin the organization of the industrial system; on the other hand, I ask the industrial class, who are the most positive, to join together so as to give their *intellectuals* the resources to conduct and publish the scientific work that they need.[9]

We know today that this was the first occurrence in writing of the term 'intellectual' used as a noun. As it was previously unknown, Saint-Simon put the word in italics. It is interesting to note that the concept figures for the first time in a public appeal to organize and intervene collectively for explicitly socio-political ends. 'Intellectual' increasingly appears as a neutral word in terms of values: it includes lawyers and philosophers, who may be perceived either 'positively' or 'negatively'.

Throughout the nineteenth century, the followers of Saint-Simon formed sects or acted as 'counsellors to the prince', seeking to give their spiritual master's prediction concrete form, but they disappeared by the end of the century. Social tensions put paid to the vision of cooperation between classes and professions: industrialization, urbanization, the advent of mass democracy and socialist parties, created a class consciousness that carried a specifically political dimension. And yet, in a rather surprising

---

9   Henri de Saint-Simon, *Du système industriel*, Paris: Renouard, 1821, pp. 151–2.

way, the idea of collaboration between the classes became fashionable again in the late twentieth century. In 1982, a hundred and sixty years after Saint-Simon's utopian appeal, new figures once again sought to give it a concrete expression.

A group of 'positive' intellectuals and personalities from civil society came together in Paris to give birth to the Fondation Saint-Simon. Its board was made up of academics (François Furet, Pierre Rosanvallon and Emmanuel Le Roy Ladurie), along with eminent journalists and communicators (Jean Daniel, Serge July, Christine Ockrent and Anne Sinclair), senior civil servants and technocrats (Jean-Claude Casanova, Roger Fauroux, Jean Peyrelevade) and leading figures from the world of business and banking (Alain Minc, Jean-Louis Beffa, Jean-Luc Lagardère). Saint-Simon had called for 'a general and definitive attack on prejudices'; his heirs proclaimed the same mission, with the only difference that a hundred and sixty years later these 'prejudices' had undergone a few changes, given that social hierarchies had been completely modified.

In 1821, Saint-Simon singled out two particular institutions for attack, both already on the decline: the dominant aristocracy, with its parasitic value system, and the clericalism of the Catholic church. He called for an egalitarian and unified world of rational and honest producers. In 1982, Furet and his associates launched an assault on the Marxist left, which had in fact already begun a historical decline though its would-be gravediggers were unaware. The new Saint-Simonians of the late twentieth century proclaimed their intention to launch a vast offensive against totalitarianism, seeing it as the great menace to the democratic values of European civilization. Their immediate objective was actually to neutralize the influence of the Communist Party, which had been in a governing coalition since the previous year, and to quash the vestiges of a revolutionary utopia that was still hegemonic, not only on the Left Bank, but in many places across France.

Saint-Simon had died in 1825, unable to witness the realization of his project. The Fondation Saint-Simon closed its doors in 1999, after the death of its initiator François Furet, and although it is hard to assess its particular contribution to the evolution of the ideological atmosphere in France, its founders could bask in a sense of satisfaction: Marxism, in all its versions, had experienced a marked decline in the last quarter of the century, and along with it radical culture as a whole. This was not of course due to the members of the Fondation, whatever their efforts, but to rather more significant factors that had modified the ideological framework of the intelligentsia in France as in other Western societies. The important point for our present subject, however, is that the weakening of critical conceptions of the world, which have always contained a utopian dimension, has been accompanied by the decline of the towering intellectual, the moral guide whose thought could give political commitment inspiration and encouragement.

We should note that this association of late twentieth-century 'Saint-Simonians' was unlike any customary group of Parisian scholars. The coalition of academics (mainly historians), media figures and big businessmen was more reminiscent of an American think tank (which led to close ties with the far more important elite association, Le Siècle) than with the traditional modes of intervention that intellectuals had practised since the late nineteenth century. The new intellectuals no longer believed in the direct effectiveness of the expression of ideas in the form of petitions, charters, articles and public debates in forums open and accessible to all. To put it another way, they sought to be nothing more than auxiliaries of capitalism, whose image had never really been restored after the Second World War. They resembled the organic intellectuals of communism that some of their number had once been: specially selected minds who gathered in closed meetings to fix the ideological guidelines they would subsequently pronounce in public. This intellectual enterprise had an exclusive character; not everyone could participate, as its continued financing depended on the goodwill of its 'positive' bosses.

No 'great' intellectuals took part in the Fondation Saint-Simon. Jean-Paul Sartre and Roland Barthes had both died two years earlier, but prominent critical thinkers such as Pierre Bourdieu, Jacques Derrida, Michel Foucault, Jean-François Lyotard and Edgar Morin, all at the peak of their prestige in the Western world, had no intention of participating in this new course. Even Raymond Aron, the new idol of the Parisian conservative intelligentsia in the late 1970s, was not invited to join the Fondation even in a symbolic capacity; he too died a year later in a halo of glory. As Pierre Nora, one of the club's founders, wrote: 'The intellectual as oracle has had his day.'[10] He was completely right: the critical man of letters in the image of Émile Zola, André Gide, Albert Camus, Jean-Paul Sartre or Michel Foucault, independent of state, capital and media, no longer occupied anything like the same rank in the Parisian public arena. It was even possible to do without such figures, and replace them collectively.

A number of well-known and talented Parisian historians, heirs of *Annales*, were happy to hobnob with big capital and the media moguls. With the exception of François Furet, however, it is difficult to classify them as initiators of new sensibilities, big ideas or particularly original modes of thought. The founding group failed to include any renowned sociologist or philosopher, or indeed any prestigious writer or scientist. The 'Saint-Simon think tank', like other more important phenomena that preceded its creation, marked the end of a certain presence of those prophetic intellectuals who had long had the upper hand in Paris. Men of letters did indeed still figure in the public sphere, but with a new kind of symbolic and moral capital, and new forms of presence.

With due precaution, it is possible to distinguish various social, political and cultural phenomena that accompanied and sometimes conditioned the avatars of the hegemonic intellectual

---

10   Pierre Nora, 'Que peuvent les intellectuels?', *Le Débat*, 1 May 1980, p. 5.

body. This is a question of working hypotheses that are hard to verify, and should be viewed as archetypes or starting points susceptible to modification and amendment. The relationship between these phenomena will not always be clear, but without them it is hard to begin to rethink the contemporary modes of presence of intellectuals.

Conflicts, myths, identities

The first hypothesis is that the central and rising status of scholars in the modern world, beyond the requirements of the division of labour, was above all a response to the demands of a nation-state in the course of its construction. Such a state had a need for a large number of cultural agents to produce and organize the new national culture. From the writer who enlivened and developed the national language to the historian who 'scientifically' invented the nation's past, a wide spectrum of men of letters contributed to laying the foundations of a collective consciousness centred on the modern state of the nineteenth century. The intellectual was not simply a fellow traveller of the expanding bourgeois class, he was a key participant in the nation's construction.

On the other hand, the collective emergence of critical intellectuals in late nineteenth-century Paris happened basically against the background of the establishment of mass political parties, in the context of a new liberal democratic system. The corollary of enduring class conflicts was the creation of socialist parties, trade unions, cooperative societies, social and cultural associations, newspapers, publishing houses, etc. Behind the national political stage a growing class of workers began to move, impelled to unite, almost despite themselves, by the process of industrialization – a process that continued for nearly a century. This class did not seek either to take over the means of production or to manage them, as its first organizers had imagined that it would, but it established solid political pressure groups within the democratic nation-state.

The working class that formed one of the axes of the historic bloc known as the 'left', supported by a notable section of intellectuals, experienced a process of regression starting in the 1970s. Automation, the transfer of branches of industry to countries with lower wage costs, the substitution of energy sources (closure of most coal mines), all considerably modified the morphology of the world of productive work. The 'working-class century' ended with the disarray of those who had dreamed of a socialist future. Without seeing here a direct connection of cause and effect, we can nonetheless propose a certain correlation between organized class struggle and the critical intellectual. The left-wing intellectuals had long drawn their ideological inspiration, with its utopian aspects, from perspectives bound up with the future of the main class of producers. Their liberation, which would be sufficient to put an end to exploitation, could only be collective and not individual, which is why the myths forged in its name always took the form of narratives bearing a collective vision.

The profound conception of progress, born in the eighteenth century and fuelled by the political vision of the bourgeoisie and its ideological outriders, was expanded in the nineteenth century by new hopes for a more socio-economically egalitarian society. And if ever since the eighteenth century humanism and the philosophy of human rights had seduced men of letters from Voltaire to Victor Hugo, in the late nineteenth century, faced with the brutal exploitation exercised by capital accumulation, socialism won over many hearts and minds within an intelligentsia whose socio-economic status was always somewhat uncertain. A section of this intelligentsia, generally dependent on the dominant classes, was driven by its numerical growth into a grey zone, a kind of no man's land between social classes, where it absorbed both scepticism towards the existing order and moral solidarity with the dominated social groups.

From Émile Zola to Anatole France, and from Jean-Paul Sartre to Michel Foucault, the class tensions that were characteristic of the century formed an object of reflection and theoretical sensitivity, whether consciously or repressed. They were also at the origin of many intellectual frictions. A fringe of scholars coming from different cultural fields took up socialist and anarchist ideas of one kind or another; some were moved by a profound ethical idealism, others were unhappy in their situation of dependence on the state apparatus and the vagaries of the market. The option of an egalitarian worldview and a universal system of values perfected the myth of progress that was already hegemonic in wide circles of the intelligentsia.

This may explain why in the wake of the First World War, that orgy of nationalism and irrationality, a strange passion emerged that viewed the revolutionary agitation in societies lacking an industrial proletariat as the starting point for a more just world, and even a revolutionary model for industrialized societies. A worldview that was both optimistic and, we have to recognize, unfounded, took hold of many critical intellectuals, lasting until the mid-1970s. It is superfluous to add that this strong 'communist' – or rather, 'Blanquist' – passion went against the materialist conception of history of Marx and Engels, according to which only a high level of capital accumulation made possible the formation of a class able to assume the direction of production. To resolve this fundamental contradiction, many Marxist intellectuals were therefore forced into an eventful 'dialectical' acrobatics that lasted at least sixty years.

If André Gorz's celebrated book *Farewell to the Working Class*, published in 1980, did not become the new 'communist manifesto', it was nonetheless a conscious and incisive expression of the closure of the 'working-class century' that had begun in the 1870s and ended in the 1970s.[11] The steady disappearance of an organized proletariat did not reduce inequalities; these even tended to increase in the 1980s, with economic stagnation, while the mass of new workers, mainly in the service sector, no longer

---

11   André Gorz, *Farewell to the Working Class*, London: Pluto, 2001.

possessed organized means of resistance comparable to those of the industrial workers of an earlier generation.

The historic bloc formed around the industrial working class, which had made it possible to achieve a consumer society, now began to come undone. On the one hand, the lower middle classes, increasingly given to consumption, abandoned this bloc as they rose up the social scale; while on the other hand, young literati, to whom this same consumer society had opened the gates of higher education, abandoned the intellectual world of the left for which they no longer saw any need.

Socialist parties were transformed into increasingly hollow electoral machines, and trade unions saw their membership fall, while the working-class culture forged in social struggles went into terminal decline. It gave way to a pseudo-liberal consumer society, with the growing atomization of the masses and their alienation from any kind of engagement and organization. The economic stagnation that affected all markets at the end of the twentieth century only aggravated this situation. With such a high rate of unemployment, and despair at the vagaries of the economy, opposition forces found themselves neutralized, while capital, embarking on globalization, celebrated its pyrrhic victory over the world of labour, not realizing that in the long run, and in terms of its profitability, it was in the process of cutting off the branch on which it was sitting.

Elections were now the only vehicle of social protest, but the ideological messages from parties claiming to represent 'discontent' were increasingly less relevant. In this new situation they had less need for intellectual auxiliaries, given that new ideas had almost evaporated from their programmes. For a growing number of observers it became clear that electoral politics might make certain things possible, but certainly not an escape from the logic of capitalism and the construction of a new society. Talented communications advisers were now entrusted with the essential task of developing the apparatuses of hegemonic political seduction.

The dissolution of the industrial proletariat has also cast light on the growing deterioration of the relationship between representatives and represented, which was the foundation of modern political culture. Since the late nineteenth century, the principle of representation lay at the core of the mentality of the democratic nation-state. This conception of national representation also involved a division of roles: the parliamentary left was supposed to represent in the main the interest of the wage-earning classes, while the right spoke for the upper and a section of the middle classes. This kind of distribution, which should be seen simply as an ideal type, was almost totally undermined in the last quarter of the twentieth century, with the decline of those images of universality that had previously surrounded the apparatus of the democratic nation-state, thanks in particular to the work of intellectuals. It now became increasingly clear that everyone has their particular interests, and that there is no universal class in society. The awareness that political elites are concerned above all with their own representation and that of the apparatuses that guarantee their hegemony, has become very widespread, being perceived well beyond the microcosm of politics.

Starting from newly posed epistemological problems, the relationship between signifier and signified, and radical deconstruction that challenges the claim of literature to express any kind of reality, doubt in the ability of intellectuals to represent universal values, scepticism and even suspicion towards any system of representation have become part and parcel of a general sensibility that invaded the public sphere.

Another historical process that cannot be ignored, given its repercussions on the status of the critical intellectual, has also marked the long century of conflict. It began with globalization and the race for colonies, and ended with the Western powers retreating from their occupation of the rest of the world, and the anchoring of globalization with the help of new instruments of domination. We should remember that the intellectual battles around the second Dreyfus affair, in 1898, took place at the same time as the Fashoda crisis and the competition between France and Great Britain for the division of territorial booty. For some sixty years, the intellectual world remained indifferent to the inequality and great injustices of the process of conquest and colonization; carried away by national pride, left and right even joined together in hymning the glories of empire-building.[12] Competition for colonies was the natural partner of the advance of democratization and the consolidation of the nation-state in the metropolises, never mind its generous contribution to triggering two great wars.

The decolonization that began after the Second World War and continued through to the 1970s combined with the communist revolutions in feeding the myth of ineluctable progress, and particularly stimulated the commitment of intellectuals opposed to the existing order. In the mid-1950s, but especially in the 1960s, the 'socialist' hopes that had been disappointed by the course of the USSR shifted to the 'proletarian nations' of the Third World. However, the complicated liberation process of these suffering and oppressed people ended up damaging the force of criticism, which has always been nourished by universal hopes and ideas.

Anti-colonial struggles came to an end in 1975, in South Vietnam, Cambodia, Laos, Angola, Mozambique and Guinea-Bissau. Yet the political independence gained by the 'revolutionary' path, often under the leadership of former intellectuals, did not lead to the building of 'progressive socialist' societies, but rather gave rise to new waves of violence, corruption, totalitarian oppression and even wholesale massacre. The action of the

---

12   In 1879, the old Victor Hugo advised: 'Pour your overspill into this Africa, and by the same token resolve your social questions, change proletarians into proprietors', *Actes et paroles: depuis l'exil 1876–1885* (available on gutenberg.org). On the eve of the Second World War, the young Marguerite Duras could co-author a book on the French Empire with the republican aim of 'teaching the French that they possess an immense domain overseas' (Philippe Roques and Marguerite Donnadieu, *L'Empire français*, Paris: Gallimard, 1940).

Khmer Rouge, or of certain Marxist liberation fronts in Africa, dealt heavy blows to the great dreams of revolution and shook the very notion of solidarity with the oppressed. All collective struggle waged under a secular socialist banner, no matter what its colour, lost its original humanist value. This was not just a defeat for abstract utopianism, but also a snub for the critical intellectuals that had maintained and cherished it.

The performances of the 'new philosophers' on radio and TV, and the creation of the Fondation Saint-Simon, were two early intellectual expressions of a break with the long century during which conflict had been intimately associated with the myth of a utopian future. It was not the books of Alexander Solzhenitsyn that provoked the 'anti-totalitarian' turn of the new Parisian intellectuals; similar accounts had been published much earlier without shaking either the basic beliefs or sensibilities of the fellow travellers of Stalinism – or later, the sycophants of Maoism.[13] Books, as we well know, do not change the world, but when something in the world does change, other books are sought.

The distressing disappearance of the proletariat, the devastating ravages of Maoism in China, the disappointing and sometimes even horrific consequences of decolonization, followed soon after by the final collapse of the communist regimes in Eastern Europe and Russia, generated a climate of ideas that prepared the ground for the advent of intellectuals with ideologies that blocked any formulation of a project for the future. Literati who feared and rejected any evocation of a new horizon beyond the present now had the upper hand.

Previously, universal and subversive intellectuals were characterized by their forceful criticism of social injustices, along with a tendency to idealize societies hostile to their own. The course of

---

13   See for example Victor Serge, *From Lenin to Stalin*, New York: Pathfinder Press, 1937; Victor Kravchenko, *I Chose Freedom*, New York: Charles Scribner's Sons, 1947; Margarete Buber-Neumann, *Under Two Dictators: Prisoner of Stalin and Hitler*, London: Gollancz, 1949.

events has now been reversed: the new intellectuals, media-friendly and consensual, acknowledge a conservatism that celebrates the existing social hierarchy and political culture while damning all those who challenge or threaten it, whether at home or abroad.[14]

As I shall explore in the next chapter, 'totalitarians', whether communists and leftists, or at a later date veiled or bearded Muslims, are in the eyes of the conservative intellectuals who now set the tone a real threat to Western culture, and consequently the culture of our good old France. From Alain Finkielkraut to Michel Houellebecq, Éric Zemmour to Renaud Camus, certain literati much fêted in the media have set out to create the myth of a stable and homogeneous past, which in fact never existed.[15] They have perfectly translated the sense of insecurity and alienation caused by the economic crisis and cultural globalization into a myth made from fear, withdrawal and fatalism. The rejection of all utopias has become a major element of intellectual sensibility.

The myth in question bears above all on the question of collective identity, and is pervaded by the obsession with a threatening future. Collective identity has always rested on a common memory that is itself the product of a historical construction. The collective memory that is built up day after day in France is fed by a paranoid imaginary, a kind of inverted mirror of the 'radiant future' that progressive milieus of a past generation

---

14   A very interesting book on these changes in the Parisian intellectual arena is Daniel Lindenberg, *Le Rappel à l'ordre. Enquête sur les nouveaux réactionnaires*, Paris: Seuil, 2002.

15   In the United States, this conservative turn took place rather earlier than in Paris. Former left intellectuals, such as Irving Kristol who undertook to hymn the 'marvels' of capitalism (just before the start of the economic crisis), Norman Podhoretz who encouraged George W. Bush to attack Iraq with its supposed 'weapons of mass destruction', and David Horowitz, author of a truly McCarthyite publication (*The Professors: The 101 Most Dangerous Academics in America*, Washington, DC: Regnery Publishing, 2006), have become popular media stars, and advisers to various leaders of the traditional right.

clung to. In contrast to imagining the future, however, the imaginary past serves above all the function of creating and reinforcing an identity that excludes the 'Other' and has no intention of understanding or mingling with him or her. The myths that drew from an Enlightenment source generally tended to integrate the 'Other', whereas conservative myths tend openly to reject difference. A politics of identity that prizes communitarian representations, whether 'ethnic', religious, moral or all three, that does not tolerate immigrants and shows hostility towards any change that bears on the ancestral 'high' culture, is the ever-more-dominant historical and political consciousness proclaimed in the public sphere.

It is interesting to note that the elitist ideologies of the new intellectuals are enthusiastically spread by the major media of 'mass culture'.

Mass media and public sphere

The distinction frequently made between the authentic intellectuals of the past and the counterfeit 'media intellectuals' is not quite exact. This widespread view needs a certain rectification.[16] To mark their presence with the public, intellectuals have always been keen to maintain close relations with the media. Before the emergence of new means of communication, intellectuals published articles in the press – no doubt to influence public opinion, but also to avoid being forgotten. It was through newspapers that intellectuals publicized their protest at the time of the second Dreyfus affair. Raymond Aron had a regular column in *Le Figaro*. Albert Camus, Jean-Paul Sartre and Simone de Beauvoir were keen on being photographed; pictures of the mandarin couple with Che Guevara or Fidel Castro confirmed

---

16   See Pascal Boniface, *Les Intellectuels faussaires. Le triomphe médiatique des experts en mensonge*, Paris: Gawsewitch, 2011. This book has a particularly fascinating chapter on Bernard-Henri Lévy.

their status as politically committed intellectuals and their popularity with radical students. When the couple sold a banned
newspaper in the street, journalists were naturally present. When
Sartre stood on a barrel to address the strikers at Billancourt,
photographers were there to immortalize his natural solidarity
with the working class. Later on, Michel Foucault was also in the
frame. In one of the last photos of Sartre, where the great existentialist intellectual is standing on the steps of the Élysée together
with Raymond Aron to demand assistance for Vietnamese refugees, the future was already behind him: in the background we
see the 'new philosopher' André Glucksmann, edging his way in
to make sure of being in the picture.

I discussed the change in the status of written communication
in the course of the twentieth century at the end of the first chapter of this book: born from the great print revolution of the
fifteenth century, it reached its apogee between the late nineteenth century and the middle of the twentieth, from which time
it has increasingly had to share its hegemonic position with
audiovisual communication. And just as changes in the means of
production modify social relations, we may say that with the
shift in means of communication, the balance of forces between
producers and consumers of communication has also changed.

If television in its early days assisted the spread of student
revolts, by broadcasting images of protests against the Vietnam
War or the demonstrations of May 1968, producers rapidly
learned their lessons, and images were framed and controlled by
more experienced producers. The supply of television grew from
one or two channels under government control to 'packages' of
several dozen channels, most of these belonging to private capital, which produced an increasing output of news, documentary
and action films, pop videos and series. But this proliferation of
output and channels, along with the intense competition between
them, did not lead to more diversity and pluralism of thought.
On the contrary, everything was done to reduce this and arrive at
a lowest common denominator, so as to attract the maximum

number of viewer-consumers. 'Ratings' became the supreme point of reference and imposed the rules of the game. Besides, the plethora of advertising that breaks up news programmes, films and even broadcast debates destabilizes the capacity for rational analysis and judgement. Concrete images, presented in a cascade of illogical disorder, not only prevailed over abstract conceptualizations; they also undermined the fundamental cognitive skills built up through free education for all in the late nineteenth century.

If we believe the American media critic Neil Postman, of George Orwell's *1984* and Aldous Huxley's *Brave New World*, the two great dystopian novels of the twentieth century, it is the latter that better anticipated the future.[17] Huxley did not fear a 'Big Brother' banning books or a thought police that would punish the least ideological deviance. He envisaged instead oppression by way of pleasure, love and desire; in other words, through a permanent and invasive entertainment that would distract consumers' attention from their fundamental interests. Huxley prophesied a capitalist world in which truth would not be repressed by an oppressive totalitarianism, as in less developed societies, but rather fragmented and drowned in an ocean of pseudo-events and trivial human interest. Viewers would be deluged with news, mostly devoid of significance; they would develop a consumerist passivity and be confirmed in a narcissistic atomization. And indeed audiovisual technologies have now taken hold of thought; the small screen, present in every household, has shaped the view of the world.

Television has poured out an endless number of distracting programmes, but it has not done away with a particular form of intellectual diversion. Like the written press, it needs reinforcements of learning from time to time, and for these it draws on those deemed to know more than others, who can dispense to a

---

17   Neil Postman, *Amusing Ourselves to Death: Public Discourse in the Age of Show Business*, New York: Penguin, 2005.

wide public a good ration of 'wisdom'. At the same time, else-where in the public sphere, in universities and research institutes, a professionalism has developed that privileges detail in every human and social respect. The last quarter of the twentieth century counted more scholars than ever in the history of human-ity, but, as Ortega y Gasset remarked, these were above all schol-ars who had learned a great deal about a very small parcel of human knowledge, and were ever less concerned with the general course of human societies. These experts in narrow fields are indeed invited to spell out specific points, but this does not confer on them any particular symbolic capital, and their names are hardly remembered.

It is hard to spread political philosophy or detailed and composite linguistic information through the visual media. (It is certainly possible, but this would mean a steep fall in the ratings.) Successful intellectuals, therefore, if they are invited to debate on the television set, must have a sense of repartee, be able to authoritatively formulate definitive generalizations and sometimes be provocative, though not going against accepted ideas, and of course possess an audiovisual charisma. It is better for them to live in Paris or its surroundings, to make sure of being in the studio at the appointed time. They must also be effective at self-promotion, understand the authorized limits precisely and anticipate what is expected of them, as to both the content and form of their performance. As a general rule, they must be personally acquainted with the interviewers or present-ers and have friendly relations with the 'competing' intellectuals whom televised debates present as their 'opponents'. In fact, the desire to give an image of the political and ideological pluralism that lies at the heart of the public sphere in liberal democracy implies being careful not to diverge from the authorized consen-sus. There are indeed places where the foundations of ideologi-cal consensus can be challenged, but this is only on marginal channels or programmes broadcast at times when the audience is small.

The second half of the 1970s saw the rise of new and particular forms of intellectuals with whom a wider public was to familiarize itself. In the past, the promotion of a book in the media was a result of either its success in the community of scholars and writers, or the scandal it had produced in the intellectual microcosm. Today it happens quite differently: journalists in the audiovisual media believe themselves justified in choosing their intellectuals as they think fit (whereas with political figures, the choice is made by the channel heads). This is less a function of the literary or theoretical value of their works than of their potential success with a wide audience and their compatibility with the dominant ideologies. Those intellectuals with an acute sense of communication make sure that they publish a string of short and light works, so as to be invited onto the Sunday show. This has led to the appearance of an increasing number of 'professionals' who think and react quickly, having learned to sell their intellectual image to gain that much more screen time. Pierre Bourdieu was quite accurate in describing these as 'fast-thinkers who offer cultural "fast food" '.[18] None of these media intellectuals has so far managed to acquire a lasting position of charismatic authority, in contrast to some television presenters.

In 1989, the weekly *Événement du jeudi* organized a poll to measure the popularity of living intellectuals. Top of the poll, with an equal number of votes, were the globally celebrated anthropologist Claude Lévi-Strauss, then aged eighty-one years, and Bernard Pivot, aged fifty-four, presenter of the television programme *Apostrophes*.[19] Pivot's impact had been so great that this result was in no way surprising. His programme, broadcast each Friday evening, attracted an audience well beyond the habitual viewers of literary programmes. The author of a new book who was not invited onto this show, whether writer, philosopher or academic, was viewed as non-existent. The power of

---

18   Pierre Bourdieu, *On Television*, New York: The New Press, 1999, p. 29.
19   *L'Événement du jeudi*, 28 February 1989.

this small-screen professional over the intellectual scene was without any precedent. He oversaw the promotion of new cultural fashions, and was among those who overturned the ideological agenda of Parisian intellectuals with a masterful hand. All other 'cultural' broadcasters in Paris would soon imitate this system, if with lesser talent.

It was quite symbolic that Bernard Pivot was elected in 2004 to the Académie Goncourt, the first 'non-writer' to be enthroned in this prestigious conclave. This was in a certain sense a great return of the figure of the journalist from the late nineteenth century. The media-world descendants of these earlier journalists had succeeded, a century later, in taking their revenge on the heirs of the moralist intellectuals, the brothers-in-arms of Émile Zola. We might cautiously suggest that the media intellectual had become the great cultural hero in the society of the uninterrupted spectacle.[20]

However, the audiovisual culture of the second half of the 'century of conflict' was not confined to the TV set. The cinema also became a great supplier of amusements and distractions, and the producers of moving images even found genuine intellectual critics in their ranks, whose works brought debate on ideas into the public sphere. Already in the age of silent film, René Clair and Charlie Chaplin proved the most incisive critics of Taylorism, at a time when the majority of literati had absolutely no idea of the inhuman situation that prevailed in the world of manual work. Later on, Stanley Kubrick succeeded in exposing the stupidity and dangers of the Cold War while almost all American scholars and journalists were persuaded of the rightness of the path taken by their leaders against the communist menace. The

---

20   On the power of Parisian journalists from the 1980s on, and their presence in the electronic media, see Serge Halimi, *Les Nouveaux Chiens de garde*, Paris: Liber-Raison d'Agir, 1997. For the attack by a battalion of German journalists, publicists and critics on the great writer Günter Grass, who had dared to criticize German reunification, see Olivier Mannoni, *Un écrivain à abattre. L'Allemagne contre Günter Grass*, Paris: Ramsay, 1996.

American director Joseph Losey, banned from Hollywood, brought the 'forgotten' Vichy regime back into the memory of the amnesiac French. In Italy, Gillo Pontecorvo depicted the brutal anti-colonial struggle with true artistry when this was still on the margins of European consciousness, while Bernardo Bertolucci reminded his country's historians that fascism had been authentically Italian. As for the films of Jean-Luc Godard, their quality is on a par with the best of writers.

It is important to recognize that, from the 1930s to the 1970s, the existence of critical films, even if many only conveyed stereotyped platitudes, played a distinct role in the development of a political sensibility of protest and disturbance. However, in parallel with the decline of the 'clerk', we have also witnessed the retreat of the innovative cineaste. The finance capital of the cinema industry no longer finds it interesting to produce works that arouse controversy, now that the community of rebel viewers that consumed these is in the process of disappearing. Nonconformist works, whether financed privately or publicly, became scarcer in the 1980s and after, giving way to lurid television series full of sex and blood.

Another shift was on the way. The 'internet revolution' would overturn the rules of the intellectual game. It may initially have seemed that this new tool of communication was re-establishing written expression and limiting the growing hold of the moving image, but the improvement of digitalization actually made possible a renewal of audiovisual diffusion on the internet, its largest providers being television channels and YouTube. It is true that forums, blogs and social networks continue to fashion a space for writing of a new kind, but as of now it is hard to know what the presence of intellectuals in this media will actually be. Something old is clearly being undone, supplanted by something radically new. Is this a democratization or an individualization, or is it rather the accelerated and momentary temporality of a fragile form of knowledge? Is Eben Moglen, professor at Columbia University, right to warn us against the danger that the internet poses to individual freedom, and the risk of seeing the domination of state apparatuses and market forces over our life and culture only strengthened?[21] Who can evaluate these changes and predict their directions?

At the time of the protest movements of 2010 in the Arab world, for example, young intellectuals used social networks to spread messages and encourage street demonstrations. Many were convinced, in this revolt against oppressive elites, that the new communication tools were the basis for a new mobilization, autonomous political movements and a virtual public sphere. The rapid restoration of the old order, however, particularly in Egypt, showed that these predictions were too optimistic; it was impossible to go beyond the spontaneous and ephemeral aspect inherent to such networks and establish a stable new political culture.

In the West, the internet initially served as a refuge for dissident intellectuals of both right and left who were excluded from televised forums. With its bold and critical journalistic sites, less dependent on big capital than most of the printed press, but also its racist, impulsive and Judeophobic blogs, the net increasingly captured young readers, who rightly saw it as the most accessible and freest source of knowledge since the invention of printing. Of course, commercial advertising also invaded the net, but it was relatively easy, compared with television, to circumvent and avoid it. New generations have become faithful consumers of various sites where they are quick to react, though most often in a confused and superficial way. The choice of sites constantly varies and displays great fluidity, with the result that it is hard to know where preferences lie.

In France, the internet opened new perspectives. If educational establishments, books, the press and television have always firmly maintained the traditional relation of forces between the centre (Paris) and the periphery (the 'provinces'), for the first

---

21   See for example his *dotCommunist Manifesto* (available on gibello.com).

time in French history the internet posed a real challenge to cultural Jacobinism. It is still impossible to get a firm idea of its potential, but even its partial expression would substantially change the options open in future to young creators in the French regions.

Perhaps Foucault's prediction concerning intellectuals who are specific and – despite everything – dissident is in the process of coming to pass. The agents of critical culture in future generations may be more like such uncommon figures as Julian Assange, founder of Wikileaks, or the former CIA and NSA employee Edward Snowden, who has influenced our knowledge of politics and diplomacy more than any other critical intellectual. Will the irony of fate have it that these 'silent' figures, whose power lies not in the words they produce but rather in the exploitation of a strategic position in the systems of diffusion of knowledge, become the guides of a new rebel generation in the cultural fields of the future? The problem is that so far the function of intellectuals has almost always consisted in delivering explicit messages, not only knowledge but also value judgements. Intellectuals have also been unable to exist without institutions, in the absence of political organizations and social movements, or, at least, of faithful customers willing to obtain their works by way of monetary exchange. And so it is the very definition of the word 'intellectual' that is challenged by new figures like the whistleblowers who have emerged from the internet.

I do not really know how to end this book. I feel full of confusion and hesitation, not only because I am unable to clearly decipher the fluid present, which stubbornly resists definition, but also because of my pessimism about the moral shifts that are currently inscribed in the culture of our age. I feel equally torn between the 'reflective' historian that I want to be, and the critical intellectual that I am. In other words, I wander and stray between, on the one hand, analyses intended to confer a reasonable level of neutrality, free of value judgments, and, on the other hand, a strong incitement to participate, despite everything, in seeking rational and humanist alternatives to contradictions that currently have no solution, whether in terms of the capitalist economy or the question of planetary ecology.

I am clearly not advising, on the basis of the reflections in this book, that we should search for or invent a new status of the intellectual, with the vocation of representing the universal and seeking to guide moral reality towards a new enlightened utopia. I do not share the idealist illusions that accompanied many intellectuals for a whole era, when they saw themselves as pure spirituality without a body. Besides, I have always believed that moral ideas do not stroll around in the streets by themselves, but only change the world because they respond to the needs of groups able to adopt them. The decisive questions bear on the social dimension of collective interests that are able to form the basis of a broad solidarity, and on the nature and quality of the values that emerge.

Will the future bring a kind of conflict yet unknown, which might fuel a new ethic, accompanied by a renewal of reflection by critical intellectuals? Will this be one that is not based on pseudo-communitarian fears and enmities towards those with different 'origins', culture or religion? Will it produce conservative, racist and xenophobic intellectuals, in the lineage of those who increasingly occupy our public sphere as economic stagnation deepens?[22]

Starting from the postulate that any modern society in motion is conflictual by definition, will the coming confrontations set the deprived against the holders of power, the dominated against the dominant, the humiliated against the humiliators? Another cardinal problem: what form will social struggles for a more egalitarian distribution of resources take? Will this distribution

---

22   The positions adopted by one wing of contemporary media intellectuals are reminiscent of their predecessors in the 1930s, but in contrast to the confusion and state of crisis of that time, they are not opposed today by an intellectual bloc solid enough to defend the historical values of the left, with all their qualities and defects.

enable us to avoid the spiral of deadly violence that has almost always accompanied the capture of natural resources? What political philosophy will interpret and accompany these struggles?

Will future intellectuals be fellow travellers of new social movements desiring to change existing reality? Will they be able to fashion, on an independent website or in autonomous popular forums, a charismatic authority that can elaborate enlightened views of the world? Where will tomorrow's intellectuals come from: the university or its margins, or even from its ruins?

It may be that we stand today at the end of a familiar civilization, and are slipping into an age whose contours are still mysterious. Should we suppose that the dynamic born with the Enlightenment is now in a permanent state of stagnation, or even approaching an end? Perhaps the intellectuals of tomorrow will definitively cease aspiring to change the world with the help of representations of the future designed to improve social existence. Will they be the traditional guides – priests, imams, rabbis (or their modern versions, desirous of restoring and refounding a traditional logic) – whose moral foundations have been perceived for centuries as offering security and consolation? Yet it is hard to imagine how the ancient religions, or those established outside the Western world in symbiosis with nationalism, can manage to bring solutions to the rifts and deep contradictions of the economic and social structures of the present time. It is undeniable, all the same, that the strong aspiration to pre-national myths is currently at a high point.

These questions are impossible for anyone to answer at this time. With the greatest caution, we can only suggest that, just as social classes and the relationships between them are today undergoing major changes, so the intellectuals who accompany future confrontations will not resemble the great Parisian luminaries who were our compass in a long previous century that has now come to an end.

PART TWO:

Islamophobia and the Intellectuals' 'Rhinoceritis'

From Houellebecq to *Charlie Hebdo*: Submission or Humour?

BERENGER: You wouldn't like to be a rhinoceros yourself, now would you?

JEAN: Why not? I'm not a victim of prejudice like you.

BERENGER: Can you speak more clearly? I didn't catch what you said. You swallowed the words.

JEAN: Then keep your ears open.

BERENGER: What?

JEAN: Keep your ears open. I said what's wrong with being a rhinoceros? I'm all for change.

Eugène Ionesco, *Rhinoceros*, 1959

The global ridicule in which the works of Foucault, Lacan, Derrida and Deleuze had suddenly foundered, after decades of inane reverence, far from leaving the field clear for new ideas, simply heaped contempt on all those intellectuals active in the 'human sciences'.

Michel Houellebecq, *Atomised*, 1998

At the start of 2015, I was staying in Nice, working on this book on the intellectuals. On the evening of 6 January, I settled down as usual to watch the news programme on France 2. To my great surprise, Michel Houellebecq was invited to speak for eleven minutes about *Submission*, his new book which would be available in the shops the next day. It was immediately clear that the unusual honour and publicity that this writer enjoyed did not come from his having received the Nobel Prize or any other major literary award. Nor was this invitation related to the fact that, in the novel in question, the France 2 presenter, David Pujadas, is immortalized under an avalanche of compliments – though we may suppose that this flattery was no obstacle to the novelist's invitation.[1]

What led the news programme to host this unusual intervention, making Houellebecq's book a media and 'intellectual' event even before its publication, was the provocative political cheek that forms the key axis of its plot. *Submission* traces the process by which France is transformed in a few years into a fully Islamic country. A substantial part of the television news was thus devoted to something that *might* happen, if we are to believe a section of the French elite, rather than what actually has happened or is happening now. But the stupefaction that came over me on watching this televised interview was by no means at an end.

The following morning, 7 January, *Charlie Hebdo* made its regular weekly appearance. Houellebecq, glorified by this satirical magazine, is depicted on the cover as a calm magus joyfully proclaiming, 'In 2015 I'll lose my teeth, in 2022 I'll keep Ramadan.' Inside is a supposedly funny cartoon of the writer, with the text, 'Scandal. Allah made Houellebecq in his image.' Also in this number is a review of *Submission* by Bernard Maris, a close friend of Houellebecq, in which he calls the book 'an extraordinary and credible futuristic projection . . . Another

---

1   David Pujadas had previously published, together with Hassan Chalghoumi, a book titled *Agissons avant qu'il ne soit trop tard. Islam et République*, Paris: Le Cherche Midi, 2013. On the positions taken by this major presenter towards Islam, see Thomas Deltombe, *L'Islam imaginaire. La construction médiatique de l'islamophobie en France (1975–2005)*, Paris: La Découverte, 2005, pp. 187–96.

magnificent novel. Another masterful work.' Sadly, this was the last article that Maris was to write.

The same morning, at 11:30, two French Islamists broke into the *Charlie Hebdo* offices and murdered eight members of the editorial team, along with a visitor, two policemen, and one of the maintenance staff. Two days later, another assassin continued their bloody work, executing four hostages in the Hyper Casher supermarket. These murderers were not just Islamist extremists, but also crazy Judeophobes. Their determination reminded me of Anders Breivik, who killed eight people at random in Oslo before going on to massacre sixty-nine young socialists who, according to him, were guilty of being too disposed toward Islam.[2] This butchery in the heart of Paris continued a long series of attacks committed in Europe that have intensified the conflict in the West between Muslims and non-Muslims.

Though, as an Israeli, I am far more accustomed than the majority of French people to attacks of this kind (I experienced one at close hand), this was a violent shock. Like millions of others, I felt an urgent need to do something; in other words, to find a way of reacting to this act of madness, with a view to preventing a repetition. As a historian, I could not prevent myself from thinking that there had not been a similar butchery in the streets of Paris since 17 October 1961 and 8 February 1962.[3] A few days later, I could also note that since August 1914 France had never known a *union sacrée* so broad and complete as in this cold month of January 2015.

---

2   The murderer Mohammed Merah showed a similarly remarkable determination in Toulouse. It was not enough for him to kill three French soldiers of Maghreb origin; he went on to murder three Jewish children and a teacher. The same phenomenon characterized the suicide attacks carried out in Paris on 13 November 2015.

3   On 17 October 1961, the Paris police attacked a demonstration by supporters of the Algerian FLN, killing at least several dozen people and throwing their bodies into the Seine. On 8 February 1962, eight people, all but one of them Communist Party members, were crushed to death at the Charonne Métro station when the police repressed a demonstration against the Algerian war. *Translator's note.*

There would seem to have been no connection between Houellebecq's appearance on television and the act of terrorism committed the next day. Despite this contingency, however, their simultaneity obsesses me. It would be no exaggeration to believe that, at this time, the relationship of France to its Muslim residents had reached a kind of boiling point; its future development and the risks associated with this are hard to evaluate at this stage. All the same, before pursuing my reflections and focusing on the relationship of the media 'clerks' to this chain of events, I would like to trace two precipitous trajectories: on the one hand, that taken by the committed intellectual Michel Houellebecq, and, on the other, that taken by the no-less-committed satirical weekly *Charlie Hebdo*: both marched side by side towards the exceptional events of January 2015. Their itineraries are eloquent testimony of the ideological evolution of a significant fringe of the Parisian intelligentsia, whom I have had great difficulty in understanding over the last few years, and have treated only superficially in the last chapter of this book.

The committed writer

Is Houellebecq a committed media intellectual? There would seem to be no writer to whom such a definition is less applicable. In his eyes, there is nothing more abominable than the notion of commitment and the generation of writers who bore this term. In 'Sortir du XXe siècle', for example, a short theoretical text dating from 2000, he peremptorily asserts:

> When we recall the crass scientific ignorance of the likes of Sartre and Beauvoir, supposedly belonging to the field of philosophy, when we consider the almost unbelievable fact that Malraux could be considered – even very briefly – as a *great writer*, we can measure the degree of stupidity to which the notion of *political commitment* has led us, and it is amazing that an *intellectual* can still be taken seriously today; for example,

that such figures as Bourdieu or Baudrillard have continued to find outlets prepared to publish their stupidities.[4]

Houellebecq does not visibly support any cause, or identify himself with anything. He opposes and detests almost everything. This is his pseudo-nihilist pose in the face of a degenerate world. And yet he does not remain silent, since like every French intellectual he is well aware that silence is also an adopted position. The authentic and singular suffering of this curious and original author is publicly displayed and goes well with the spirit of the time: his particular anxieties, when they are not too perverse, connect at least in part with those of everyone. And if (like other neo-conservatives) he is horrified by the leftists of the 1968 generation, if (like others contemptuous of the hypocrisy and ideology of progress) he is repelled by humanists, and if (like other misogynists) he is afraid of feminists, his greatest fear (in common with many French people) is of the latest 'foreigners' of the late twentieth and early twenty-first century – in other words, Muslims. These appear as the real enemy threatening the novelist's traditional and fragile identity, 'indige-nous French' yet unfortunate enough to be born of a 'pied noir' mother in an overseas department. This anxiety towards Islam has aroused in him a literary commitment of a unique kind.

If we are to believe the evidence of Houellebecq's mother, it was in 1991, just after the first Gulf War, when he was not yet a writer, that he began to express his obsessive repulsion towards Arabs and Muslims.[5] Initially, this hatred hardly

---

4   Michel Houellebecq, *Lanzarote et autres textes*, Paris: J'ai Lu, 2002, p. 74. His contempt for committed intellectuals, however, did not prevent Houellebecq, for publicity purposes, from publishing a narcissistic volume of epistolary exchanges with Bernard-Henri Lévy, the contemporary caricature of the committed intellectual and the 'heir of Malraux' (Bernard-Henri Lévy and Michel Houellebecq, *Public Enemies: Dueling Writers Take on Each Other and the World*, New York: Random House, 2011).

5   Lucie Ceccaldi related in an interview with *L'Express* of 29 April 2008 her last meeting with her son: 'We talked about the Gulf War. This set him off on a crazy diatribe about the Arabs, how we should burn them all . . . And then he continued: "It's the fault of their stupid religion."'

appeared in his books, apart from a pointed reference to the attacks committed by Arab terrorists on the Champs-Élysées in his first novel of 1994.[6] Ten years later, ten years in which a steadily rising Islamophobia had acquired increasing media legitimation, he felt more comfortable in publicly expressing his hostility.

In his novel *Platform*, published in 2001, one of the characters (an Egyptian) says, 'Islam could only have been born in a filthy desert, among filthy Bedouins who had nothing better to do – pardon me – than bugger their camels.'[7] While the hero goes on to declare, 'Every time I heard that a Palestinian terrorist, or a Palestinian child or a pregnant woman, had been gunned down in the Gaza strip, I felt a quiver of enthusiasm at the thought of one less Muslim in the world.'[8]

These are of course words spoken by fictional characters in a novel, and do not necessarily commit their author to them (a distribution of roles that Houellebecq always hides behind). However, when Michel the writer is asked why he puts such harsh words into the mouth of Michel his hero, he replies, 'But in the situation in which he finds himself, it is normal for Michel to want as many Muslims as possible to be killed . . . Yes . . . Yes, revenge does exist. Islam is a dangerous religion, it has been so ever since its origin.'[9]

When, in the same interview, Houellebecq is asked, 'Isn't it not just contempt for Islam that you express, but actually hatred?' the writer is quite frank in his response: 'Yes, indeed, you could say hatred.' And he continues in the same tone: 'After all, the most stupid religion is Islam. When you read the Koran, it's shattering!'[10] The previous day, in *Le Figaro*, Houellebecq had already displayed his profound 'acquaintance' with the holy book

---

6   Michel Houellebecq, *Whatever*, London: Serpent's Tail, 2011, p. 20.

7   Michel Houellebecq, *Platform*, New York: Knopf, 2003, p. 251

8   Ibid., p. 349.

9   *Lire*, 1 September 2001.

10   Ibid.

of Islam: 'It's disgusting to read the Koran. Right from the birth of Islam, it signalled its desire to subjugate the whole world. Its nature is to subject . . . It's a warlike, intolerant religion, which makes people unhappy.'[11]

These expressions and others led to Houellebecq being prosecuted, but he was acquitted with the particular help of self-proclaimed defenders of freedom of expression, Philippe Sollers at the head of them. It is well known that in Paris there is still a reluctance to punish famous intellectuals. Although Houellebecq's fear and hatred had not disappeared, he had learned a lesson and now paid greater attention to what he said in public. In his 2005 novel *The Possibility of an Island*, he only touches on the subject: 'Relying on massive and unending immigration, the Muslim religion became stronger in the West . . . targeting as a priority the people of the Maghreb and of black Africa, it had no less success with some "indigenous" Europeans, a success that owed itself uniquely to machismo.'[12]

These assertions are clearly not those of a prophet or clairvoyant. A few months before the publication of this book, the Islamophobic propaganda that began in 1989, with the case of the three girls from Creil,[13] reached a paroxysm, and to the great joy of all true 'secularists', the law banning the wearing of religious emblems in state schools was passed in 2004. From this historic date on, Muslim girls wearing a headscarf were no longer allowed in state schools. Despite the number of these actually being now

---

11   *Le Figaro*, 31 August 2001. Houellebecq added in another interview, in his capacity as a specialist on Islam: 'It's quite extraordinary. People have started saying in some papers what I had been thinking for a long while, that Islamic fundamentalism isn't particularly a distortion of the Koran, it's there already' (*L'Opinion indépendante*, 7 November 2001, quoted in Vincent Geisser, *La Nouvelle Islamophobie*, Paris: La Découverte, 2003, p. 44).

12   Michel Houellebecq, *The Possibility of an Island*, London: Weidenfeld & Nicolson, 2014, p. 264.

13   In September 1989, three girls in the town of Creil were expelled from school for wearing Islamic veils. *Translator's note.*

on the decline,[14] the French Republic, like many parents, is more concerned with what covers its students' heads than what goes into them in the context of secular education. A few centimetres of cloth, in other words, seem more important than their first encounter with Voltaire and Rousseau, an enriching acquaintance with the theory of evolution, the Dreyfus affair or other secular subjects, which are clearly deemed less important in the eyes of the legislature than wearing a scarf. To this end, the republic was prepared to refuse entry to these girls, who were thereby forced into private religious schools, and the fact that more girls started to put on veils at the school gate, as a sign of protest, did not particularly bother them.[15]

In an inverted mirror, the relationship of the secular French Republic to the Islamic veil has begun to be reminiscent of that of the Islamic Republic of Iran. The weakness and lack of confidence in secular national identity revealed by this obstinacy over the veil made a particular contribution to the adoption of this aggressive and excessive law. Houellebecq perfectly sensed this dialectic of reciprocal fear and radicalization.

In 2011, visiting Israel, a country he admires particularly for the way in which it treats its Palestinian Muslims, Houellebecq expressed a warm support for his hosts, and could not prevent himself from adding about France: 'There is however an excessive demand made by Muslims in the last few years, it's impossible to

---

14   See on this subject the excellent book by Alain Gresh, *L'Islam, la République et le monde*, Paris: Fayard, 2004, p. 263. I was opposed to this law right from the start, for two main reasons. First, while I could understand the ban on state employees wearing religious emblems (the principle of separation of church from state), I was quite unable to understand how this law could be applicable to the consumers of state culture. Secondly, I knew that my two grandmothers from the Lodz ghetto had been gassed in 1941 while wearing Jewish religious head covering. Both were traditional believers, like the majority of Jewish women of their age from the common people.

15   See Pierre Tevanian, *Le Voile médiatique. Un faux débat*, Paris: Liber-Raison d'agir, 2005; Ismahane Chouder, Malika Latrèche and Pierre Tevanian, *Les Filles voilées parlent*, Paris: La Fabrique, 2008. Joan Wallach Scott, *The Politics of the Veil*, Princeton: Princeton University Press, 2007, is only now due to appear in French.

deny this . . . The mindset of collaboration with a dangerous power, in this case Islamic fundamentalism, the tendency to collaboration, is dominant in France today, you find it in many milieus.'[16] And he attacked the French Green Party for behaving towards Islam like 'people collaborationist by nature'.[17] At the time, the writer was probably in the process of writing his new novel, *Submission*.

We do not know whether it was his lawyers, his collaborators or his friends who advised him on this occasion not to present Islam as 'the most stupid religion'. Unlike Jacques Prévert, Houellebecq is 'not stupid', and even proves himself a very clever marketer of his books, as shown by the effective tactic he adopted.[18] Accordingly, *Submission* is free of the vulgarity characteristic of Houellebecq's previous publications. There is no swearing, no blasphemy, and he even gives the impression at some points that the Koran is a 'convincing' book. But we should not be deceived! The committed writer has well judged the spirit of the time and the rising strength of Marine Le Pen's electorate, directly correlated with the unemployment curve. *Submission* is one of the most manifestly Islamophobic books published in France so far this century. Its capacity to shock is reminiscent of certain other xenophobic dystopias: Émile Driant's *L'Invasion noire* and *L'Invasion jaune*, published a little more than a century ago under the pseudonym of Danrit.[19]

---

16   'Houellebecq accuse les écologistes de "collaboration" avec l'Islamisme', *Libération*, 4 April 2011.

17   Ibid. See also *Le Point*, 31 March 2011.

18   I am alluding to a contemptuous article by Houellebecq in 1992, 'Jacques Prévert est un con' (reprinted in Michel Houellebecq, *Interventions*, Paris: Flammarion, 1998, p. 12). This is an opportunity for me to admit that when I began to love French culture at an early age, this was among other things through the poems of Jacques Prévert, translated into Hebrew. Today, thanks to Houellebecq and his friends, I understand that the writers I liked above all were anti-authoritarian rebels and those who refused to submit to the hegemonic politics.

19   The first of these, published in 1895, narrates an attempted conquest of France and Europe by Africans, with the support of the Ottoman Empire. The second, which followed ten years later, describes the victory of a Sino-Japanese army over the West, and the invasion of Europe that follows. Both books were published by Flammarion.

This explains Houellebecq's invitation to appear on the eight o'clock news, which enabled this mediocre book, the second part of which is frankly boring, to become a bestseller not only in France but also in Italy, Germany and of course Israel.

The narrative focuses entirely on typical Parisian intellectuals. The narrator and principal character is a professor of literature at the Sorbonne. He falls for Myriam, a 'Jewess', who is not the mother of Jesus, nor anything like the rich Jewish Myriam in Drieu La Rochelle's novel *Gilles*. On the contrary, she is a young and sexy woman with black hair and dark eyes, more or less corresponding to the stereotype of the exotic Jewess in German anti-Semitic fantasies of a not-so-distant past. The narrator is also a specialist on Joris-Karl Huysmans, a 'decadent' writer of the late nineteenth century. Himself an admirer of Huysmans, Houellebecq does not feel the need to explain to his readers that this faithful reader of *La Libre Parole* was also Judeophobic.[20]

The narrator's peaceful life in the Latin Quarter where he works, and the Chinese Quarter where he lives, grateful that there are few Blacks or Arabs here, is interrupted by his discovery of terrorist attacks that the public authorities and media are trying to cover up. In the Paris universities, pressure from ever-growing cells of Islamic students is making itself felt. According to rumour, an agreement made with them blocks Jewish organizations from access to the campus, and they rapidly disappear.[21] At the same time, the presidential election takes place. A moderate Islamic party, which has put behind it an 'anti-Semitic' past,

---

20   In an interview given to *La Libre Parole* on 4 February 1898, in the wake of the publication of Émile Zola's 'J'accuse', Huysmans, a staunch Catholic, declared: 'Zola took the side of the Jews out of hatred for the church and love of the golden calf.' Four years later, in the same newspaper, he explained the reasons for the Dreyfusard victory as follows: 'I believe, in fact, in a universal movement organized by the Jews, who are the freemasons' bankers, as Drumont has said ... The Jews arranged the rehabilitation of their traitorous co-religionist' (*La Libre Parole*, 24 July 1902). See on this subject the excellent article by Jean-Marie Seillan, 'Huysmans, un antisémite fin-de-siècle', in *Romantisme*, vol. 27, no. 95, 1997, pp. 113–26.

21   Michel Houellebecq, *Submission*, New York: Farrar, Straus and Giroux, p. 21.

arrives in second place behind the movement of Marine Le Pen. This breakthrough leads to an atmosphere of latent civil war. The Front National organizes a demonstration of two million on the Champs-Élysées, with placards bearing the simple and unaggressive slogan: 'This Is Our Home.'[22] But this giant and restrained demonstration is no use. The defeated Socialists, and even the UMP, decide to collaborate and call on their supporters to vote for the cunning and ingenious Ben Abbes, who is elected president of the republic.

At this point, Houellebecq tricks his readers by giving the impression of being actually Islamophilic. Apparently, things settle down in the best way possible. Calm and order reign in the new democratic realm, especially in the poor districts. Crime falls dramatically, there is a significant drop in unemployment (due to women returning to the household), and France soon becomes hegemonic within the European Union, which expands southward. All the Arab countries of the Mediterranean shores become members of a great and prosperous power resembling the Roman Empire of antiquity.[23] A moderate Islamic party also comes to power in Belgium, while similar movements appear in all other European countries. And, perhaps the most attractive point for Houellebecq and his character in the novel, the new regime seductively proposes polygamy. Men can marry two women or even more. Women are educated according to Islam to be devoted and submissive, with the result that everything becomes very agreeable for the dominant males, and particularly for the intellectuals among their number.

The novel's protagonist is initially reticent towards the conquering religion. The Sorbonne has become, like other establishments, an Islamic university, purchased by money coming from the Middle East, so he leaves Paris for a town by the name

---

22   Ibid., p. 95.
23   Houellebecq draws his scant knowledge of the Islamic world from the superficial book by the British Arabophobe Bat Ye'or, *Eurabia: The Euro-Arab Axis*, Madison, NJ: Fairleigh Dickinson University Press, 2010.

of Martel (as usual, a clumsy allusion).[24] He finally succumbs to the lure of an attractive salary, the 'enchanting' spirituality of the Koran and the plurality of wives, and so returns to the capital, converts to Islam and becomes once more a respected lecturer. His submission to Islam is complete and entire. This supposedly utopian novel comes to a happy end with a new and sensual life in a great and strong France.

It needs to be added that the symbolic figure of the collaborating and subjected intellectual is not the narrator caught up in his prevarications, but another brilliant and committed professor answering to the name of Roger Rediger. One of the very first to convert to Islam, he becomes president of the Sorbonne, then minister for universities and the right arm of the president of the republic. He began his process of 'Pétainist' conversion and opportunist rise very early, making a reputation as a pro-Palestinian who called for a boycott of Israel and as the editor of the *Revue d'études palestiniennes*. Under his editorship, the university offices are decorated with panels inscribed with verses from the Koran. All the secretaries and women students wear the veil. Student numbers however decline, as girls are now educated for domesticity and pressed to marry at an early age. All the study programmes in the universities, and even the schools, are adapted to the teaching of the Koran. Women not only wear the burka in the streets of the capital, but also stop working and retreat to the household.

French Jews are forced to emigrate to Israel for fear of persecution, as 'it is well known' that they have never lived in peace under the oppression of Islam (Houellebecq says nothing to his readers about the far more crushing Judeophobia under the medieval Christianity that he so admires). The narrator's beloved Myriam, with her black hair, dark eyes and quivering backside,

---

24   Martel, in the département of Lot, was supposedly founded by the Frankish leader Charles Martel, who defeated the Arab invasion at Tours in 732. *Translator's note.*

emigrates with her parents to her 'natural' country of refuge, where she feels better despite the crazy kamikazes who blow themselves up every day. The novel's protagonist must now take his pleasure with simple and submissive Muslim women; initially these are prostitutes, but they go on to become his legitimate wives.

The story is hardly amusing, apart from one detail. Though Islam penetrates every cell of life, both public and private, of the indigenous French, the limit where it stops for Houellebecq is that of wine. The novel's characters continue to consume alcohol without any problem. The author was aware that a ban on wine would be perceived by his French readers as an impossible fantasy lacking any credibility.

Given all of this, the book's triumphant reception is hardly surprising. David Pujadas was not alone in his enthusiasm. Other fellow travellers of Houellebecq immediately mobilized to echo it as much as they could in both audiovisual and written media. We have already seen how, in the last number of *Charlie Hebdo* before the massacre, Bernard Maris gave it a eulogistic review.[25] Alain Finkielkraut, the 'philosopher' who had just been elected to the Académie Française, immediately congratulated the author, whom he called a 'great novelist of the possible'.[26] Another well-known 'philosopher', Bernard-Henri Lévy, hastened to write on his blog, on 6 January 2015: '*Submission*, in other words, is a fable. It is a cruel and bitter tale. It is a satire whose extremism and bad faith are only equalled by the way in which it captures various episodes of striking topicality.'[27]

In *Le Monde*, the writer Emmanuel Carrère compared Houellebecq to George Orwell and Aldous Huxley, before adding, with a rather immodest French pride: 'He is a more

---

25   *Charlie Hebdo*, 7 January 2015, p. 13.

26   'Pourquoi Alain Finkielkraut a aimé le livre de Houellebecq', *Causeur*, 5 January 2015.

27   Bernard-Henri Lévy, 'Houellebecq, écrivain', Laregledujeu.org, 6 January 2015.

powerful novelist than either of these.'[28] On 21 January, in the course of an interview on the Swiss TV channel RTS, Hélène Carrère d'Encausse, permanent secretary to the Académie Française, proposed its election of Houellebecq on the grounds of this important book. This distinguished historian added: 'What he describes makes you say to yourself: he's not wrong.'[29]

Soon after, another venerable historian, Jacques Julliard, asserted that this was in no way a book on the danger that Islam presented, and certainly not Islamophobic, but rather a criticism of the inclination to collaboration with any imported totalitarianism (Nazi, Stalinist . . .) that was latent in French intellectuals. And he concluded, with a certain admiration: 'Houellebecq's novel is a powerful discriminator: it may well be that in the immediate future it contributes to reshaping the geography of intellectual passions in French society. People's reactions to their reading of this book say a great deal on their respective sensibilities: there is now a Houellebecq test on political questions.'[30] Perhaps Julliard exaggerated, but he was not mistaken: there is indeed a Houellebecq test, which can help us better understand the Islamophobic and conformist tendencies of a significant section of the French intelligentsia at this point in the twenty-first century.[31]

Ultimately, and contrary to the view of his admirers, there is not an ounce of utopianism in Houellebecq's novel, which actually comes across as a pure dystopia. The novel is a heavy black

---

28   *Le Monde*, 6 January 2015.

29   'Soumission: Hélène Carrère d'Encausse donne raison à Houellebecq', Rts.ch, 21 January 2015. As for Houellebecq, he immediately declared himself ready for an Académie chair (*Le Figaro*, 27 January 2015).

30   *Marianne*, 24 January 2015.

31   The first to fail this test was J. M. G. Le Clézio, winner of the Nobel Prize for Literature in 2008, who declared: 'I do not much like the title of this book and I shall probably not read it, since I do not think it is a good message to give to French people, to tell them that they should be so afraid of Islam. I believe there is already a tendency in France to give in to fear, which I do not think is a good idea' (*Metronews*, 2 February 2015).

cloud wrapped in perfumed cotton wool to give consistency to the fragile identity of a nationalism in crisis. Common sense shows that the theory of France becoming an Islamic state in 2022 is simply an insubstantial spectre. The idea of a Muslim minority, today rather low on the social ladder, coming to exercise omnipotent domination over an absolute majority of subjected French people is explicitly designed to exploit sentiments of fear within a culture that has lost confidence in itself somewhere along the line. To quote Ayatollah Khomeini, as Houellebecq repeatedly does, to the effect that 'if Islam is not political, it is nothing',[32] in a state that has perhaps six million 'Muslims'[33] but where there is not a single member of parliament of Islamic faith, is equally designed to stimulate book sales. We might say, paraphrasing Khomeini, that if *Submission* is not a political (anti-Islamic) book, it is nothing. And if we were to replace Muslims with Jews, the book's message would certainly be one of what a century or so ago was called the 'beautiful hatred': Judeophobia.

On reading this book, I asked myself whether a well-known French novelist would have dared to write, in 2015, a book on France becoming a Jewish state. An imagination similar to Houellebecq's, for example, could conjure up a president of the republic by the name of Pascal Strauss-Lévy, a cunning Jew but a moderate politician, linked to international financial groups, who with the help of the Conseil représentatif des institutions juives de France (CRIF), the Le Siècle club, the Socialist Party, Les Républicains, Israel and the pro-Zionist lobby in Washington, succeeds in the presidential election.

---

32   Michel Houellebecq, *Submission*, p. 181.

33   I say 'perhaps six million' as there are no official statistics of the number of believers in France. The 'number of Muslims' includes both those born in Islamic countries and also their descendants. Ironically, this number would accordingly seem to include Houellebecq himself, as well as Éric Zemmour, Bernard-Henri Lévy, Elisabeth Lévy, Shmuel Trigano, Fréderic Haziza and other well-known 'admirers' of Islam.

Strauss-Lévy immediately appoints the philosopher Alain Gluckskraut as minister of national education. Intellectuals start convincing themselves of the superiority of ancient Jewish morality, and many in the media demand that the mortal remains of Emmanuel Levinas be transferred to the Panthéon. Heading this campaign is the satirical weekly *Beni Hebdo*, whose editor is now appointed head of French broadcasting. Many people begin looking for Jewish parents or ancestors, and indeed finding them. Genetics laboratories specializing in DNA research, helped by Israeli institutes, provide certificates for those who request them.

Everyday life also undergoes changes. Complete silence sets in on Friday evening and Saturday (the Sabbath): work stops and public transport is interrupted, the same as in Israel. Only religious marriages are authorized by the state, with the result that non-Jews cannot marry Jews except if they convert to Judaism, again just as in Israel. The population at large may still be Christian or non-religious, and pig-breeding remains legal in France (in contrast to Israel, where this is allowed only in places remote from the holy sites), but everyone is taught in school the tragic fate of the chosen people and their full right to evacuate from the Biblical homeland the remainder of the Palestinian population.

While these changes are underway, a soft Jewish stranglehold over France is being pursued. Certain districts of Paris come to be inhabited exclusively by well-to-do Jews. All proprietors of the major media networks are Jews, and it is necessary to be circumcised in order to hold a high position in a bank or university. Circumcised Muslims, however, unless employed in construction and maintenance, are forced to leave France. Just before the end of the novel, Israel, now a large and rich country thanks to the flow of Jewish-American capital by way of Goldman Sachs, joins the European Union, whose Council of Ministers is transferred from Brussels to Jerusalem. European unemployment falls, while growth increases and overtakes that of China.

Jews show the world once again how to govern a flourishing economy.

This 'utopian' description is of course crazy, but it is neither more excessive nor less dangerous than the dystopian perspective depicted by Houellebecq. 'Thank God' (and never mind which one), no one could today publish in France or anywhere else in Europe such a diabolical political fiction, and then be invited with full honours onto the eight o'clock TV news the day before the book's publication.[34] Only Alain Soral, in his stubborn perversity, could make the noxious and influential pamphlet by Édouard Drumont available on his internet site *La France juive*, now particularly aimed at frustrated and distraught young people on certain *banlieue* estates. This book that was viewed as legitimate, 'normal' and interesting in 1886, 1938 and 1943, to the point of becoming a resounding bestseller, is rightly perceived today as unacceptable. The price to pay for this change in political mentality towards the Jews has been, as we know, very high. No one is yet in a position to predict what we may have to pay for the manufacturing of fear of Muslims in present-day Europe.

The 'libertarian' weekly

The journalists and cartoonists of *Charlie Hebdo* were certainly not guilty of Judeophobia. Despite the anti-Judaism that was typical of the French tradition of caricature, *Charlie* had more in common with *L'Assiette au beurre* of the early twentieth century (nothing like its imitation of 1943–4) than with *La Libre Parole*, Drumont's popular newspaper, which also published a great many caricatures. At the time of its creation, in 1969, the satirical weekly was permeated by a leftist anarchism, fully matching

---

34   I should point out here that *Submission* is not the only anti-Muslim novel to have been published recently in Paris. *Dawa* by Julien Suaudeau (published by Robert Laffont in 2014), *Les Événements* by Jean Rollin (P.O.L., 2015) and *2084* by Boualem Sansal (Gallimard, 2015) have likewise sought to exploit popular fear of the twenty-first-century 'Moors'.

the spirit of contestation of the young intelligentsia of the time. From the late 1960s until 1981, when it broke off publication for want of readers, it well embodied the "68 generation', complete with its retreat and dissolution.

In 1992, a new team of journalists and cartoonists took up the title and launched a completely new version of the weekly. For its first decade, this quite diverse group took as its targets above all right-wing politicians, conservative and religious institutions, even if the respectable left was also sometimes put in the pillory. We should note that the paper took up the cause of the *sans-papiers*, and in 1996 even launched a petition to ban the Front National. However, the conformism that affected a whole generation of former oppositionists in the 1980s and '90s ended up reaching the doors of the realm of caricature.

Among the new editors of the weekly was Philippe Val, who soon became its editor-in-chief. Over the years, his hold on the paper steadily grew, and he became its director in 2004, with the power of decision over the paper's orientation. In 2009, when Jean-Luc Hees, also a contributor to *Charlie*, was appointed head of Radio France by Nicolas Sarkozy, he chose his close friend Philippe Val to direct the flagship France Inter station.[35] To take up this prestigious role, the ambitious director resigned from *Charlie*, but his political spirit continued to hover over it.

Val had been from the start a firm editor-in-chief, with very little tolerance for the free expression of his colleagues (even earlier, he had had no hesitation in supporting the *loi Gayssot*).[36]

---

35   Already in 2007, Val was invited to the 'summer university' of Medef, the employers' association – something quite unimaginable in the oppositional 1970s, or even in the '90s.

36   This 1990 law, named after its communist sponsor, makes it a criminal offence to question the existence or scale of crimes against humanity as defined in the London Charter of 1945 under which Nazi leaders were convicted. It did not however prevent the French Constitutional Court from overturning a subsequent law that defined the First World War massacre of Armenians as genocide. *Translator's note.*

His opponents had nicknamed him 'the Kim Il-sung of the rue Turbigo'. In 2000, he succeeded in dismissing Mona Chollet from the paper, a brilliant writer, who had dared to criticize an article in which he had described Palestinians as 'uncivilized'. The following year, the journalist Olivier Cyran proved to be too independent and leftist for his taste. And in 2004, having become the omnipotent boss of the paper, he crossed swords with the critical sociologist Philippe Corcuff, who was forced to put an end to his articles for the weekly. It was in 2008, however, that the purge conducted by Philippe Val reached its zenith: the eviction of the cartoonist Siné was the most significant and most publicized in the history of the paper, and deserves our dwelling on it here for a moment.[37]

Siné, the pseudonym of Maurice Sinet, was one of the pillars of the group as well as one of its most talented cartoonists. He had drawn for the old *Charlie Hebdo*, and joined the new edition in 1992. He remained a stubborn libertarian, perhaps an artifact of his belonging to an earlier generation, as if he had not understood that the world had changed. He thought he could take on the whole world, and make fun of all religions and believers equally. On 2 July 2008, he wrote sarcastically:

Jean Sarkozy, a worthy son of his father and already a member of the UMP's leading body, emerged almost with applause from his court case for failing to report an accident with his scooter. Even the prosecution requested his acquittal! It has to be said that the plaintiff was an Arab. Not only that: he has just declared that he wants to convert to Judaism before

---

[37] On his arrival at France Inter, in 2009, Val was directly involved in the sacking of Didier Porte and Stéphane Guillon, two humourists who were too independent and critical for his taste. For more on the evolution of Val's mental universe, and the ideology imposed on *Charlie Hebdo*, see Mathias Reymond, 'Une histoire de *Charlie Hebdo*', Acrimed.org, 8 September 2008; and Sébastien Fontenelle, *Même pas drôle. Philippe Val, de Charlie Hebdo à Sarkozy*, Paris: Libertalia, 2010.

marrying his Jewish fiancée, the heir to the founders of Darty. The kid is going places![38]

An immediate storm followed. Philippe Val, a friend of Jean-Luc Hees, himself close to Nicolas Sarkozy, mobilized his intellectual friends, from Bernard-Henri Lévy to Alexandre Adler, against this uncontrolled 'Judeophobe'. On 15 July, the weekly's director, who was perfectly aware of the limits to freedom of expression in the French Republic and the essential difference between Jews and Muslims, sacked the impertinent cartoonist.[39] The story is a simple one: the 'anachronistic' Siné had not understood that in the twenty-first century it is precisely not permissible to make a correlation between Judaism or Jews and money. On the other hand, the equation between Islam, Muslims and terrorism posed no problem, either for Siné, the editorial board of *Charlie Hebdo* or a large section of the French intelligentsia.

On 30 September 2005, the right-wing Danish paper *Jyllands Posten* published a series of cartoons about Islam and Muslims. Some of these made fun of Islam and the intolerance of many of its adherents. Other more cutting caricatures directly identified Islam and Muhammad with terrorism. One drawing by Kurt Westergaard particularly stood out: the Prophet was shown with a turban on his head in the shape of a bomb. In Denmark, Westergaard was immediately idolized by the far right. A salient fact about this country is that the (Lutheran) church is not separate from the state, which pays salaries to its priests, but it does not seem that *Jyllands Posten* has ever seen this as a problem.

In France, certain newspapers, after some hesitation, published a few of the more moderate Danish cartoons, but on 8 February

---

38   On 11 June of the same year, Siné had written in his weekly column: 'I confess that increasingly I find Muslims intolerable, and the more I cross paths with the veiled women who proliferate in my quarter, the more I want to kick them violently in the butt!' This sentence failed to arouse any storm in the media, it was quite within 'normal' bounds.

39   Siné launched a successful lawsuit against his dismissal and the motives for it.

2006 *Charlie Hebdo*, the 'libertarian' organ, hurried to publish them in full, even adding some of its own. Against a backdrop of violent protest in the Islamic world, its sales rocketed from the usual 40,000 copies (or even less, according to some sources) to half a million. Philippe Val and his former leftist fellow editors drew a lesson from this: nowadays, as far as Islam is concerned, there is no longer a distinction between a good marketing move, freedom of expression and radical secularism. While President Jacques Chirac described the cartoons and their publication as 'a manifest provocation of Muslims', a large part of the Paris media milieu, with joyous irresponsibility, made the Prophet into a kind of new Hitler or Stalin for the twenty-first century.

Flipping through the back issues of *Charlie*, from 2006 to 2015, is a stupefying experience. Although the place devoted to Islam is not central, it is certainly far from marginal; Islam is far more than a 'detail' in the paper's weekly existence. We get the impression that, when Islam is concerned, all brakes are off: Muslims are always repugnant, repulsive, and even, most of the time, menacing and dangerous. The *Charlie* cartoonists take particular interest in the Prophet's backside, his scrawny testicles and his manic desire to fornicate with pigs and camels. Faithful Muslims certainly did not buy or subscribe to this weekly, but they could not escape its covers, exposed in full view in all kiosks.

There was more than ugliness in this despicable and contemptuous representation of the belief of a religious minority. The constant slippage between Islam, Muslims and radical fundamentalism was seen as only 'logical', and was never the object of any sharp distinction. I have a sad memory of another cartoon imported from Denmark, by Rasmus Sand Høyer. Here we see Muhammad, a cruel-looking bearded figure wrapped in a white jellaba, his eyes hidden and holding a long pointed knife, and alongside him two veiled women in black niqab of whom all we see is their desperate look. This caricature is remarkably like those that were published in Drumont's *La Libre Parole*, which always showed ugly Jews carrying large bags full of money.

It is surprising to see how much the 'Semitic' Jews of the past resemble the 'Semitic' Muslims of today: the same ugly face and the same long and fat nose. True, *Charlie* could also mock Jews and Christians, in a more restrained and reasonable way, but it would never have published a caricature showing a bearded Jew wearing a kippah in the role of a street-corner moneylender, nor an American Jewish banker pulling the strings of the world economy. We have also been spared the backside of Moses, along with that of the pope and the president of the republic – this is not seen as a subject for laughter by today's 'anarchists', and indeed, so much the better.

And further, when the Muslim man is not a terrorist, he is at least a polygamist or a lazy scrounger benefiting from state handouts. I have in mind a cartoon published in *Charlie* showing an Arab worker stopping in front of a prostitute, while a bearded preacher lectures him: 'My brother! You're going to pay 40 euros a time, when you can buy yourself a wife for the same price.' This repugnant cartoon is published in a country where polygamy is forbidden, and where many Muslim men have a very hard time setting up home with one wife. A cartoon of this kind is not directed against fundamentalists or oil-state princes, nor is its intention to defend women. It amalgamates ordinary Muslims, those you meet every day cleaning the streets or on building sites, with the 'danger of polygamy' that hovers over this famously monogamous and devout country.[40]

On 3 July 2013, the Egyptian army, under the command of General Fattah el-Sisi, carried out a coup d'état against the legitimately elected president, Mohamed Morsi – with the backing

---

40   Similarly, the cartoon representing veiled women showing their thighs while praying to 'mother Mecquerelle' is not just a mockery of religion or jihadists, but also of ordinary Muslims. See Olivier Cyran, '*Charlie Hebdo* pas raciste? Si vous le dites . . .', Article11.info, 5 December 2013.

of Saudi Arabia, a great friend of the French Republic. The army then violently repressed the crowds of demonstrators supporting the government of the Muslim Brotherhood and opposed to the military dictatorship. On 10 July 2013, *Charlie Hebdo* appeared with a red cover and the banner headline: 'The Koran is shit.' This is explained by a cartoon in which a bearded man uses the holy book as a shield to protect himself from bullets fired by Egyptian soldiers; with his eyes wide open, he exclaims when the bullets pierce the Koran and strike him: 'It doesn't stop bullets!'[41]

General Abdel Fattah el-Sisi triumphed over these crowds with machine guns, thereby strengthening fundamentalism and radical terrorism in Egypt.[42] *Charlie Hebdo* has so far triumphed by way of laughter and the help of the French law. In all the cases brought against it, it has regularly been acquitted, just like Houellebecq; those who felt themselves injured and lodged complaints have always been dismissed. The unreserved support of such intellectuals as Élisabeth Badinter, Claude Lanzmann and Bernard-Henri Lévy, and political figures including Nicolas Sarkozy and François Hollande, has created a climate of sympathy for the accused. Many Muslims and non-Muslims alike have seen this as a weakness of French legislation, and regularly criticized it for this. Radical Islamists, frustrated, disoriented and with a very fragile faith, decided in revenge to react with deadly folly. On 2 November 2011 they set fire to the magazine's offices. On 7 January 2015 they moved up a notch, breaking into the same building, opening fire and massacring those inside.

---

41   Could one imagine a cover page with the headline 'The Talmud is shit', and beneath it a cartoon representing the rabbi and three religious students shot by Mohammed Merah outside their school in Toulouse? Such a thing is rightly impossible in contemporary France.

42   The military coup in Egypt recalled a rather similar intervention by the Algerian army in 1991, against the Front islamique du salut (FIS) which had won the first round in that year's elections. This intervention gave birth to a radical fundamentalism and a deadly cruelty on both sides, which claimed nearly 100,000 victims.

Unhappily, it is not just the Koran that fails to stop bullets, but also the pages of a satirical paper.[43]

President François Hollande immediately declared three days of national mourning, and called on all French people to demonstrate for freedom of expression. At the same time, Joachim Roncin, artistic director of the magazine *Stylist*, posted the phrase 'Je suis Charlie' on Twitter. The combination of these two initiatives had an immediate effect; 11 January saw more than four million demonstrators respond to the president's appeal – most of them under the banner 'Je suis Charlie'. Hollande himself, together with the prime minister, appeared at the head of the Paris demonstration, flanked by heads of state, ministers and ambassadors from all over Europe and the rest of the world. These included the Israeli head of government Benjamin Netanyahu and his then foreign minister, Avigdor Lieberman. Also present were Sergei Lavrov, the Russian foreign minister, the Turkish prime minister Ahmet Davutoğlu, Abdullah II, king of Jordan, Sheikh Abdullah bin Zayed, foreign minister of the Arab Emirates, and Nizar Madani, head of foreign relations in Riyadh. The identification of *Charlie* with freedom of expression and defence of secularism was international and total. On account of the horrible action of two wretched little murderers, educated in the schools of the republic and probably not great believers, for a moment Paris became the epicentre of the 'free world'.

Throughout my life, I have been reticent towards demonstrations organized by the state and public authorities; but despite everything, I was hoping to join a calm gathering, so as not to

---

43   The last discussions at *Charlie Hebdo*, just before the killings, were about French jihadists. 'Tignous [a cartoonist who was murdered] did not actually justify them, but as a true kid from the *banlieue* who had escaped a life of poverty there, he asked what France had really done to avoid creating such furious monsters . . . Bernard Maris replied that France had done a great deal, spending heaps of money' (account by a survivor, reported by Philippe Lançon, 'J'allais partir quand les tueurs sont entrés . . .', *Libération*, 13 January 2015).

feel too isolated and powerless. I had imagined the demonstration would be above all against terror and fear, but after this harsh ordeal I had also hoped we would express our solidarity with immigrants and foreigners. I would have liked representatives of the three communities, Christians, Muslims and Jews, to march at the head, together with trade-union leaders and figures of non-political voluntary associations. The last thing I expected was a demonstration of hypocritical politicians and representatives of oppressive states, proudly parading in the streets of the capital and facing spectators with the smiles of victors.[44]

In Nice, where I was staying at this time, the mayor Christian Estrosi paraded at the head of the demonstration, holding a large banner with the words 'Je suis Charlie'; you could see on his face that he felt more justified than ever. For this reason, I stayed away from the demonstration, but I must confess that the deeper reason why I refused to get carried away by the crowd of demonstrators was the slogan 'Je suis Charlie' itself. I told myself right away that, if a nutcase from the Jewish Defence League tried to kill the Judeophobic 'humorist' Dieudonné, I would denounce the crime and demand that its authors were judged with due severity, but I would never demonstrate with a banner inscribed 'Je suis Dieudonné'.[45]

As for Houellebecq, and many of his kind who immediately proclaimed 'Je suis Charlie', I knew that their identification with the magazine implied a basic agreement with its contents.[46] I have always believed that freedom of expression is a priority, and I have

---

44   The presence of Ahmet Davutoğlu in the front of the demonstration struck me as still more intolerable than that of Benjamin Netanyahu. Just two years earlier, on 9 January 2013, three Kurdish militants had been murdered in Paris with the active complicity of the Turkish secret services (MIR).

45   See my article 'Shlomo Sand: "Je ne suis pas Charlie"', *Mediapart*, 13 January 2015.

46   For example André Glucksmann, in *Le Figaro* of 12 January 2015: 'The Islamic terrorists were not wrong in their choice of target; *Charlie Hebdo* is the heir of Voltaire, of the *Roman de Renart*, of that irreverent and free France that we love so much.'

fought for it in my own country throughout my adult life. But I
have equally been aware that it has limits. No one has the right to
incite an attack on others, just as it is forbidden to call for a group
of people to be stigmatized on account of their origin, sex, sexual
orientation or religion. As against customary (and mistaken) interpretations of the republican principle, I am favourable toward the
freedom to express religious views in a public space, naturally so
long as those values and requirements to worship are not imposed
on me. I have always been anti-clerical in political terms and anti-
religious in philosophical ones, but I have also always sought as far
as possible to avoid confusing the two. Such in my view is the
quintessence of enlightened thought. I am the offspring of parents
and generations who long suffered hatred, contempt, insult and
persecution. My ancestors and their ancestors, who lived in
Christian civilization, suffered harshly – not on account of their
'race', but because of their stubborn belief and the religious practices that went together with it.

It is necessary to dwell on this point for a moment, in order to
clarify a disturbing semantic and ideological question. The owner
of *Libération*, Laurent Joffrin, seeking to justify Val's dismissal of
Siné, defended his friend Val in the following terms: 'Attacking
Islamic fundamentalism and denouncing the supposed power of
the Jews are not the same thing. In the first case you are anti-
fundamentalist; in the second case you are racist. People choose
their religion, but not their race.'[47] Certainly he immediately regret-
ted his words and sought to repair the linguistic slippage, but this is
symptomatic of the Paris intellectual climate in the early twenty-
first century. Joffrin is neither racist nor Judeophobic, and his intentions were good (and not just towards Val). In his deep ignorance,
however, he wanted to say that hostility towards Jews is racism,
whereas hostility to Muslims is a question of religion; and he clum-
sily made Jews into a race, as otherwise Judeophobia could not be
racist! However, the age-old hatred of Jews did not come from any

---

47   *Libération*, 25 July 2008.

racial theory or a different DNA; it was the result of a long train of prejudices against the believers in a different religion.

In the famous plays of Christopher Marlowe and William Shakespeare, neither of whom were personally acquainted with Jews, Judeophobic stereotypes do not bear on a race, but attack members of a 'greedy' religious community who stubbornly refuse to receive Christian grace. Anti-Jewish prejudice is also abundant in French culture, from Voltaire to Proudhon; this comes from a view of Judaism as a religion of the golden calf, a foreign cult whose followers, dispersed from Asia, are hereditary money-lenders. (We should point out that Judeophobes made no distinction between the religion and its followers.) In the Russian Empire, in the late nineteenth and early twentieth century, the people perpetrating pogroms were not racist, but had learned to hate the Jews as 'foreigners' who, according to rumour, cooked their Passover matzos with the blood of Christian children. Only in the second half of the nineteenth century, a modern, secular and scientific age, did Western Europe gradually start to racialize the Jews, in other words, to apply to them a concept of race. This popular term, however, had no genuinely biological connotation; what it denoted above all was a human, religious or 'ethnic' group, arriving from elsewhere and apparently not belonging to the nation.

From the late nineteenth century, massive waves of Jewish migrants from the Russian Empire – some 2.7 million people – reached the cities of Central and Western Europe (for the great majority of them, these cities were only a stopover on the way to North America). This immigration further inflamed the traditional rejection encountered by these bearded and repugnant descendants of the killers of Jesus Christ.[48]

---

48   We still lack any serious study on the impact of Jewish immigration on the emergence of Judeophobia in the late nineteenth and early twentieth centuries. On the mass emigration itself, a major research work is Gur Alroey, *The Quiet Revolution: Jewish Emigration from the Russian Empire, 1875–1924*, Jerusalem: Zalman Shazar, 2008 (in Hebrew).

Why did more than 4 million French people parade under a slogan that identified them with a totally irresponsible and Islamophobic magazine? Should we see this as a great sensitivity to the question of freedom of expression? Was it a courageous republican impulse to preserve the legacy of the Enlightenment? There certainly were demonstrators for freedom, though far less so for fraternity. Some came to the parade in shock from a cruel and barbaric act, but I also fear that far too many were demonstrating against the 'Other', different but present among them. Under the consensual slogan 'Je suis Charlie', was also hidden a very un-fraternal way of saying, 'Je suis français'.[49]

At a time when Frenchness is experiencing an acute crisis, when a political party that mobilizes against 'foreigners' is in the process of becoming the 'first party of France', the wave of hysteria and *union sacrée* suddenly reminded me of the rejection of the 'non-Jew' characteristic of the political climate in Israel. The only difference is that in France this is all done under the sign of the Enlightenment, the republic and Voltaire.

It is worth drawing attention to the fact that the majority of demonstrators were not supporters of Le Pen, whose movement was almost officially kept away from the parades. Emmanuel Todd has made a pertinent analysis of this subject: in the towns where the Front National obtained a high proportion of votes, the number of demonstrators was very low (for example Marseille, Nice, Béziers, in contrast to Paris, Lyon, Grenoble). The majority of 'Je suis Charlie' demonstrators did not come from the poor districts; they were not manual workers but belonged mainly to the middle class, for whom voting Le Pen remains illegitimate and

---

49   Many intellectuals expressed the populist thirst for a vanished collective pride. Jean-Pierre Le Goff, for example, wrote in inflamed tones: 'We have seen here the pride of being French, we have seen the crowd sing the *Marseillaise* and applaud the police, the assertion of a people who rise to defend the Republic' (*Le Parisien*, 13 January 2015).

vulgar.[50] All the more so, in that the far-right party today expresses a national conception that is retrograde and anti-European, and was until quite recently tinged with Judeophobia.

For the majority of 'Charlies', separatism vis-à-vis the 'Other' was less marked. It insisted that the rejection it expressed was not directed against Arabs, and was consequently not racist. This new code, however, established the complete legitimacy of hating Islam and Muslims. The war against Islam was seemingly not essentialist but cultural. The division of labour to exclude the 'Other' was complete and effective, between the vulgar and the timid, the ignorant and the semi-intellectuals. Euphemism has always been the most effective method of perpetuating racism.

The collective identity of many 'Charlies', though clearly not all, thus assumed a relatively new character. They adopted a pseudo-national – or, more precisely, 'zombie nationalist' – identity which, promoted for many years in the Paris media, and in semi-philosophical and pseudo-historical essays, came principally from 'above' and not from 'below'. They did not take up the populist electoral discourse pronounced in the working-class suburbs. The contours of this identity proclaimed themselves very French, but they are not exactly those of classic France. They were shaken and fragmented, and to a large extent already modelled on the imaginary frontiers of a white Europe, to which the fashionable Parisian imperative had already attributed the distinguished and very widespread appellation of 'Judeo-Christian civilization'.

This term, a pure media product of intellectual circles, was the new expression of an old cultural hypocrisy. It caused confusion about the history of Christian civilization. This received a new baptism that made it 'Judeo-Christian', something it had previously been unaware of. Jews, likewise, after living for a thousand

---

50   Emmanuel Todd, *Who Is Charlie? Xenophobia and the New Middle Class*, Cambridge: Polity Press, 2015. Without necessarily sharing all this author's 'scientific' shortcuts, particularly between anthropology and politics, we have to recognize the originality of a courageous historian and demographer.

years in Christian Europe, had sadly been unaware of living in a symbiotic 'Judeo-Christian' culture. The participants in the Crusades, who killed a large number of non-Christian believers, never saw themselves as coming from a 'Judeo-Christian' world. The harsh agents of the Inquisition, whose autos-da-fé interrogated descendants of the 'people of the deicide' along with heretics and apostates, never imagined themselves for a moment to be 'Judeo-Christian'. And likewise, until the late 1950s, successive popes never introduced into their Sunday prayers any word in praise of the Jews, whom they preferred to refer to as *perfidis Judaeis*.

Five million individuals who were murdered in Europe during the Second World War, whether Jews or their secular descendants, did not realize they were Judeo-Christians, and lacked the opportunity to become such. But the followers of *Charlie Hebdo*, the admirers of Houellebecq, and the media and book people in Parisian salons, feel very much at ease with this purifying term.[51] The important point is that the imaginary frontiers of the new 'Judeo-Christian atheists' correspond to the state of mind that has become hegemonic in France in the early twenty-first century: those persecuted yesterday have been integrated, but the frontiers keep out the rejected and humiliated of today.

In actual fact, no one knows how many of the demonstrators were familiar with the *Charlie* cartoons. Despite the sharp drop in sales that the weekly had registered, it is probable that in the age of the internet many discovered them in the three days that followed the massacre. The fact that their ugliness and clear incitement to hatred of Muslims did not dissuade the demonstrators may well be disturbing, but there was nothing fortuitous about it. Shocking as it might appear, identification with Islamophobic messages was very likely a stimulus to demonstrate, and to

---

51   It is by no means accidental, therefore, that intellectuals like Alain Finkielkraut, Élisabeth Lévy and Éric Zemmour hastened to sign the petition 'Touche pas à mon église' [Hands off my church] published on 15 July 2015 in the conservative weekly *Valeurs Actuelles*. This petition called for the protection of empty churches, to avoid – God forbid! – their falling into the hands of Islamic invaders.

purchase the seven million copies of the issue published just after the events.

Identification with the magazine's contents is regularly justified in the name of the valiant national battle for secularism in the face of all religions. Despite myself being secular and atheist, I did not want to join the number of my friends who flocked to this great troupe. Identification with *Charlie* seemed to me a kind of 'rhinoceritis' as described so well in Eugène Ionesco's play. One after another, several of my close friends were transformed into conformists, with a thick European epidermis and threatening 'Judeo-Christian' horns. According to Ionesco, becoming a rhinoceros is quite normal and natural when everyone is doing it and happy about it. And the more rhinoceroses there are, the stronger 'rhinocerite' feeling grows, and the more its victory is assured.[52] Ever since 1967, I have constantly experienced this phenomenon in my own small Middle Eastern country.

It may be that one of the reasons why I could not be *Charlie* is because I grew up in a country where devout atheists, basing themselves on a theological text and in the name of a god already dead in their mind, took over the land of people who had the misfortune to believe in a still living god. This immunized me against the excess of trust sometimes extended to those who, despite being non-believers, devote to their icons a cult just as religious as the rest. I knew that the secular Nazis in Germany and the atheist Fascists in Italy were no less deadly than the long Christian and Islamic oppressions. The bitter experiences of Stalinism and Maoism should also serve as a warning sign to restrain the aggressive anti-religious tendencies that have long lost their raison d'être in the French Republic, just as they have in the People's Republic of China.

---

52   I may point out here that one of the few not to allow themselves to be swept up in the 'secular republican' torrent, and to have had the courage to criticize the irresponsibility of *Charlie Hebdo* towards Islam, is Loränt Deutsch, author of the bestseller *Métronome*. This is not accidental: he is a Catholic and a royalist. See his interview in *Nice-Matin*, 23 January 2015.

CHAPTER 7

From Finkielkraut to Zemmour:
Decadence or Xenophobia?

*I shall never forget the moment when I experienced and understood
for the first time the tragedy of colonization . . . Ever since that day
I have been ashamed of my country. Ever since that day, I cannot
meet an Indochinese, an Algerian or a Moroccan without the desire
to ask their pardon. Pardon for all the pains, all the humiliations,
that they have been made to suffer, that their people have been made
to suffer. For their oppressor is the French state, which acts in the
name of all French people, and so for a small part in my name.*

Simone Weil, 'Qui est coupable
des menées antifrançaises?', 1937

*But don't deceive yourselves. It's not thugs you're dealing with, it's
soldiers. And even if they actually are thugs, these thugs are an army,
the armed wing of conquest. Whether they are conscious of this or
not, and in fact I think they are far more so than people believe.*

Renaud Camus, *Le Grand Remplacement*, 2011

I have always been clear that traditional religions have to be
opposed wherever they are dominating and oppressive. Having
lived the greater part of my life in a state where an atheistic

though not secular government uses institutionalized religion not to inculcate a belief but mainly to mark a separation between populations, I have always fought intransigently against religious compulsion in all its forms; I find it horrific.

I always thought that in the liberal democratic West, anyone with a moral conscience should offer support and encouragement to anti-clerical protests and revolts in the oppressive Islamic states: whether Saudi Arabia or Iran, Pakistan or Kuwait. However, since coming to France I have been convinced that venting hostility towards Islam, in parts where it is not an established state religion, is not only futile but above all dangerous, as it recurrently generates perverse and unforeseen reactions that fuel hatred.

On 11 September 2001, nearly 3,000 Americans were killed by a network of Islamic terrorists. This was the greatest and most dreadful attack in the Western world for many years. The Patriot Act, which came into effect in 2002, enabled the US government to undermine both the position of immigrants and many civil and human rights. President George W. Bush also used the pretext of this terrorist act to attack in 2003 an oil-rich state that had nothing to do with the September attack, to destroy its economic, political and cultural infrastructure, and cause the death of several hundred thousand Iraqis.

The United States of America, it is worth recalling, is alone in having used atomic weapons against a civilian population, and is still a deadly imperialist power. But it can also boast particular traditions of resistance and opposition to the authoritarian tendencies inherent in its national culture.[1] On 4 March 2015, the liberal mayor of New York, Bill de Blasio, announced that from now on the city's public schools would be closed for the two Islamic holidays Eid al-Adha and Eid al-Fitr, just as they are

---

1   Despite the terrible episode of McCarthyism, the United States is perhaps the nation that has produced the strongest and widest opposition to an imperialist war while this was still on-going.

for Christian and Jewish festivals. This aroused great enthusiasm in the Islamic community (8 per cent of New York's population), and American Muslim intellectuals stressed their fidelity to the country and its liberal democratic values. This was not the start of a submission to Islam, as in Michel Houellebecq's menacing vision, nor an 'attack on secularism', as *Charlie Hebdo* and Philippe Val would certainly have interpreted it if the mayor of Paris had adopted a similar measure.

There is a separation between church and state in the United States, but in contrast to France, the state there has not taken the place of the church. There is also an identity politics of a kind that Parisian intellectuals, on the right and left alike, have never understood (with the exception of a short list of atypical thinkers, from Alexis de Tocqueville to Tzvetan Todorov). It certainly took a great deal of time for this identity politics to lead to legal equality for African Americans, but once this was finally acquired, it did not suppress recognition of plurality and difference in American culture – or Anglophone culture more generally. The French Republic, on the other hand, was born in the shadow of an egalitarian totalitarian terror, and a part of the collectivist uniformity resulting from this was absorbed into French national culture from the start of its construction. Universal man, sublime radiant archetype of the Revolution, was not just an egalitarian model; he also unfortunately became to a large extent a one-dimensional prototype.

There have been few fascist intellectuals in France (the nationalist Jacobins and their revolutionary republican legacy certainly played a large role in this). And yet, it is no accident that, in contrast to Great Britain and the United States, there have been a large number of Judeophobic intellectuals (from Maurice Barrès to Louis-Ferdinand Céline), frightened of exception and difference. Later on, Maoist intellectuals and their followers (from Benny Lévy to André Glucksmann) found it natural to reject political or cultural pluralism, with an aggressiveness that was completely 'popular-republican'. Both Judeophobia and

Maoism have very fortunately declined, but something of their intolerant temperament remains, deeply anchored in the culture of a part of the Paris elites.[2]

The twenty-first century began with a period of deep economic stagnation, combined with a particularly acute identity crisis that followed European unification and cultural globalization. At surprising speed, a powerful media intelligentsia arose whose most striking hallmark was stigmatization of the different and noticeable Other. Detestation of the Islamic religion, and firm opposition to its free public expression on French soil, have effectively become the new opium of the 'anti-totalitarian' intellectual.

Intellectuals and Saracens

In 1979, the Soviet army invaded Afghanistan, and the genie escaped from the lamp. The Soviet occupation generated the first emergence of a national Islamic resistance movement, which would later influence the formation of the Taliban and the birth of al-Qaeda. This was also more or less simultaneous with the birth of a jihadi movement whose ideology was based on Saudi Wahhabi doctrine and which made terror its principal weapon. Before the 1980s, no one would have envisaged a correlation between terrorism and Islam. The terrorism of Islamic extremists did not find its origin in the Koran, any more than the greed of rich Jews comes from the Talmud (contrary to what Charles Fourier, not to mention Karl Marx, may have thought). Rather, during the years of decolonization, it was secular movements that resorted to terrorism, whereas devout Muslims were perceived as relatively more docile and tranquil. Closer to us, Palestinian terrorism came from the Palestine Liberation Organization and its secular fronts, whereas the imams were

---

2   The long intellectual and political indulgence displayed towards Soviet Stalinism is also understandable against the background of this Jacobin tradition.

generally collaborators who kept their distance from national politics.[3] The German Red Army Faction (RAF), the Japanese Red Army, the Italian Red Brigades and the Basque Euskadi Ta Askatasuna (ETA), all secular, also resorted to terrorism. The worst terrorist actions, until the end of the twentieth century, were carried out by the Tamil Tigers of Sri Lanka, who were certainly not Muslims.

However, something happened in the Arab and Islamic world in the wake of the total collapse of the secular socialist alternative. While in Paris the vision of a socialist future disappeared from the intellectual imaginary to give way to conservative ideologies based on communitarian identities in the context of the great 'Judeo-Christian' civilization, national religious fundamentalism became the bearer of a new challenge to the dominant West that began to emerge in 'Judeo-Islamic' civilization.[4] The corruption and repression practised by the most secular and 'Western' regimes, whether that of the Shah in Iran or the FLN in Algeria, aroused new symbioses of revolt, of which one axis was popular-nationalist Islam, and the other terrorist Islamic fundamentalism. The readiness for sacrifice, the contempt for material existence and waste, the egalitarian temperament of Islamic militants and fighters, in contrast to the 'secular' leaders, increasingly seduced the masses.

One of the first to have recognized the anti-communist potential that this new kind of 'revolutionary' Islam contained was Bernard-Henri Lévy, typically the quickest to react among

---

3   In the 1970s, Israel encouraged Islamic organizations in the occupied territories, and even helped to establish the first structures of Hamas, with the objective of weakening secular nationalism and the Palestinian left. The results went well beyond its hopes, and the same is true of the Americans in Afghanistan.

4   The concept of 'Judeo-Islamic' is very little used, and yet relatively more adequate than that of 'Judeo-Christian' civilization, not only in theological terms (for example, Muhammad was a prophet, not the son of God) or linguistically (there was Jewish philosophy written in Arabic, but not in Latin), but also in cultural practices (circumcision, dietary prohibitions, the position of women in the house of worship, etc.).

Parisian intellectuals. In 1981, he visited the borders of Afghanistan to assist the Mujahideen, in the same year that these were joined by dozens of volunteers from the Arab world, including Osama bin Laden. At this time, Bernard-Henri Lévy's obsession was still communism and not yet Islam, whose mutation into an anti-communist fighting force he was quick to encourage.

However, his vigorous support for Zionism and Israel (Lévy may well be a universalist Malraux in France, but in Israel he is a very nationalist Barrès) soon cooled his enthusiasm for Islamic resistance, which he completely abandoned as soon as it turned its rage against the West.

In 2002, Oriana Fallaci's well-known Islamophobic book *The Rage and the Pride* was published in French. Bernard-Henri Lévy immediately reacted in an extremely critical tone, proclaiming that the book 'will make the most extreme Le Pen followers green with envy'.[5] A rapid reading of the Italian journalist's hysterical text clarifies Lévy's point: Fallaci thanks the Soviets for having invaded Afghanistan in order to bar the way to the Muslim barbarians, and insults all those who came as volunteers to support 'the heroic Afghan people'. On the new Parisian spectrum of sensibilities, the reserve that Lévy displayed on this occasion was rather exceptional. The publication of Fallaci's book marked an acceleration in the mental and verbal volleys of secularist pen-pushers against Islam. What Houellebecq had permitted himself to say a couple of years earlier began to become the norm among media personalities and their intellectual sidekicks.

Alain Finkielkraut, despite a minor reservation, was the first to hail the success of this hateful book:

> It is to Oriana Fallaci's great credit that she does not let herself be intimidated by the virtuous lie. She doesn't flinch, but seeks

---

5   *Le Point*, 24 May 2002.

to look reality in the face. She rejects the penitential narcissism that makes the West guilty of what it is actually the victim. She takes the speech and acts of its adversaries at their word. But in her distress she goes too far. She writes in heavy block letters.[6]

Pierre-André Taguieff is not simply a serious scholar, he is also an adviser to the CRIF.[7] He has no time for Judeophobia, and has devoted his life to opposing it. He did, however, like *The Rage and the Pride*, not hesitating to write: 'Fallaci sees things correctly, even if some of her expressions may shock.'[8] A little while later, a no-less-serious researcher, Robert Misrahi, was invited by Philippe Val to express his view on Fallaci in *Charlie Hebdo*. Under the headline 'Intellectual Courage', this Sorbonne professor and expert on Spinoza had no compunction about lauding a book in which we learn, among other things, that Muslims 'breed like rats'. This man of culture considered that there is no xenophobia or racism in Fallaci, whom he sees as a courageous writer for her boldness in breaking the silence, in a cowardly Europe where 'people are unwilling to clearly see or condemn the fact that it is Islam that has embarked on a crusade against the West, and not the other way round'.[9]

This was indeed just a year after the shock of 11 September 2001, but also a year after the occupation of Afghanistan by the US army, with the support of NATO. In March 2003, the United States and Great Britain launched a crusade against Iraq, which, as everyone knows, was 'building up weapons of mass destruction'. What is allowed for the 'grown-ups' is forbidden to the 'little ones'. France did not join this war, which caused no small irritation in circles of the Paris intelligentsia, concerned at the

---

6 Ibid.
7 Conseil représentatif des institutions juives de France, an umbrella organization of Jewish institutions. *Translator's note.*
8 *Actualité juive*, 20 June 2002.
9 *Charlie Hebdo*, 3 November 2002.

decline in the status of Europe as a significant actor in the international balance of forces.

While mass demonstrations were held throughout the world against the war, a petition was published in *Le Figaro* to censure these anti-American defeatists and give fervent support to the invasion.[10] Its signatories included Robert Redeker, Pierre-André Taguieff, Shmuel Trigano and other prestigious scholars. Since this failed to have much resonance, a louder militarist appeal was published with the backing of well-known philosophers and historians, in particular Pascal Bruckner, Chantal Delsol, Denis Lefebvre, Mona Ozouf and Stéphane Courtois.[11] Pascal Bruckner and André Glucksmann had already published an article in support of George W. Bush, whom they praised for freeing the Iraqi people from a totalitarian tyrant.[12]

Others, such as Bernard-Henri Lévy and Alain Finkielkraut, were a little more cautious, but deemed the war moral and did not oppose it in principle. Of course, as always with wars, these intellectuals sat comfortably in their armchairs, not having to go and fight: their intention was that young French men and women should be dispatched to join those of 'friendly' countries, with a view to giving concrete expression to their view and conception of the world.

Hesitation towards Western neo-imperialism, which had been given new impetus by the fall of the USSR, was still apparent in 2003, but it would completely disappear in the course of the following decade. Thus, when France did send troops 'for a very short term' to zones of its former colonial empire in Africa, with a view to 'pursuing the jihadists' and taking the opportunity to repress Tuareg insurgents, too, there was no more question of critical public debate on the right or reason to re-engage in a neo-colonial policy. France's right to maraud Africa with a view

---

10   *Le Figaro*, 15 February 2003.
11   *Le Figaro*, 4 April 2003.
12   'Saddam doit partir, de gré ou de force!', *Le Monde*, 4 March 2003.

to managing the tragic territorial legacy whose frontiers it had arbitrarily fixed is similar to the Anglophone world's right to trample over the Middle East and dictate its wishes.

Perhaps we also need to recall that the riots of young people from the ghetto estates in November 2005, in the suburbs of Paris and other cities, were one of the elements that triggered the instauration of the new intellectual climate. As is well known, the first generation of immigrant workers, brought to France during the economic miracle of the 1960s, were submissive and obedient, whereas the mentalities of the second and third generations are very different. The children and grandchildren of immigrants, most of whom have become citizens, believe they are entitled to equal and identical consideration as their 'indigenous' neighbours receive from the state. They have been educated in the schools of the republic, and in a certain sense this teaching has succeeded beyond all hope, making them impertinent challengers. In a society in which solidarity is on the decline (the immigrants' local neighbours formerly voted Communist, whereas a large number of them now support the Front National), in which the welfare state is crumbling and leaving its last workers and their children shut up in ghetto districts with no future, the republic and its symbols have lost a significant amount of their prestige. Retreat to the traditions of their forebears, and the search for a community outside the state, has been the response in these social margins deprived of a future.

Demonstrations and riots of this kind further raised the level of popular disquiet over the Islamic threat, which now received legitimation from the government. Nicolas Sarkozy, then interior minister, promised the 'indigenous' inhabitants of these districts: 'You've had enough of this gang of scumbags, haven't you? Ok, we'll get rid of them.' Alain Finkielkraut, a little more intellectual, proposed a 'philosophical' basis for the condemnation of the rioters: 'The problem is that the majority of these young people are Blacks or Arabs with a Muslim identity . . . So, it is clear that this is a revolt with an ethnic-religious character . . . I believe that we are at the stage of an anti-republican pogrom. There are people in France who hate France as a republic.'[13]

Who is responsible for this menacing 'Muslim' and 'anti-republican' awakening? Finkielkraut points his finger at the failure of the educational system, which has lost faith in itself and whose teachers 'teach colonial history as something exclusively negative'. And he adds: 'We no longer teach that the colonial project also sought to educate, to bring civilization to savages. They talk about it as just an attempt to exploit, dominate and pillage.'[14]

Without admitting it, Finkielkraut identifies one of the paths that have fuelled this new-old phobia. Self-flagellation about the colonial past must cease; it lies at the root of national weakening and the decline of republican prestige. From the words of these new voices, of whom this media 'philosopher' is one of the most visible, we might conclude that the ferocious oppression in Algeria should be more or less forgotten, as well as the circumstances of painful defeat there. France was driven out of Algeria at the end of an exhausting and bloody war, but in the historical imaginary of many conservatives the battle is not over. All the less so in that, according to certain of their number, a reverse colonization has begun: the Arab enemy, continuing to harass the soldiers of the republic, has reached the gates of the capital. The paranoia that equates Islam with a threat against France has become a major intellectual currency.[15]

On 1 March 2006, *Charlie Hebdo*, in association with the Danish conservative newspaper *Jyllands Posten*, published an appeal under the heading: 'Together against the new

---

13   Interview with *Haaretz*, 18 November 2005.

14   Ibid.

15   On the republican ambivalence towards French Muslims after the end of the Algerian War, see the interesting book by the American scholar Todd Sheppard, *The Invention of Decolonization: The Algerian War and the Remaking of France*, Ithaca: Cornell University Press, 2006.

totalitarianism' (also known as the 'Manifesto of the 12') at the initiative of Philippe Val, Bernard-Henri Lévy, Caroline Fourest and other intellectuals, some of whom were of Arab or and Islamic origin. This text begins with the following words: 'After defeating fascism, Nazism and Stalinism, the world is facing a new global threat of a totalitarian type: Islamism. We, writers, journalists, intellectuals, call for resistance to religious totalitarianism.'

The signatories abstained from spelling out that when some of their number, after abandoning their revolutionary Maoist phase, transformed themselves into young 'anti-totalitarian' intellectuals, Stalinist totalitarianism, the target of their vehemence, had already long since ceased to constitute a threat. And they omitted to include in their charge sheet the terrible exactions perpetrated by colonialism or the bloody policies of pro-Western dictatorships in Latin America and Africa.

Marx ironically said that history always repeats itself, the first time as tragedy, the second as farce. This perfectly applies to the French version of the Rushdie affair that developed around Robert Redeker. This episode illustrates very well the creation process of the new 'Islamist' enemy, designed to replace the old 'communist' one. On 19 September 2006, *Le Figaro* published an article by this philosophy professor, working in Toulouse, who was already one of the most vocal champions of French participation in the war waged by George W. Bush in Iraq. Titled 'What should the free world do against Islamist intimidation?', it spelled out the dangers that, according to Redeker, Islam posed to Europe: specific food for Muslim children, the demand to wear the veil in schools, etc. To believe this 'philosopher', France was already experiencing 'a more or less conscious submission to the dictates of Islam':

As previously with Communism, the West finds itself under ideological surveillance. Islam presents itself in the image of this now defunct Communism, as an alternative to the

Western world. Like Communism, Islam plays on a sensitive chord in order to conquer minds. It boasts a legitimacy that troubles the Western conscience, attentive to others: that of being the voice of the planet's poor. Yesterday, the voice of the poor claimed to come from Moscow, today it comes from Mecca! Today again, intellectuals embody this eye of the Koran, as they yesterday embodied the eye of Moscow. They excommunicate on grounds of Islamophobia, as they did yesterday for anti-Communism.

We should not deceive ourselves. For the new 'philosopher', Islamism is neither a distortion nor an interpretation of Islam; it is well anchored in the Koran, and its founding prophet was a mass killer, especially of Jews. If 'Jesus is a teacher of love, Muhammad is a teacher of hate', Redeker proclaims. And this odd specialist in Islam concludes, so as to remove any shadow of doubt: 'While Judaism and Christianity are religions whose rites reject violence, delegitimize it, Islam is a religion that, already in its sacred text as well as in some of its everyday rituals, exalts violence and hatred.'

This stupefying assertion deserves clarification. We may doubt right away that its author has ever read the Old Testament. If he had done, he would be aware how fierce and strong violence is in the Torah, the most sacred Jewish text. Various contradictory passages in the Old Testament are at the origin of theological developments that are present in the Talmud, the New Testament and the Koran. These three sacred books have integrated, using various rhetorical means, a part of the aggressive messages contained in the more ancient texts. And if it is indeed true that the New Testament is marked by a significant attenuation of biblical violence, the new 'Judeo-Christian' Redeker must be familiar with Jesus's words: 'I have come not to bring peace, but a sword' (Matthew 10, 24). Quite logically, this peremptory expression did not restrain a Christianity that had become omnipotent from behaving as one of the most oppressive religions in history. We need only recall that there were no Muslims left in the zones under Christian domination in Europe, whereas Christians continued to live under Islamic power in the Middle East (less so in North Africa) until the modern age.

It is interesting to note here that the kind of excitement and lack of culture exposed in Redeker's article was formerly characteristic of writers in the far-right press. Now, however, it came from a member of the editorial board of *Les Temps modernes*, associated with Sartre and today presided over by Claude Lanzmann. And if even *Le Figaro* found itself obliged to express certain reservations about this article, the same was not true on the part of the new secular intelligentsia, including those coming from the left. Soon after the publication of Redeker's article, rumours circulated, spread in particular by Caroline Fourest, that a fatwa against Robert Redeker had been broadcast on the Al Jazeera TV channel. In due course the rumours proved baseless, but only after they had had time to arouse the fury and wide mobilization of intellectuals.

On 3 October 2006, an 'Appeal in support of Robert Redeker' was published in *Le Monde*. Its signatories included the leading standard-bearers of the struggle against the 'new totalitarianism', along with a few new recruits.[16] As well as Philippe Val, Bernard-Henri Lévy, Alain Finkielkraut, André Glucksmann and Pascal Bruckner, there were also the editors of the neo-conservative periodical *Le Meilleur des mondes*, who had all supported the war on Iraq. Another petition of the same type appeared in *ResPublica*, supposedly an organ of the 'republican left', also attracting wide support.

If the concern for Redeker's safety was understandable, and fully justified the effort to protect him from real or imaginary threats, it is significant that neither petition distanced itself from

---

16   Among them, Alexandre Adler, Laure Adler, Élisabeth Badinter, Michel Deguy, Élisabeth de Fontenay, Romain Goupil, Olivier Rolin, Élisabeth Roudinesco, Guy Sorman and Pierre-André Taguieff.

the incitement to xenophobia in relation to Islam and Muslims that had been expressed in such a leading newspaper as *Le Figaro*.[17] It had already become so commonplace to attack a religion and its believers, to sully its holy books and glorify one's own hegemonic culture, that many no longer saw this simply as a right but also a duty: any precaution was interpreted in conservative milieus as a form of submission.

A suicidal identity

The radicalization of discourse in wide circles of the Parisian elite prepared the ground for the publication of writings in the following decade that were still more aggressive. 'Daring' ideas that twenty years earlier were expressed only by a marginal far right now attracted public attention, arousing reactions that were initially hesitant but soon increasingly favourable. One of the first of these, Renaud Camus's *Le Grand Remplacement* published in 2011, was not a great success in the bookstores, and attracted a good deal of criticism (his previous comments on Jews had not served him well).[18] *Langue fantôme, suivi d'Éloge littéraire d'Anders Breivik* by Richard Millet, published the following year, despite its provocative title and the fact that its author had edited a series for Gallimard, was received badly and did not enjoy substantial sales.[19] But it was a different case with two subsequent books that were acclaimed by the media and soon beat sales records. 2013 saw the appearance of Alain Finkielkraut's *L'Identité malheureuse*, followed a year later by Éric Zemmour's *Le Suicide français*. Quite likely, no polemical essay had reached

---

17   See Pierre Tevanian, 'La faute à Voltaire? À propos des usages racistes de la liberté d'expression', *Revue internationale et stratégique*, vol. 65, 2007, pp. 181–8. On the rise of anti-Muslim phobia, see the essential book by Raphaël Liogier, *Le Mythe de l'islamisation. Essai sur une obsession collective*, Paris: Seuil, 2012.

18   Renaud Camus, *Le Grand Remplacement*, Paris: Éditions David Reinharc, 2011.

19   Richard Millet, *Langue fantôme, suivi d'Éloge littéraire d'Anders Breivik*, Paris: Pierre Guillaume de Roux Éditions, 2012.

such an impressive readership since Drumont published *La France juive* in 1886 (with the possible exception of Mao Zedong's *Little Red Book*). It is clear, in any case, that the context and causes of the success of these essays were astonishingly similar. History may well not repeat itself, but to look for scapegoats in a time of economic stagnation and social crisis rather than investigate the operation of the socio-economic structure as a whole has always been an intellectual and political accompaniment to the evolution of capitalism. It is ironic that when capitalism prospers it attracts virulent critics that do not bother it, while when it is in trouble and seems to have lost the ability to overcome its contradictions, criticism is directed against other targets.

Finkielkraut's and Zemmour's books differ from one another in terms of both style and mode of argument: the first is more intellectual, while the second is more political; the first deals with 'high culture', the second with 'popular culture'; the first turns out to be banal and unsurprising, while the second is both coherent and audacious. In the last analysis, however, they are united by the same diagnosis and the same enemy: the French Republic is in full degeneration. The cause of this misfortune, for Finkielkraut, is the collapse of the educational system and high culture; for Zemmour it is a society that is too feminized, hedonistic and individualistic. However, the main reason for the unhappy identity of the nation-state and its political suicide lies in the massive immigration that brings with it the domination of Islam. These two books prepared the ideological ground for the enthusiastic reception of Houellebecq's *Submission*, and perhaps indirectly the identification of many who marched on 11 January 2015 under the 'Je suis Charlie' banner.

Both authors can themselves be cited as examples of successful immigration. Finkielkraut was born in Paris, but his parents came from Eastern Europe and were naturalized as French in 1950. Zemmour was born at Montreuil in the Paris suburbs, of parents who came from Algeria while the war of national liberation was in progress. Both grew up and were educated during the *trente glorieuses*, a period when France experienced a strong economic growth and the welfare state functioned properly. The phenomenon of immigrants – or children of immigrants – themselves very well integrated but expressing a negative or even aggressive attitude towards later and 'less successful' immigrant groups is in no way exceptional (Nicolas Sarkozy, for example). In modern history, almost with every wave of immigration there have been strident voices of criticism from earlier arrivals.

What is perhaps surprising with these two writers, in terms of their careers as public intellectuals, is that their symbolic capital comes simply from writing essays for a broad public that are widely relayed in the dominant media. Finkielkraut is certainly presented in the media as a philosopher – doubtless because he uses countless quotations from various thinkers – but he has not produced any serious philosophical work of his own.[20] Zemmour has certainly tried to build up symbolic capital by writing novels, but their mediocrity prevented him from recognition as a novelist. The time when intellectuals first acquired prestige and authority in the field of creation and research, only then appearing in the public sphere, belongs to a bygone past. The directors of the mainstream media can nowadays do without public figures with their own charismatic authority, whom they see as uncontrollable. They are satisfied with manufacturing their own intellectuals, in other words 'clerks' who refrain from direct criticism of today's real ruling elites, who know perfectly well where power really lies, and are always ready to accuse and crucify the *misérables*. Victor Hugo is long since dead, but Sartre, Foucault and Bourdieu still need to be forgotten.

Finkielkraut and Zemmour, in the wake of Bernard-Henri Lévy, Pascal Bruckner and Philippe Val, perfectly represent the

---

20   In a former time, those presented as philosophers were people like Bergson, Sartre, Derrida or Foucault. The 'philosophers' of today are Bernard-Henri Lévy, Alain Finkielkraut, Pascal Bruckner and the like. This is striking evidence of the sad state of the media, though not of philosophy.

new balance of forces between the controllers of communications and the masters of the word. These two newer essayists, much in the public eye, undoubtedly possess an appreciable talent for writing, a determinant criterion for positioning oneself in the hierarchy of Parisian culture, but above all they have an impressive presence on radio and television. They have also succeeded in capturing attention thanks to their direct treatment of political and cultural actuality. Their capacity to intuitively sense the age, and to go with the shifts in public opinion, is what has given them their name; both were well aware of this from the start of their careers. They perceived, more quickly than others, the dissolution of the 'political correctness' associated with the late great thinkers and the defeat of the ageing leftists who stood in their shadow. They perfectly deciphered the disintegration of the humanist value system of embourgeoised pacifists and libertarians.

They were also aware that the media bosses welcomed them because their discourse aroused dormant instincts, pleasing a large public of readers and viewers who wanted to be anti-racist and anti-immigrant at the same time, ardently pro-Jewish and self-legitimized anti-Muslim. They thus succeeded in making a large contribution to the emergence of a new 'political correctness' that is in the process of winning a dominant position. Their writings may be superficial and basically insignificant, but their contribution to the formation of a 'political correctness' shamelessly proclaiming its elitist and pseudo-national personal egoism proves irreplaceable.

The two authors constantly lament France's cultural and intellectual decline. The fact that their writings have enjoyed such great resonance despite the mediocrity of their arguments at least proves that their contention is not totally erroneous. We can only be stupefied by their superficial conception of history, the lack of historical sense that spoils their understanding of the nation-state, their ignorance of economics, the candour in their analyses of the balance of political forces and the primacy they give to trivial incidents rather than to the statistics and analyses of specialists.

The very fact of focusing on France without the least serious comparison with other countries borders on a provincialism that we might have believed went out with Charles Maurras, Édouard Drumont, Julien Benda, Alfred Fabre-Luce and similar writers who belong to a bygone past.

The ardent aspiration of these two talented children of immigrants to be recognized as indigenous 'true-born French' is itself suggestive of a certain unease, and perhaps admiration. In the last analysis, it should not be surprising that their writings were so favourably received by readers plunged into confusion by the genuine mirages and blind alleys of identity politics in these early years of the century. Our two authors want to be very French, without really understanding the significance of the acute crisis that 'Frenchness' is undergoing. They cling to a 'France of yesteryear' that is totally imaginary, yet which they would have us believe existed for a thousand years before finishing in the joyous carnival of May 1968. How ironic that these two sons of immigrants are nostalgic for an educational system in which all students recited 'our ancestors the Gauls'. And is it not pathetic to see a son of Jewish Poles and a son of Jewish Berbers fantasize about the 'great nation' that has vanished forever?

The writings of these new 'true-born French' are full of what at first sight looks like a profusion of 'history', but soon turns out to be a very selective collation of episodes from the past, presenting this as a lost paradise, authoritarian and statist. The simple reason for this is that in a world where the present is so fluid, and the future so uncertain and disquieting, it is attractive to play to the maximum on the strings of nostalgia for a past stability and national greatness. As we know, however, nostalgia is most often no more than a melancholy regret for what has never really existed. The nostalgia expressed by Finkielkraut and Zemmour is not an aspiration to return to any real past; it is rather the embrace of a series of selected scenes designed to give the impression of a national homogeneity, forever unchanged, but which is now decaying into a kind of multiculturalism. In fact, these two essayists conflate a certain homogeneity of the intellectual and political field in Paris, which produced an eminent literature and created an impressive system of uniform education, with a homogeneity of the whole nation, which never existed.[21]

Here is an amusing example, among many others, that illustrates Éric Zemmour's ideas of 'historicity': 'To integrate Islam, France would have to renounce a thousand years of history, to deny Philip the Fair, Richelieu, Louis XIV, Napoleon, de Gaulle; we would move bit by bit from a multi-ethnic [sic] society to a multicultural one, which would become multi-confessional in the Lebanese manner.'[22]

The new Parisian prophet does not threaten us with the British, American or Brazilian models of pluralism, although he does not like them; they are not sufficiently frightening for his readers, the descendants of 'French' peasants from the time of Philip the Fair. He brandishes the anxiety-arousing 'multi-confessional' model that French colonialism imposed in its time on the protectorate it established in Lebanon. He simply forgets to remind us that the terrible civil war that broke out there in the 1970s did not have at its origin differences of belief or culture, but was due above all to the structural political inequality inscribed in the mode of political representation, which gave permanent supremacy to Christians. It is a supreme irony that it should be precisely the 'terrifying' Shiites who at that time demanded the application of the democratic republican principle of one man, one vote.

---

21   I have sometimes hesitated to criticize the unhistorical statements of the two authors on the development of nationalist sensibility. One should read for example *The Identity of France* (3 vols, New York: HarperCollins, 1988–92), which Fernand Braudel wrote at the end of his life, to understand the depth of the great illusion of an eternal France, not only on the part of intellectuals with a ready pen, but also among serious historians.

22   Éric Zemmour, *Le Suicide français*, Paris: Albin Michel, 2014, p. 330.

Just like Zemmour, Finkielkraut dreams of a single France, united, centralized and uniform, that will live forever. This leads him to maintain with confidence: 'The state does not limit itself to defending the principles of fraternity, secularism and equality . . . It defends a way of being, a form of life, a type of sociability – in short, we can risk saying, a *common identity*.'[23]

Here we find ourselves at the heart of the new 'statist's' work. True, this is not yet fascism: it lacks a good many elements for us to apply such a term. But like many former leftists, particularly those of Maoist tendency, Finkielkraut has never understood or adopted political liberalism, nor known the limits of intervention by the nation-state in public life and culture. The reasons for this aspiration towards a muscular authoritarianism become quickly clear. The 'philosopher' Finkielkraut, like Renaud Camus, Zemmour, Houellebecq and other 'declinist' intellectuals of recent years, is full of fear over the risk of Islamic domination, which leads him to accuse the recent past: 'For the first time in the history of immigration, the guest refuses his host, whomever this may be, the faculty of embodying the host country.'[24]

I am certain that the writer, who well deserves election to the Académie Française on the grounds of his xenophobic and anti-modern work, has walked the streets of Brooklyn and seen there the half million or so descendants of immigrants dressed completely in black, the women covering their heads with a scarf (and with the highest birth rate in the United States), who reject in disgust any assimilation into the American melting pot. It only remains to be hoped that Finkielkraut does not

---

23   Alain Finkielkraut, *L'Identité malheureuse*, Paris: Gallimard-Folio, 2013, p. 81.

24   Ibid., p. 111. Finkielkraut goes on to add: 'Muslims are asked to share a certain heritage, like everyone else. Instead of this, the more moderate of their number calmly envisage the transformation of empty churches into full mosques' ('Exclusif: la rencontre Michel Houellebecq–Alain Finkielkraut', *Le Figaro*, 13 August 2015).

believe that the United States should have opposed this 'unfriendly' immigration and left every Jew in the clutches of the Nazis.[25]

> At the summit of society as in the depth of the provinces, in the order of morality as in the material order, in the commercial, industrial, agricultural world and even on the construction sites where he competes with French workers, the foreigner poisons us like a parasite. An essential principle for conceiving a new French politics must be to protect all nationals against this invasion . . . The Jewish question is bound up with the national question. Though assimilated with indigenous French by the Revolution, Jews have maintained their distinctive character.[26]

This text, which resonates with the present day, was not written by Finkielkraut or Zemmour – its Judeophobia forewarns us against any risk of confusion. The author was Maurice Barrès, in 1898. He was then at the peak of his fame, in a decade marked by economic instability. Barrès was not the first to claim that Jews, clinging to their particular characteristics, could never become really French (Drumont and others had preceded him), but he was one of the first secular 'indigenists' to sincerely fear the loss of France's republican identity due to the strengthening

---

25   In 1924, following American voices similar to those of Finkielkraut and Zemmour, the Johnson-Reed Act was passed, drastically restricting immigration from Eastern Europe and thus obstructing the rescue of the Yiddish people. Without this law, it is likely that a large number of Jews could have been saved. (Very probably, too, the state of Israel would not have been created, as the United States remained closed to survivors of the genocide after 1945.)

26   Maurice Barrès, 'Programme de Nancy (1898)', in *Scènes et doctrines du nationalisme*, Paris: Félix Juven, 1902, pp. 432–3. Barrès launched his battle against immigrants in the early 1890s. In 1893 he published three articles in *Le Figaro*, under the heading 'Contre les étrangers, étude pour la protection des ouvriers français' (ibid, p. 457). See also 'Les Droits de l'Homme et du Citoyen, et la question des étrangers' (ibid, pp. 474–7).

of Judaism and the arrival of immigrants who would soon dominate the country.

The early twenty-first century, with its specific kind of cultural
crisis, is not the first time that public discourse has been obsessed
and poisoned by fear of foreign immigration. In periods of
economic stagnation, hostility towards foreigners accused of
'submerging' France has almost always intensified, among the
public at large and also among intellectuals. During the last
decade of the nineteenth century and in the 1930s, xenophobia
reached a peak. In the south of France, hatred of the Italians was
particularly widespread, well before the appearance of contemporary Islamophobia. At a time when the labour force had some 19
million wage-earners, 1.7 million immigrants came from Italy
between 1876 and 1913.[27] Fear of this invasion of 'Ritals' reached
a paroxysm in 1893, with the murder of eight Italian immigrants
by an angry crowd in Aigues-Mortes. The Italian press spoke of
150 deaths at this time. Many were forced to return to Italy or to
leave for the New World. The large mass of Polish immigrants
(half a million in 1931) suffered likewise. Mostly working in the
mines of the Nord, they lived in isolation on the periphery of
urban centres, and because of their fervent Catholicism were
sometimes confronted with the hostility of secular workers.[28] In
1935, when the economic slump was at its worst, many of them
were sent back to Poland by the French government.

From the late nineteenth century to the Second World War,
close to a hundred thousand Jews from Eastern Europe passed
through – and lived in – the Marais quarter in the heart of Paris.
They spoke a foreign language, wore strange clothes, and many
remained attached to their religious tradition. They had their sons

---

27   See Bertrand Blancheton and Jérôme Scarabello, *L'Immigration italienne en
France entre 1870 et 1914*, Cahiers du GRETHA, 2010–13.

28   See Gabriel Garçon, *Les Catholiques polonais en France (1919–1949)*,
doctoral thesis, Université Lille-3, 2003; and Janine Ponty, *Polonais méconnus. Histoire
des travailleurs immigrés en France dans l'entre-deux-guerres*, Paris: Publications de la
Sorbonne, 1988.

circumcised, the women covered their hair, they ate kosher food, and on their religious holidays they also worshipped in the street. When a Parisian entered the quarter (the *pletzel*, as it was called in Yiddish), he did not feel 'at home'. Robert Brasillach described the intolerable Jewish 'stranglehold' over the quarter: 'Suddenly we perceive that the ghettos of Central Europe have spilled out here their Jews with fur hats, their dirt, their jargon, their shops, their kosher butchers, their cheap restaurants, for a rapid clean-up before the commercial ghettos of the faubourg Montmartre and the luxurious ones of the avenue du Bois de Passy.'[29]

Given this hostility, not only from 'true-born French' but also from established French Jews, many of these immigrants continued their odyssey in the direction of the United States, to establish themselves en masse particularly in Brooklyn and the Bronx. Some 25,000 immigrants who remained in the Marais were deported to death camps by the German Occupation, under the blinkered eyes of Parisians.

Emmanuel Berl, a writer of Jewish origin and a brilliant intellectual, was friendly with the major writers of the 1930s. He was not a fascist, but for a long period could be classed as belonging to the circles that defined themselves as 'neither right nor left'. More than anyone else, he set out to convince his readers not to be racist Judeophobes but simply to oppose cultural immigration. In his view, the refugees and immigrants of the 1930s were an 'immigration of cast-offs' who risked degrading France. The republic should accordingly modify its immigration laws that were far too generous, and accept only those who were prepared to definitively renounce their original culture. Berl's firm conclusion was that it was impossible 'for France to let her country and her capital be invaded by the undesirables of every land'.[30]

---

29   Robert Brasillach, *Notre avant-guerre (1939–1940)*, Paris: Le Livre de poche, 1992, p. 114.

30   Emmanuel Berl, 'Les Pavés de Paris', 9 December 1938, quoted in Michael R. Marrus and Robert O. Paxton, *Vichy and the Jews*, Stanford: Stanford University Press, 1995, p. 43.

With the defeat of France and the Occupation, Berl hoped like many other French Jews that the new regime would not attack them, but only Jews who were immigrants, rootless, powerless and without French citizenship.[31] This may explain why he was so keen to write speeches for Marshal Pétain, the new head of state. And it may also explain why Éric Zemmour, likewise blindly moved by love for the tradition of a France 'one and indivisible' and by his obsessive repugnance for immigrants, has sought to minimize the part played by Vichy in the deportation of Jews, and give new currency to the old argument that 'the strategy adopted by Pétain and Laval in the face of German demands was to sacrifice foreign Jews to save French Jews'.[32]

Berl's close friend Drieu La Rochelle, like other intellectuals of the 1930s, felt deep disgust towards refugees and immigrants, seeing them as a major cause of French and European decadence. Drieu was the heir of Barrès and Huysmans, and not being Jewish like Berl, he remained coherent in expressing an unbridled hatred of Jews. Addressing the Germans in 1941, he wrote: 'Four million foreigners in France, including a million Jews, gave me the sense of occupation long before you.'[33] He summed up in this way a decade of escalation in the intellectual discourse about foreigners, characteristic of the pre-war years and prefiguring the xenophobic climate and legislation of Vichy.

Drieu La Rochelle's last remaining hope evaporated with the victory of the Allies and the 'Jews', and he committed suicide in 1945. Despite their profound pessimism and their obsession

---

31   See Maurice Rajsfus, *Des Juifs dans la collaboration. L'UGIF 1941–1944*, Paris: EDI, 1980.

32   Éric Zemmour, *Le Suicide français*, pp. 89–90. Zemmour exhibits a crude anti-Americanism towards Robert Paxton, and passes over in silence the anti-Jewish legislation of the Vichy government (in particular the abrogation of the Crémieux decree, which directly affected Zemmour's own family), which was not promulgated under German pressure. The deportation of children was likewise a purely Gallo-Catholic initiative.

33   Pierre Drieu La Rochelle in *Nouvelle Revue Française*, August 1941, quoted in Charlotte Wardi, *Le Juif dans le roman français*, Paris: Nizet, 1973, p. 57.

with French decadence, the authors of *L'Identité malheureuse, Le Suicide français* and *Submission* seem to believe that their writings might contribute to the new Reconquista that is needed to halt the Saracens of the twenty-first century and put an end to their occupation of Europe. They thought for a moment, along with many other 'intellectuals' inspired by the same obsessions, that the *union sacrée* of 11 January 2015 would give a new impulse. They were very soon disappointed.

The following September, France began to bomb the bases of the Islamic State in Syria. On 13 November, Daesh responded by perpetrating a series of particularly horrible attacks. A hundred and thirty-two innocent victims were killed in the heart of Paris. And while French aircraft immediately set out once again to bomb the strongholds of the terrorist organization in Syria, the president of the republic, François Hollande, decreed a state of emergency and called for the national union of all French people. This time, however, the consensus was less complete than after the attacks of January.

Six days after the terrible massacre, Michel Houellebecq published in an Italian newspaper an article titled 'I accuse Hollande and defend the French people'.[34] His words were immediately reproduced by the entire French press. This article sought to be an echo of Zola's 'J'accuse'. Despite his declared aversion for committed intellectuals, this successful writer of the early twenty-first century manifestly positioned himself as their direct heir. Just as Zola had fiercely attacked the heads of the French army, so Houellebecq launched an unprecedented assault on successive French governments, blaming them for the tragedy, and starting with 'the insignificant opportunist who occupies the seat of the head of state' and 'the mental defective who performs the functions of prime minister'.[35]

---

34   *Corriere della Sera*, 19 November 2015.
35   Ibid.

What Houellebecq reproaches them for, along with their predecessors, is 'having made inauspicious cuts in the police forces, to the point of reducing them to exasperation and rendering them almost incapable of performing their task', as well as 'having for years inculcated the idea that frontiers are an outdated absurdity, the symbol of a sickening nationalism'.[36] If he pours public scorn on the leaders of the state, Houellebecq seeks on the other hand to flatter his compatriots: 'The French population has always maintained its trust in the army and the forces of order: it has received with disdain the preachings of the "moral left" on the reception of refugees and migrants.'[37]

In a certain sense, this column can be seen as the tragi-comic end of a long cycle of moral commitment of Parisian intellectuals in public affairs. From one 'J'accuse' to another, from Zola to Houellebecq, everything that made for the nobility of the 'French intellectual' seems to have definitively evaporated.

For its entire existence as a kingdom, and for a further hundred years after the Revolution, France was marked by a rich cultural and linguistic pluralism. Breton, Provençal, Occitan and Alsatian continued to be vehicles of everyday communication. Neither the law of 1884 on compulsory education, nor the construction of railways across the country, put an end to this linguistic and cultural richness. In the twentieth century, Italians, Poles, Eastern European Jews, Spaniards and Portuguese immigrated in waves and continued to diversify the spectrum. Varied subcultures coexisted, and their specificities were absorbed into the great national whirlpool. Contrary to appearances, certain components of these diverse cultures resisted the

---

36　Ibid.

37　We should recognize that in the same breath Houellebecq stigmatized the French government's irresponsible foreign policy as contributing to the wave of terrorism. Michel Onfray also denounced France's interventions in the Middle East (see the interview with him in *Le Point*, 15 November 2015).

erosion of time, and form part of the wealth and attraction of France today.[38]

The marks of imported material that conservatives find it hard to digest are equally visible in high culture, among intellectuals. From Tristan Tzara who produced Dadaism (so far from Cartesianism) to Aimé Césaire who coined the concept of negritude (so foreign to republican uniformity), from Georges Politzer who introduced psychoanalysis into a country dominated at that time by 'psychology', to Emmanuel Levinas who imported Talmudism (so remote from the Pascalian tradition), immigrants have enriched France with multiple sensibilities, making the country a pluralist and exciting land in cultural and intellectual terms.[39] True, France has always viewed itself as 'one', in direct descent from Louis XIV and Napoleon, but in its depths a rebellious multiculturalism has persisted, and almost always succeeded in difficult moments (except during the short Vichy period) in restraining the nationalist furor that rejects difference and diversity. In France, a country of immigration par excellence, difference and diversity have never been weaknesses, but on the contrary sources of vigour and renewal, as in the United States and indeed Israel.

On reading Finkielkraut, Zemmour and again Houellebecq, I could not keep from thinking in my usual way of the very opposite. I remembered one of the heroes of my youth, Missak Manouchian, the Armenian intellectual, poet and immigrant (as

---

38   Anyone wanting to learn about immigrants in France and their socialization should read the pioneering book by Gérard Noiriel, *The French Melting Pot: Immigration, Citizenship and National Identity*, Minneapolis: University of Minnesota Press, 1996. See also Edgar Morin and Patrick Singaïny, *La France une et multiculturelle*, Paris: Fayard, 2012.

39   In the world of the visual arts it is almost impossible to speak of French painting in the late nineteenth and early twentieth century. The presence of 'foreigners', from Van Gogh to Dalí by way of Modigliani, Picasso, Soutine, Chagall, Foujita and Giacometti, made Parisian painting a colourful tower of Babel. With the exception of the proto-Nazis who rejected 'degenerate art', this led no one to complain of a foreign occupation.

myself the son of Yiddish-speaking immigrants and not a 'true-born sabra', I have always been inclined to revere 'exotic' and remote heroes).

In the early months of 1944, the Nazi occupiers and their Parisian collaborators put up the famous 'red poster' across the city. They knew what they were doing in not naming on this poster any 'true-born French', but rather the names of ten immigrants and sons of immigrants, stateless and internationalist. The words on the poster read:

> Here is the proof. If Frenchmen loot, steal, sabotage and kill, it is always foreigners who give the order. It is always unemployed and criminals who carry it out. It is always Jews who inspire it. This is the army of crime against France. Banditry is not the expression of injured patriotism, it is a plot of the foreigner against the life of French people and against the sovereignty of France. It is the plot of anti-France. It is the world dream of Jewish sadism. Let's strangle it before it strangles us, our women and our children!

This xenophobic agitation by the Nazis was not completely arbitrary. The battalion of 'foreign' communists organized in the FTP-MOI[40] was effectively the spearhead of the Resistance in Paris. The twenty-three 'terrorists' under the command of Manouchian included two 'indigenous' communists; all the others were immigrants: Italians, Spaniards and above all Poles and Hungarians of Jewish origin. Some scarcely spoke French and had not been naturalized. Manouchian, whose parents had survived the Armenian Genocide, arrived in France in 1925 as an illegal immigrant. Lacking education, he became a manual worker, but he wrote poems in his mother tongue. Set on maintaining his original culture at any cost, he published a review in

---

40   'Francs-tireurs et partisans – Main d'œuvre immigrée' (Irregulars and partisans – immigrant workers' movement).

Armenian, enrolling at the same time as a free student at the Sorbonne and translating Rimbaud and Baudelaire into Armenian. The Communist Party actively helped and supported immigrant workers, and Manouchian became a fervent militant. Under the Occupation he went underground and became one of the leaders of the Resistance in the Paris region. He was shot on 21 February 1944, along with twenty-two of his comrades-in-arms.

What was the percentage of foreign immigrants in the armed Resistance that fought the Nazi occupiers? And what was the percentage of readers and followers of Édouard Drumont, Maurice Barrès, Joris-Karl Huysmans and Pierre Drieu La Rochelle among those who risked their lives to inflict defeat on 'true-born Germans'? We do not have figures, and so have to leave this to the historical imagination. The future, however, will depend on whether the heirs of yesterday's 'decadent' nationalists, so popular in recent years, become tomorrow's moral references.

As a historian, I know that in the modern age the designation of an imaginary 'foreign enemy' always makes it possible to unite all hearts, and in this way reinforce authority and stabilize the existing hierarchical order. In the past, the French nation was welded together against England, then against Germany, sometimes also with the help of Judeophobia.

Today Europe is seeking to assert itself by accusing 'Muslim foreigners' of wishing to conquer the 'Judeo-Christian' continent. Fear and hatred, whatever their motives, have always been one of the most explosive cocktails in human history. But if we know how rejection of the Other begins, we are incapable of predicting how it will end. Everything suggests that the world market, despite economic stagnation and persistent unemployment, will continue to move and toss people around, and that the migrations of refugees fleeing war and mass butchery will continue to overturn frontiers and walls. In the face of these phenomena, and despite the real difficulties, the complexity of solutions, the authentic frustrations and imaginary fears, to take a stand will be a genuine criterion of civilization. No one – neither republican, socialist, nor even persecuted minorities and their descendants – is a priori immune from the contagious plagues of fear and rejection of the Other.

I would like therefore to end this book with the simple poetic words of Missak Manouchian, the migrant intellectual, the refugee who had escaped from one genocide before exchanging the pen for the gun in order to confront the fomenters and executors of another genocide:

> When I wander the streets of a metropolis,
> All the misery, all the destitution,
> Everywhere both lamentation and revolt,
> My eyes gather them, my soul houses them.[41]

---

41   'Privation' (translated from the Armenian by Gérard Hekimian). The image of Manouchian continues to upset certain 'true-born French'. At the end of 2014, a monument in his memory was profaned in Marseille (*Le Monde*, 24 December 2014).

Acknowledgements

I would like to express my thanks here to everyone who helped me bring this book through to publication. Above all to my French translator Michel Bilis, thanks to whom the book is clear and precise, and still more Cartesian than it originally was.

Two close friends, Richard Desserme and Julien Lacassagne, extended me their valuable help. Our discussions in Nice enabled me to clarify points that were not self-evident, and I owe them a great debt for this.

I also thank those of my students who, by their pertinent questions, refined the questioning that formed the basis of this book.

Finally, I also owe many thanks to Alain Gresh, Dominique Vidal and the team at Verso (especially to David Fernbach), for their commitment in giving this book its final form.

Tel Aviv and Nice, 2017

Index

Abbes, Ben, 213
Abdullah II, 226
Abellio, Raymond, 157
Abetz, Otto, 163
Abramsky, Alexandre, 153
Académie Française, 148
Académie Goncourt, 194
Action Française, 140–2, 148–50,
    155, 164
Age of Enlightenment, 3, 69
Al Jazeera (TV channel), 247
al-Qaeda, 238
Alsatian Auguste, Scheurer-
    Kestner, 55
Althusser, Louis, 2, 170
*Ancien Régime and the Revolution,
    The* (de Tocqueville), 79
Andreu, Pierre, 150
Animal Farm (Orwell), 31
anti-colonial wave, 19–20
anti-Dreyfusards, 56, 60
anti-intellectualism
    anti-totalitarianism and, 33
    Britain and, 29–31

anti-Semitism, 60, 155. *See also*
    Judeophobia
Apostrophes (TV programme), 193
Aragon, Louis, 22
Aron, Raymond
    Fondation Saint-Simon
        and,180
    published writing of, 189–90
    quoted, 91–2, 111,136, 171
    sociological approach of, 93
Aron, Robert, 145–6
Arthuys, Jacques, 160
Assange, Julian, 197
Auden, W. H., 30
Aufklärung, 17
automation, 182
Aymé, Marcel, 165

Bacon, Francis, 103
Badinter, Élisabeth, 225
Bagatelles pour un massacre, 155
Balthasar, Victor, 154
Barrès, Maurice
    Dreyfus affair and, 60

Ligue de la patrie français and, 56–62
political intervention and, 48
'Protest of the Intellectuals, The' and, 43
quoted, 39, 255
readers of, 263
Barrès, Philippe, 160
Barthes, Roland, 180, ix
Basque Euskadi Ta Askatasuna (ETA), 239
Belin, René, 159
Bell, David, 168
Benda, Julien, 82–7, 90–1
Beni Hebdo (weekly), 218
Benn, Gottfried, 21
Benoist-Méchin, Jacques, 161
Benoit, Pierre, 141
Béraud, Henri, 149
Bergery, Gaston, 159
Berl, Emmanuel, 257–8
Bernard, Claude, 50
Berth, Édouard, 27
Bertolucci, Bernardo, 195
Beuve-Méry, Hubert, 141
bin Laden, Osama, 240
bin Zayed, Abullah, 226
Blanc, Louis, 81
Blanchot, Maurice, 150
Blond, Georges, 155
Bloomsbury Group, 29
Blum, Léon, 31, 55, 121
Bolshevism, 157, 160
Bonaparte, Napoleon, 127
Bonardi, Pierre, 151
Bonnard, Abel, 141, 151, 161
Bonnier, Charles, 111
book banning, 191
book burnings, 20
boulangiste episode, 142

Bourdieu, Pierre
advent of technocrats and, 98
quoted, 94, 95, 97, 193
sociology of culture and, 68
Bourget, Paul, 55–6
Bourgin, Hubert, 141
Brasillach, Robert
Action Français and, 155–6
execution of, 163–4
Je suis partout and, 161
Nazism and, 148–50
quoted, 135, 165, 257
Brave New World (Huxley), 191
Brecht, Bertolt, 22, 32
Breivik, Anders, 205
Brogan, Denis William, 29
Bronx
emigration to, 257
Brooklyn
emigration to, 257
Bruckner, Pascal, 23
Brunetière, Ferdinand, 55
Burke, Edmund, 30, 32, 79
Bush, George W., 236, 242, 245

Calas affair, 48. *See also* Dreyfus affair
Calvin, Jean, 75
Cambodia, 33
Camus, Albert, 180
Camus, Renaud, 188, 235, 248
Candide (Voltaire), 69
Carrel, Alexis, 154
Carrère, Emmanuel, 215
Cartel des Gauches, 140
Cartesian legacy, 3
Castro, Fidel, 25, 189
Catholicism, 30, 92, 137, 142, 145, 178, 256
Céline, Louis-Ferdinand, 155

Césaire, Aimé, 261
Chack, Paul, 149, 151
Chaplin, Charlie, 194
Charle, Christophe, 54–6, 58–9
Charlie Hebdo
    attack against, 34
    Houellebecq and, 204–6
    Judeophobia and, 219–25
China, 23, 111, 187, 218. *See also*
    Maoism
Chirac, Jacques, 223
Chollet, Mona, 221
Chomsky, Noam, 16, 27, 67, 169,
    171
Christian culture, 60, 253
church
    clerics of, 89
    decline of, 77, 129
    power of, 118
    state separation from, 237
Clair, René, 194
Clemenceau, Georges, 43, 65
Cocteau, Jean, 165
Cold War, 170, 194
collective identity, 188, 231
Collini, Stefan, 29
colonialism, 17, 147, 245, 253
Combat (magazine), 149–150, 155
Communards, 62
Communism, 19, 22–3, 30, 179,
    240, 262. *See also*
    Communist Party
Communist Manifesto (Marx and
    Engels), 102, 109, 120
Communist Party, 152–3, 158,
    178. *See also* Communism
Comte, Auguste, 75–8, 90–1,
    97–9, 118
Conseil Représentatif des
    Institutions Juives de France

(CRIF), 217
conservative sociologists, 93
Coppée, François, 55
Corcuff, Philippe, 221
'Corporatism of the Universal,
    The' (lecture), 96
Courtois, Stéphane, 242
critical intellectuals, 16, 89,
    168–71, 182–7, 197–8
Critique of Dialectical Reason
    (Sartre), 168
cultural hegemony, 125–6
Cyran, Olivier, 221

d'Encausse, Hélène Carrère, 216
Dadaism, 261
Dandieu, Arnaud, 145
Danrit, 211
Danton, Georges, 81
Darnton, Robert, 72
Daudet, Léon, 55, 56
Davutoglu, Ahmet, 226
de Beauvoir, Simone, ix, 24, 189
de Blasio, Bill, 236
de Bouhélier, Saint-Georges, 55
de Châteabriant, Alphonse, 149
de Fabrègues, Jean, 146, 148, 150
de Jouvenel, Bertrand, 151, 160,
    163
de Lamartine, Alphonse, 81
de Man, Henri, 146
de Montherlant, Henry, 165
de Rougemont, Denis, 145
de Sade, Marquis, 2
de Saint-Simon, Claude Henri,
    10, 177
de Tocqueville, Alexis, 75, 76, 78,
    81
Déat, Marcel, 159
Debray, Régis, 167

Declaration of the Rights of Man and the Citizen, 61
decolonization, 186, 187
deep symbols, 12
Degas, Edgar, 48
de Gaulle, General Charles, 2
Delsol, Chantal, 242
democratism, 73
Der Judenstaat (Herzl), 42
Derrida, Jacques, 180
Dictionnaire philosophique, 70, 72
Diderot, Denis, 2
'Die Intelligenz und die Sozialdemokratie' (essay), 105
Discourse on Inequality (Rousseau), 73
Distinction (Bourdieu), 94
Doriot, Jacques, 150, 158
double voting, 29
Dreyfus affair, 29–31, 39, 41, 53, 64, 68, 106, 121, 148, 185
   first defenders of, 50
   innocence of, 48–9
   intervention of intellectuals, 52–3
   judeophobia and, 60
   retrial of, 45
   second Dreyfus affair, 46, 63, 117–18, 121, 148, 189
   Zola's petition of support, 112
   See also Dreyfusards
Dreyfus, Alfred, 7, 10
Dreyfusards, 56, 61, 62, 68. *See also* Dreyfus affair
Driant, Émile, 211
Drieu, 164
Drumont, Édouard, 64, 219, 224, 252
du Gard, Roger Martin, 143

Durkheim, Émile, 49, 89–90, 105

École libre des sciences politiques, 164
École normale supérieure, 164
Ehrenburg, Ilya, 22
Eiffel Tower, 45
eighteenth century, 28, 30, 68–9, 71–3, 169
Eisenstadt, Shmuel, 58
Eisenstein, Sergei, 22
el-Sisi, Fattah, 224
Encyclopédie, 176
End of Ideology, The (Bell), 168
Engels, Friedrich, 101, 183
Enlightenment, 51, 199, 230. *See also* Age of Enlightenment
Esprit (periodical), 144
Estrosi, Christian, 227
Ethiopia, 147, 149
European socialism, 106
Évenement du jeudi (weekly), 193
existentialism, 6

Fabian Society, 110
Fabre-Luce, Alfred, 151–2, 252
Fabrègues, 149
facismo, 140
Faisceau, 140, 142
Fallaci, Oriana, 240
Farewell to the Working Class (Gorz), 183
fascism, 52, 148, 166
Fégy, Camille, 151
Fernandez, Raymond, 151–2, 160
Feuer, Lewis S., 13
Fichte, Johann Gottlieb, 84
financial capital, 14
Finkielkraut, Alain
   as revolutionary, 23

L'Identité malheureuse, 248
  position on the war, 242, 247
  quoted, 215, 240, 243
First World War, 49, 83, 136–7, 183
Fondation Saint-Simon, 178–80, 187
Fontenoy, Jean, 151
Forain, 141
foreign enemies, 263
Foucault, Michel
  as spiritual guide, 170–3
  death of, 95–6
  political choices of, 24, 94
  prediction of, 197
  'specific intellectual' defined by, 98
Fourest, Caroline, 245, 247
Fourier, Charles, 238
Fourneau, Ernest, 154
France, Anatole, 48, 56, 58, 182
Francis, Robert, 150
Franco, General Francisco 150
Frederick II of Prussia, 72
French Green Party, 211
French Revolution, 103
Front National, 213, 220, 230
Front Populaire, 148
Furet, François, 179, 180

Geistmenschen, 11
Gémier, Firmin, 55
gens de lettres, 68
German Red Army Faction (RAF), 239
German Social Democracy, 112
Gide, André, 55, 60, 143, 180
Gilles (La Rochelle), 212
Giono, Jean, 165
globalization, 185

Gluckskraut, Alain, 218
Glucksmann, André, 23, 190, 242, 247
Godard, Jean-Luc, 24, 195
Goethe, Johann Wolfgang von, 17
Goldman Sachs, 218
Gorky, Maxim, 22
Gorz, André, 183
Gramsci, Antonio, 57–8, 125, 152
Great War, 143
Guevara, Che, 189
Guizot, François, 76

Habermas, Jürgen, 170
Hamon, Hervé, 7
Hauptmann, Gerhart, 21
Hees, Jean-Luc, 220, 222
Hegel, G. W. F., 90
Heine, Heinrich, 1
Hemingway, Ernest, 32
Herzl, Theodore, 42
Heterodox Marxists, 124
Hitler, Adolf, 19, 21
Hobsbawm, Eric, 30
Hofstadter, Richard, 28–9
Hollande, François, 225–6, 259
Homo sovieticus, 22
Houellebecq, Michel
  myth creating, 188
  prosecution of, 209–11, 225
  quoted, 203, 208
  response to massacre, 259–60
  Submission, 204, 212–16, 249
  terrorism and, 206–7
Høyer, Rasmus Sand, 223
Hugo, Victor, 2, 45, 182, 250
Huxley, Aldous, 191, 215
Huysmans, J.-K., 55

Ibsen, Henrik, 32

immigrants, 250, 254–7, 262
intellectual proletariats, 106
intellectuals
   defined, 10, 102
   vs intelligentsia, 12
intellectuels
   advent of term, 43
   British mistrust of, 29
intelligentsia, 10–12, 102
intelligentsia, 44
Intelligenz, 105
internet revolution, 195
Ionesco, Eugène, 203, 233
Isherwood, Christopher, 30
Islam, 208–9, 222, 239, 248–9.
      See also Islamophobia
Islamism, 245. *See also* Islam
Islamophobia, 35, 208
Italian Communist Party, 125,
      132
Italian Fascism, 125, 138
Italian Marxists, 127
Italian Red Brigades, 239
Izard, Georges, 145

'J'accuse' (Zola), 42–3, 49, 55,
      259–60
Jacobinism, 197
Jacoby, Russell, 175
Jamet, Claude, 157
Japanese Red Army, 239
Jaurès, Jean, 31, 60, 107
Je suis Charlie, 226–7
Je suis Dieudonné, 227
Je suis français, 230
Je suis partout (weekly), 154, 156
Jean-Christophe (Rolland), 83
Jeantet, Claude, 151
Jesus Christ, 229
Jeune Droite, 146, 148

Jewish Defence League, 227
Jews. *See also* Judeophobia
   hatred of, 258
Joffrin, Laurent, 228
Johnson, Paul, 32, 33
Jouvenel, 152
Judeophobia
   battle against, 35
   Catholic culture and, 137
   Charlie Hebdo and, 219
   Dreyfus affair and, 41–2, 53,
      60
   in nineteenth century, 40–1,
      65
   Nazism and, 153–6, 164–6
   Submission and, 217
   Voltaire and, 71
   See also anti-Semitism;
      xenophobia
Judt, Tony, 171
Julliard, Jacques, 216
Jünger, Ernst, 21
Jyllands Posten (newspaper), 222,
      244

Kästner, Erich, 21
Kathedersozialisten, 110
Kautsky, Karl, 57–8, 104–8
Khmer Rouge, 187
Khomeini, Ayatollah, 217
Kissinger, Henry, 13
Koran, 214, 238, 246
Kriegel, Blandine, 23
Kristeva, Julia, 23
Kubrick, Stanley, 194

L'Assiette au beurre (newspaper),
      219
L'Aurore (newspaper), 43, 64
L'Émancipation nationale

(periodical), 151

L'Identité malheureuse
(Finkielkraut), 248, 259

L'Insurgé (weekly), 149

L'Invasion jaune (Driant), 211

L'Invasion noire (Driant), 211

La Croix (newspaper), 64

La France juive (Drumont), 64,
219, 249

La Gerbe, 161

La Libre Parole (newspaper), 64,
212, 219, 224

La Revue du siècle (periodical), 144

La Rochelle, Pierre Drieu, 135,
148, 151–2, 160–3

La Trahison des Clercs (Benda), 143

Labour Party, 31

Lafargue, Paul, 111

Lagardelle, Hubert, 111, 121

Lamour, Philippe, 141

Langevin, Paul, 143

Langue fantôme, suivi d'Éloge
littéraire d'Anders Breivik
(Millet), 248

Lanzmann, Claude, 225

LaRochelle, Drieu, 258

Last Intellectuals, The (Jacoby), 175

Laubreaux, Alain, 155

Lazare, Bernard, 40, 50, 55, 60

Le Devenir social (periodical), 105

Le Figaro (newspaper), 64, 189,
208, 242, 245, 247–8

Le Grand Remplacement (Camus),
248

Le Journal (newspaper), 43

Le Monde (periodical), 141, 215,
247

Le Mouvement socialiste (journal),
121

Le Nouveau Siècle, 141

Le Pen, Marine, 211, 213, 230,
240

Le Suicide français (Zemmour),
248, 259

Le Temps (newspaper), 64, 147

Le Trahison des clercs (Benda),
82–3

Ledru-Rollin, Alexandre, 81

Lefebvre, Denis, 242

Left Bank intellectuals, 8

Lenin, Vladimir Ilyich, 92

Les Chiens de garde (Nizan), 82,
125

Les Méfaits des intellectuels (Berth),
27

Les Temps modernes (journal), 247

Lévi-Strauss, Claude, 193

Levinas, Emmanuel, 218, 261

Lévy, Benny, 23

Lévy, Bernard-Henri
Communism and, 240–2
Islam and, 239–40
Judeophobia and, 222
Submission and, 215
support for the war, 247

liberal democracies, 15–16

Liberation, 166

Libération (newspaper), 228

Lieberman, Avigdor, 226

literary field
three groups of, 54

Literary Underground of the Old
Regime, The (Darnton), 72

Losey, Joseph, 195

Loti, Pierre, 55

Louis XIV, 72

Lutheran church, 222

Luxemburg, Rosa, 102

Lyotard, Jean-François, 174, 176,
180

Machajski, Jan Wacław, 101, 133
Machiavelli, Niccolò, 130
Madani, Nizar, 226
Magic Mountain, The (Mann), 17
male suffrage, 1
Mallarmé, Stéphane, 50, 55
Malraux, André, 143
Mann, Thomas, 17–18, 20
Mannheim, Karl, 105
Manouchian, Missak, 261–2, 264
Maoism, 23–5, 187. *See also* China
Marc, Alexandre, 145
Marcuse, Herbert, 170
Marinetti, Filippo, 143
Marion, Paul, 151
Maris, Bernard, 204, 215
Marlowe, Christopher, 229
Marx, Karl, 4, 32, 84, 101, 183, 238
Marxism
  advance of, 88–90
  anti-intellectual approaches to, 28–30, 34
  collective memory of, 134
  decline of, 179
  Jan Wacław Machajski on, 101
  Karl Kautsky and, 104–6
  Raymond Aron and, 93
  state intellectual and, 111–12
Marxist–Leninist doctrine, 145
materialism, 145
Maulnier, Thierry, 148–9, 155, 160
Maurras, Charles, 62, 158, 252
Maxence, Jean-Pierre, 148–9
Mayakovsky, Vladimir, 22
McCarthy, Joseph, 52
McCarthyism, 52
media, 66, 97

Mikhailov, Nikita, 22
Mill, John Stuart, 29
Millet, Richard, 248
Milner, Jean-Claude, 23
Mirbeau, Octave, 55–6
Misrahi, Robert, 241
Moglen, Eben, 195
Morin, Edgar, 180
Morsi, Mohammed, 224
Mounier, Emmanuel, 145
Muhammad, 222–3
multiculturalism, 253
Muslims, 243–4, 248
Mussolini, Benito, 140, 150

national socialism, 137, 150, 157
Nazi ideology, 156, 255
Nazi propaganda, 154
Nazism, 20–1, 26, 52, 148, 160, 166, 245
negritude, 261
neo-conservatism, 24
Neruda, Pablo, 22
Netanyahu, Benjamin, 226
Neue Zeit (periodical), 105
New Statesman (weekly), 32
new totalitarianism, 247
Ni droite ni gauche (Sternhell), 135–6
nineteenth century
  as scientific age, 229
  collective consciousness during, 181–2
  free education in, 191
  journalists in, 194
  representation in, 185
  Saint-Simonians in, 179
  written communication in, 190
  xenophobia in, 256
1984 (Orwell), 31, 191

1930s nonconformists, 145
Nizan, Paul, 82, 85–7, 125
Nobel Prize, 204
Noiriel, Gérard, 50
nonconformists, 147, 149
Nora, Pierre, 180
nostalgia, 252
Nouvelle Revue Française, 161

Old Testament, 246
Oppenheimer, Robert, 173, 174
Order nouveau (periodical), 144
Ordre Nouveau, 146
Ortega y Gasset, José, 51
Orwell, George, 16, 31, 191, 215
Ozouf, Mona, 242

Palestine Liberation Organization,
    238
Paris
    publishing in, 5–6
Parisian culture
    hierarchy of, 251
Parnassians, 55
Parti Populaire Français, 150
Patriot Act, 236
patriotic Communism, 166
Péguy, Charles, 27, 40, 50, 55,
    121
Pétain, Marshal, 258
Petit Parisien (newspaper), 161
Peyrefitte, Alain, 2
Philip, André, 146
Philosophe, 70
Philosophical Reflections on the
    Science and Scientists
    (Comte), 77
pig breeding, 218
Pinter, Harold, 30
Pivot, Bernard, 193, 194

Platform (Houellebecq), 208
'Plea for Intellectuals, A' (lectures),
    88
Pol Pot, 33
political commitment, 206
Political Marxism, 133
political modernization, 15
Politzer, Georges, 261
Pontecorvo, Gillo, 195
Popper, Karl, 32
Positivist Society, 78
Possibility of an Island, The
    (Houellebecq), 209
Postman, Neil, 191
Prévert, Jacques (quoted), 19, 211
Prison Notebooks (Gramsci),
    125–6, 132
proletarian intellectuals, 123
Protestantism, 30
'Protest of the Intellectuals, The'
    (article), 43
Proust, Marcel, 50, 55
public intellectuals, 29
public sphere
    defined, 4
    publishing, 5–6
Pujadas, David, 204, 215

Radical Party, 151
Rage and the Pride, The (Fallaci),
    240, 241
Réaction (periodical), 144
Rebatet, Lucien, 155
Red Guards, 23
Redeker, Robert, 242, 246–7
Rediger, Roger, 214
Reflections on Violence (Sorel), 112
Reinach, Joseph, 55
Renan, Ernest, 10
Renoir, Auguste, 48

republicanism, 61
ResPublica (periodical), 247
Revolt of the Masses, The (Ortega y Gasset), 51
Revolution of 1789, 77–8
Revolution of 1848, 78, 81
revolutionary bourgeois, 102
Revolutions of 1848, 102
Revue d'études palestiniennes (newspaper), 214
Robespierre, Maximilien, 81
Rochefort, Henri, 60
Rod, Édouard, 55
Rolland, Romain, 16, 83, 143
romanticism, 18
Roncin, Joachim, 226
Rotman, Patrick, 7
Rousseau, Jean-Jacques, 2, 32, 69, 72–5
Roy, Claude, 150, 160
Russell, Bertrand, 16–19, 30–2

Sakharov, Andrei, 22
Sarkozy, Nicolas, 220, 225, 243
Sartre, Jean-Paul
   background of, 16–18
   as conservative sociologist, 93–5
   Critique of Dialectical Reason, 168
   lectures of, 90–1, 97–8
   photographs of, 189–90
   'Plea for Intellectuals, A', 88–9
   quoted, 1
   refusal to serve, 2
   Intellectuals, The, 32
Saudi Wahhabists, 238
Schmitt, Carl, 21
scholars
   professionalization of, 51
second Dreyfus affair, 46, 63, 185, 189
Second International, 105
Second World War
   anti-colonial wave, 19
   decolonization after, 186
   migration of Jews during, 256
   murdered individuals during, 232
   radical nationalism during, 60
   'specific intellectual' after, 173
Section français de l'Internationale ouvrière (SFIO), 31
September 11, 2001, 236, 241
SFIO, 31
Shakespeare, William, 229
Shaw, George Bernard, 22, 29
Shelley, Percy Bysshe, 32
Shiites, 253
Shils, Edward, 58
Sicard, Maurice-Yvan, 151
Sinet, Maurice, 221
Snowden, Edward, 197
Social Contract, The (Rousseau), 69, 74
Social Democratic Party, 110
Socialist Party (SFIO), 159
Société Positiviste, 78
sociology
   new scientific principles of, 49–50
Sollers, Philippe, 23
Solzhenitsyn, Alexander, 22, 187
Sombart, Werner, 21
Soral, Alain, 219
Sorel, Georges, 27, 40, 84, 111
Sortir du XXe siècle (Houellebecq), 206
Soviet Communism, 140, 144
Spinoza, 83, 241
Stalin, 25, 33, 92. *See also*

Stalinism
Stalinism, 133, 169, 187, 245. *See also* Stalin
state socialism, 15
Sternhell, Zeev, 135
Strauss-Lévy, Pascal, 217
structuralism, 6
Stylist (magazine), 226
Suarez, Georges, 141, 151
Submission (Houellebecq), 204, 211, 215, 217, 259
surrealism, 6, 143
symbolic capital, 14
symbolism, 6
Symbolist poets, 50

Taguieff, Pierre-André, 241, 242
Taliban, 238
Talmud, 246
Talmudism, 261
Tamil Tigers of Sri Lanka, 239
Taylorism, 131, 194
terrorism, 205–8, 236, 238
Thatcher, Margaret, 32
Third International, 132
Third Reich, 139
Third Republic, 158, 164–5
Thompson, E. P., 30
Thorez, Maurice, 158
Thousand-Year Reich, 20
Tolstoy, Leo, 32
'Tomb of the Intellectual, The' (Lyotard), 174
totalitarian democracies, 15, 191
trente glorieuses, 250
Trigano, Shmuel, 242
twentieth century, 13, 15, 17, 25–8, 54, 137
Tzara, Tristan, 261

Ulmann, André, 145
union sacrée, 259
USSR, 242

Val, Philippe, 220–3, 237, 241, 245–7
Valéry, Paul, 48
Valois, Georges, 140–1, 142, 158, 160
Vélodrome d'Hiver, 143
Verne, Jules, 56, 58
Vidal-Naquet, Pierre, 135
Vielé-Griffin, Francis, 55
Vietnam, 26, 190
Vincent, René, 150, 155
völkisch racism, 150
Voltaire
    anti-Jewish prejudice of, 229–30
    as champion of moderate liberalism, 69
    Enlightenment optimism, 70–1
    life lessons of, 72
    quoted, 70, 71

Watchdogs, The (Nizan), 88, 125
Webb, Beatrice, 22
Webb, Sidney, 22
Weber, Max, 105
Weil, Simone, 235
Weimar republic, 143
Wells, H. G., 29
Westergaard, Kurt, 222
White Rose group, 26
Wilde, Oscar, 2
Wilhelm Pabst, Georg, 21

xenophobia, 241, 248, 254–8, 262. *See also* Judeophobia

y Gasset, Ortega, 192

Yeats, W. B., 67
Young Communists, 151

Zedong, Mao, 249
Zemmour, Éric, 188, 248–50
historicity ideas of, 253
Zionism, 39, 42, 240
Zola, Émile
    class tensions and, 180–2
    as Dreyfusard, 56, 62, 111–12

imprisonment of, 2
'J'accuse', 41–3, 55, 259
as scientific intellectual, 45–8,
    50
social logic and, 58
zombie nationalist identity, 231